AMERICAN INQUISITION

American Inquisition

THE HUNT FOR JAPANESE AMERICAN DISLOYALTY IN WORLD WAR II

Eric L. Muller

The University of North Carolina Press : Chapel Hill

This book was published with the assistance of the H. Eugene and Lillian Youngs
Lehman Fund of the University of North Carolina Press. A complete list of books
published in the Lehman Series appears at the end of the book.

Designed by Michelle Coppedge
Set in Quadraat and Quadraat Sans by Keystone Typesetting, Inc.

The paper in this book meets the guidelines for permanence and durability of the
Committee on Production Guidelines for Book Longevity of the Council on Library
Resources.

Library of Congress Cataloging-in-Publication Data
Muller, Eric L.
American inquisition : the hunt for Japanese American disloyalty in World War II /
Eric L. Muller.
p. cm.
Includes bibliographical references and index.
ISBN 978-0-8078-3173-1 (cloth : alk. paper)
1. World War, 1939–1945—Japanese Americans. 2. Japanese Americans—
Evacuation and relocation, 1942–1945. 3. Internal security—United States—
History—20th century. 4. United States—Politics and government—1933–1945.
I. Title. D769.8.A6M85   2007
940.53′1773—dc22   2007011436

A Caravan book. For more information, visit www.caravanbooks.org.

cloth   11 10 09 08 07   5 4 3 2 1

for **LESLIE**
with love and loyalty

and

in memory of my grandparents
HERBERT and **ANN DICKMAN**
and their wartime sacrifices

One of the greatest barriers to a smooth operating security program was . . . that our own [C]onstitution extended certain protection to American-born citizens who are not morally entitled to that benefit.

Japanese-American Branch,

Office of the Provost Marshal General,

1945

The notions of "segregation" and "disloyalty" around which the [War Relocation Authority's] program has been conceived would, if allowed by the Courts, become the juristic formulation in terms of which future Fascist persecution of racial and political minorities will be justified.

Attorney Maurice Walk to War Relocation

Authority solicitor Philip M. Glick,

September 1943

CONTENTS

ILLUSTRATIONS

ABBREVIATIONS

CAD   Civil Affairs Division (of the Western Defense Command)

IERB   Industrial Employment Review Board

JACL   Japanese American Citizens League

JAJB   Japanese American Joint Board

JERS   Japanese Evacuation and Resettlement Study

MIS   Military Intelligence Service

ONI   Office of Naval Intelligence

PMGO   Provost Marshal General's Office

WCCA   Wartime Civilian Control Administration

WDC   Western Defense Command

WRA   War Relocation Authority

AMERICAN INQUISITION

1:
INTRODUCTION

ASKED TO NAME a time when the government judged the loyalty of large numbers of American citizens, most people would probably cite the period often called "the Second Red Scare." By this they would mean the time in the Cold War when the government subjected all Executive Branch employees and job applicants to FBI investigation to determine whether there were "reasonable grounds" to believe that they were "disloyal to the Government of the United States." This "loyalty-security" program led to some four million investigations, more than 12,000 hearings by "loyalty boards" within federal agencies, and adverse findings in the cases of more than 500 Americans. It was the most expansive government program to assess the loyalty of citizens that the country has ever known.[1]

But it was neither the most burdensome such program nor the most suspicious of the loyalty of American citizens. Those dubious honors go to a system that preceded the Red scare by five to ten years: the multi-agency apparatus that judged the loyalty of American citizens of Japanese ancestry during World War II. This program condemned more than one out of every four Americans whose cases it reviewed. And it imposed some very severe consequences: a finding of disloyalty could lead not just to the loss of a job but to exclusion from a broad swath of the country and even to prolonged incarceration.

This study examines the mechanisms that the federal government created to judge the loyalty of tens of thousands of American citizens of Japanese ancestry during World War II. This story is not well known, even in the sizable literature on the Japanese American internment.[2] To the extent that that literature has focused on issues of loyalty, it has principally explored the demoralizing effects of the loyalty questionnaire that the government required all internees to fill out while behind the barbed wire of the so-called relocation centers in early 1943. What scholars have not done, however, is to follow those completed questionnaires into the bowels of the wartime bureaucracy, where midlevel government officials actually used them to pass judgment on the loyalty of the incarcerated Americans who had filled them out. That is what this study does.[3]

This focus on the loyalty machinery within the government bureaucracy is an invitation to a somewhat new direction in the study of the Japanese American internment as a system of legalized racial oppression. Unlike the scholarly study of the Holocaust, which passed through an important phase of debate over whether the engine of Nazi oppression lay mostly in the will of Adolf Hitler or in the vast governing structure beneath him,[4] the study of government responsibility for the Japanese American internment has attended principally to a handful of men at the top. The nature and degree of President Franklin Roosevelt's responsibility have been extensively and usefully examined, as have, to a lesser extent, the contributions of a few top military and civilian officials.[5] Yet these top figures had little to do with some of the episode's most defining features. Consider, as just one example, the barbed wire, armed sentries, and searchlights that surrounded each of the ten Japanese American camps. It is not just that these measures were not the brainchild of President Roosevelt or any of his top civilian advisers or military commanders. It is rather that these measures were not the original idea of *any federal official at all*. The governors and attorneys general of the states where the camps were to be located were the ones who demanded "concentration camp"–like confinement for the West Coast's Japanese and Japanese Americans.[6] A focus on just the top echelon of federal officials misses that fact.

This study of the loyalty bureaucracy for Japanese Americans demonstrates that many of the forces that shaped important features of the episode we call the Japanese American internment moved deep within the government rather than atop it. In shifting attention downward, from top- to midlevel officials and from headline-grabbing decisions to the more mundane business of processing loyalty cases, the study invites attention to the importance of the quotidian decisions and conflicts that pushed the government through months and years of systematized repression.[7]

The wartime loyalty bureaucracy was not a single agency. In fact, four distinct agencies or boards made loyalty findings at one time or another between 1943 and 1945 in cases involving Japanese Americans. One was the Western Defense Command (WDC), the army organization responsible for the defense of the West Coast of the continental United States and Alaska. It was the WDC that ordered the exclusion of all Japanese Americans from the coast early in 1942 on mass suspicion of disloyalty, and it was the WDC that decided which individual Japanese Americans were still not loyal enough to return to the coast when mass exclusion ended late in 1944. A second agency that scrutinized the loyalty of Japanese Americans was the War Relocation Authority (WRA), which ran the Japanese American camps and decided which internees deserved release and which deserved confinement. The third organization that passed upon Japanese American loyalty or disloyalty was the army's Provost Marshal General's Office (PMGO), which was responsible for military policing and domestic industrial security. And the fourth loyalty tribunal for Japanese Americans was an organization called the Japanese American Joint Board (JAJB or the Joint Board), an interdepartmental council that made loyalty findings in cases of Japanese Americans between March of 1943 and May of 1944.

The JAJB was to have been the meeting point for these other agencies, a place where the various government units with an interest in the loyalty of Japanese Americans could collaborate and reach consensus. The hope was that coordinated decision-making by the JAJB, with intelligence information supplied by the WDC and the FBI, would avoid duplicative work and allow for the development of a coherent standard for judging the loyalty of Japanese Americans. But it did not turn out that way. Rather, the story of the Joint Board's brief life became a story of conflict between the primary civilian and military powers that sent information or representatives to it: the civilian WRA and the military PMGO and WDC. By 1943, these civilian and military agencies had such vastly different missions and motivations, and such vastly different experiences with Japanese Americans, that consensus was impossible. Each agency did its best to maintain an illusion of JAJB authority while the Joint Board operated, but each quietly made and implemented its own decisions about Japanese American loyalty in those settings where it could claim final authority.

At times these rival judgments conflicted with each other in embarrassing ways. But the real problem ran deeper than embarrassing interagency conflict; it resided in each agency standing alone. In truth, neither the WRA nor the PMGO nor the WDC ever managed to settle on a coherent definition of loyalty *even for itself*. Japanese American disloyalty became a chimera for each of these agencies, a wall on which each organization projected a constantly shifting show of its own motivations, needs, and experiences. The WRA's process was ultimately a good deal more perceptive about Japanese Americans than were the PMGO's and especially the WDC's, which invariably projected the most paranoid possible image of Japanese American disloyalty. The important point, though, is that nothing in the actual allegiances of the observed people themselves produced the different characterizations. The government agencies produced them on their own. Each agency's conclusions about Japanese American loyalty ultimately reflected much more about the agency and the context in which it operated than about the American citizens whose cases it was judging.

Consideration of a sixty-year-old government apparatus for gauging the loyalty of American citizens is regrettably not a matter of interest just to students of World War II and the Japanese American experience. Similar sorts of mechanisms cropped up a few years later in the loyalty investigations of the second Red scare.[8] And now, attacked by terrorists and beset by internal controversy over an unpopular war, the United States again finds itself at a moment when the loyalties of some American citizens are coming under suspicion. The attackers on September 11, 2001, were all aliens. But in the wake of the attack, American citizens—most of them Muslims of Arab ancestry—have been convicted of providing support to terrorist organizations and of conspiring to levy war against the United States.[9] This is a worrisome contrast with World War II, when no person of Japanese ancestry was ever convicted of pro-Axis spying or sabotage.[10] Furthermore, the airwaves and bookstore shelves have been full of loose accusations of disloyalty and even treason against those who oppose government policy, especially military policy. To be sure, we have not yet heard calls for mass loyalty screening of citizens. But there is no telling what the future holds. Renewed terrorist attacks on the United States would surely trigger anxiety and escalate fears of disloyalty, especially if, as in the London transit bombings of July 2005, the attackers were revealed to be citizens.

The basic lesson of the government's program of judging the loyalty of tens of thousands of Japanese Americans in World War II is that the program never managed to reach anything like a satisfactory definition of loyalty. The agencies responsible for making the judgments went looking for the line between loyalty and disloyalty and instead mostly found their own agendas and preconceptions. In an era of renewed worries about the loyalties of American citizens, that is a valuable and timely lesson.

THIS IS PRIMARILY a book about government. Japanese Americans play an important role, as does the story of their eviction from the West Coast and their prolonged detention behind barbed wire. But Japanese Americans and the internment story are not the book's direct focus; the government's loyalty bureaucracy is. For this reason, the book assumes familiarity with the circumstances that led to the forced removal and detention of Japanese Americans and with the many tragic losses and difficult choices that Japanese Americans faced during the war years. Readers who wish to familiarize themselves with the internment story more deeply have an outstanding array of books from which to choose.[11]

Some background is, however, essential, because the various loyalty bureaucrats all attached great (if varying) significance to the cultural and religious identities of American citizens of Japanese ancestry before the war. The following chapter (Chapter 2) therefore briefly summarizes some key aspects of the prewar lives of Japanese Americans along the West Coast. It focuses on the lives of the American citizens of Japanese ancestry born in the United States in the first third of the twentieth century, rather than on the lives of their immigrant parents.[12] The chapter is hardly a comprehensive account of prewar life; it zeros in mostly on those attributes and attachments that loyalty investigators later found suspicious.

Chapter 3 provides a concise account of the views about Japanese American loyalty that prevailed in the various halls of power just before and just after the Japanese attack on Pearl Harbor. It contrasts the intelligence that President Roosevelt was receiving to the effect that American citizens of Japanese ancestry were overwhelmingly loyal with the conviction of some in the military, particularly WDC commander John DeWitt, that Japanese Americans all posed a racially determined threat of subversion. It was, of course, the latter view that prevailed, and that resulted in the mass exclusion of Japanese Americans from the coast in the spring of 1942. As with Chapter 2, this chapter does not purport to document the intricacies of the government's process of deciding for mass exclusion and long-term detention; other works do this ably.[13] The focus is instead on how a presumption of Japanese American disloyalty came to dominate the thinking that led to exclusion and indefinite detention in the spring, summer, and fall of 1942.

That presumption did not go unchallenged for long. By late in the fall of 1942, the government began to feel pressure from various quarters to release some Japanese Americans from confinement and to confine others more closely. All of the debates and conversations about freedom and confinement shared a common phrasing; they all turned on "loyalty" and "disloyalty." Chapter 4 documents these debates and conversations about parole and segregation, emphasizing the fixation of all government agencies on loyalty as the determining criterion. Those debates and conversations eventually led the government to administer a questionnaire to all adult internees to assess their loyalty to the United States. The disastrous tale of these loyalty questionnaires is the subject of Chapter 5.

Resentfully and unhappily, the internees did fill out their forms, which cast on the government the responsibility of processing them. At this point in the war, the loyalty screenings were to serve several purposes: to determine who was loyal enough to leave camp to relocate to a community in the interior; to determine who was loyal enough to take a job in a plant or facility engaged in sensitive war production; and to determine who was so disloyal that he or she should be transferred to more restrictive confinement. The JAJB was set up with the optimistic mission of accomplishing all of those goals; its civilian and military members were to process the volumes of intelligence information about Japanese Americans, including their answers to the loyalty questionnaire, and make these important decisions about freedom, confinement, and employment. But as Chapter 6 demonstrates, this plan quickly failed. The JAJB's voting members had such different needs and objectives, and such different visions of Japanese American loyalty, that the Joint Board fell apart within a year of its creation.

Once the JAJB moved toward irrelevance, its two primary voting members —the WRA and the PMGO—took up the task of doing their own loyalty assessments for their own purposes. The WRA evaluated the loyalty of those internees who wished to leave camp and of those who were candidates for transfer to a segregation facility for the disloyal. The PMGO, for its part, assessed the loyalty of Japanese Americans who wished to take jobs in plants doing war production work. Chapters 7 and 8 describe and contrast these two agencies' methods of evaluating Japanese American loyalty. Chapter 7 spotlights the PMGO and finds its atmosphere to be nearly as noxious on questions of loyalty as the atmosphere in which the WDC had initially ordered the mass exclusion of Japanese Americans from the West Coast in the first place. Chapter 8 evaluates the WRA's loyalty screening system and finds an approach that was at once less hostile toward the idea of Japanese American loyalty than the PMGO's and more shaped by the agency's own rather desperate needs.

By the spring of 1944, with Japan's military fortunes inexorably failing, important voices both inside and outside the military began calling for an end to the mass exclusion of Japanese Americans from the West Coast. But President Roosevelt knew that 1944 was an election year, and he did not wish to harm either his own chances at the polls in California or those of his favored House and Senate candidates by allowing Japanese Americans to return to the coast before the election. It was therefore not until December of 1944, on the eve of an adverse decision from the U.S. Supreme Court, that the government announced the end of mass exclusion, to be replaced by a program of individual exclusion that the WDC would administer. Chapter 9 explains the rather tortured process by which this change in policy came about, and then details the three quite different approaches that the WDC developed for evaluating the loyalty of those Japanese Americans who were candidates for continued individual exclusion from the coast. Given that the war was well on its way to an end by the time the WDC began devising its program, it is astonishing that the first system that the WDC proposed was the most demanding and suspicious system that any government agency had used at any point during the war. That rather bloodthirsty program never got off the ground, however; various pressures forced the WDC to implement rigid and fairly arbitrary screening criteria whose only virtue was that they would produce no more than 10,000 findings of disloyalty.

Alone among all of the loyalty screening systems for Japanese Americans in World War II, the WDC's was tested in federal court. A feisty Japanese American dentist from Oakland named George Ochikubo decided in mid-1944 to challenge his continued exclusion from the West Coast. With the help of a leading civil rights attorney, he filed a lawsuit against the commanding general of the WDC seeking to enjoin the WDC commander from enforcing an exclusion order against him. This lawsuit, which is the subject of Chapter 10, brought the WDC's system of individual exclusion under direct judicial scrutiny. But in a duplicitous move, the WDC chose not to mount a courtroom defense of the rigidly (and arbitrarily) constrained screening program it was actually using. Instead, the WDC defended a system of unfettered military discretion that it was not really using but that it wanted a court to validate in order to free the hands of future military commanders in future conflicts.

The federal government's enterprise of evaluating the loyalty of Japanese Americans in World War II began with racist presumptions and ended with distortions and misrepresentations under oath. And the path from beginning to end, from agency to agency, was for the most part charted not by reference to anything real or true about the allegiances of Japanese Americans but by reference to the preconceptions, needs, and desires of the agencies themselves. As Chapter 11 concludes, this was an enterprise that can teach us a number of valuable lessons. But it is not an enterprise to emulate.

JAPANESE AMERICANS
BEFORE THE WAR

AT THE MOMENT when the Imperial Japanese Navy attacked the American fleet at Pearl Harbor, Japanese Americans were a tiny minority. According to the 1940 census, 126,948 people of Japanese ancestry (Nikkei)[1] lived in the contiguous United States, less than one-tenth of one percent of the population of the mainland. Eighty-nine percent of the Nikkei lived along the Pacific Coast; of those, 83 percent lived in California.[2]

Just over a third of America's Nikkei in 1940 were "Issei"[3]—Japanese immigrants who retained their Japanese citizenship because American law at the time forbade any Asian from naturalizing as a U.S. citizen. Most of the remaining two-thirds of the Nikkei were the children of the Issei, the "Nisei."[4] Born in the United States, they were American citizens by operation of the first clause of the Fourteenth Amendment, which provides that "all persons born in the United States . . . and subject to the jurisdiction thereof, are citizens of the United States."

It was this latter group, the Nisei, whose loyalties became a matter of special interest to a variety of government agencies once the United States went to war with Japan. The loyalties of the Issei were, of course, also a matter of concern, but they seemed to present little complexity: security officials simply presumed that the Issei, as enemy aliens, retained their loyalty to Japan. The FBI and the Office of Naval Intelligence (ONI) had surveilled the Issei in the years before World War II, and when the Japanese attacked at Pearl Harbor, the FBI quickly arrested any Issei who presented even the remotest risk of subversive action. The Nisei, however, as U.S. citizens, were not on the FBI's arrest lists. In the months and years that followed, security officials, concerned about potential subversive acts, looked to the loyalty of the Nisei as a proxy for their dangerousness, and looked largely to the degree of their perceived cultural assimilation as a proxy for their loyalty.[5]

The years leading up to Pearl Harbor saw the Nisei on a complex trajectory toward assimilation. Most Nisei attended predominantly white public schools, where they followed the standard curriculum and distinguished themselves with above-average grades and below-average truancy rates. They spoke English everywhere outside the home, including with other Nisei; many spoke as much English as they could even at home. They dressed exclusively in Western attire, as, indeed, did most of their immigrant parents. Many of the prewar memories of the Nisei resemble those of any American of that time period: school plays, homework, athletic events, dances, church functions, and the like.[6]

In addition, some of the key political and religious organizations that kept the Nisei's parents connected with Japan had decreasing influence in the years leading up to the war, especially among the Nisei. For example, the Japanese Associations, which had played an important role in the lives of the Issei in the first part of the twentieth century, meant little to the Nisei. Japanese Associations were quasi-governmental organizations in the major West Coast cities of the United States, formed under the auspices of the Japanese consulate, that performed bureaucratic functions for expatriate Japanese citizens, especially in matters dealing with immigration to the United States from Japan, travel to and from Japan, and the Japanese military draft. By the mid-1930s, most Issei had much less use for the Japanese Associations than they had had in earlier decades: American law had forbidden immigration from Japan in 1924, and the military draft was a diminishing concern for the aging Issei. S. Frank Miyamoto's 1939 study of Seattle's Japanese community reflects widespread disengagement from, and even disaffection toward, that city's Japanese Association.[7] Naturally, the Japanese Associations were largely irrelevant to most Nisei, who, as U.S. citizens, had no formal need at all for the Japanese bureaucratic functions the associations performed. Indeed, in the late 1920s, a handful of Nisei created a civil rights and social organization just for U.S. citizens called the Japanese American Citizens League (JACL). Ardently assimilationist in its rhetoric and program, the JACL grew in membership and influence throughout the 1930s.[8]

Similarly, a distinctively Japanese religious influence waned in the years leading up to the war. Roger Daniels has noted the "strong and striking propensity [of the Japanese] to adopt the religion of the local majority in their diaspora to the New World,"[9] and this was certainly the case in the American diaspora. Conversion to Christianity was quite common among Japanese families in the first part of the twentieth century. Even for those who did not convert from Buddhism, Christianity had an Americanizing influence on Buddhism, making it more and more Western in its practices.[10]

In basic ways, then, the prewar world of the Nisei resembled that of any other second-generation Americans in the process of assimilation. Yet there

Just two weeks before the Japanese attack at Pearl Harbor, the Japanese Association of Los Angeles holds its annual meeting. The Association has invited white businessmen to attend. Second from left is U.S. Navy commander Kenneth D. Ringle, a naval intelligence officer who would later evaluate the loyalty of the Japanese American community and consult with the War Relocation Authority. (Courtesy of University of Southern California, on behalf of the USC Specialized Libraries and Archival Collections.)

were also certain features of Nisei life that kept them connected to their parents' motherland—or would be seen by others as doing so.

Chief among these, for at least some of the Nisei, was dual American and Japanese citizenship. American law follows the principle of jus soli, which confers citizenship on anyone born in the United States. Thus, all Nisei were birthright citizens of the United States. Many of those born before 1924 were, however, also citizens of Japan. This is because Japanese law, at least until 1916, rigorously followed the principle of paternal jus sanguinis, under which any person born to a Japanese father was Japanese. Thus, a Nisei born before 1917 held both American and Japanese citizenship, unless he later renounced one or the other. In 1916, Japan amended its citizenship laws to permit young Nisei (or their parents or guardians) retroactively to renounce Japanese citizenship, and in 1924, Japan again amended its laws to abolish entirely the principle of automatic Japanese nationality for foreign-born children of Japanese fathers. After 1924, a Nisei obtained Japanese citizenship only if his parents applied for it with the Japanese government within fourteen days of his birth.[11] Many Nisei, of course, never even knew that they held Japanese citizenship. But whether they knew it or not, some number of Nisei—especially those born before 1924—held dual American and Japanese citizenship.[12]

Another aspect of life that was designed to sustain some sense of Japanese identity in the Nisei was the network of Japanese schools that some of them attended after their day at public school was over. These schools, funded partly by the Japanese government, offered instruction in Japanese language, history, and geography. In the 1930s, responding to growing concerns within the Issei community about reports of Nisei hooliganism, the schools also emphasized a program of moral education grounded in a sense of Japanese racial and cultural pride. Typically, students attended these schools for an hour or so each afternoon after public-school instruction concluded, and perhaps a few hours on Saturday mornings.[13]

The primary purpose of the schools was to help bridge the language gap that had opened between the Issei, many of whom spoke little English, and the Nisei, most of whom spoke little Japanese. Although the schools were designed to "instill a positive Japanese identity" in the students, they reflected a basic decision on the part of Issei Japanese educators and parents that the Nisei should be prepared for life in America rather than life in Japan, and that a strong "Japanese spirit" would be a benefit to the Nisei as they confronted American racism.[14] Issei parents undoubtedly hoped that a Japanese education would help the Nisei find jobs in the ethnic economy, where language and cultural skills would be an advantage. Much of the effort was, however, lost on many of the Nisei youngsters, who took to the extra hours of schooling with predictable boredom and disaffection. Attendance at these schools waned appreciably during the 1930s.[15]

The Issei's commitment to "Americanize" the Japanese experiences of their children also appeared in another after-school program in which some Nisei boys participated. These were Japanese martial arts programs—especially kendo, which is the art of Samurai swordsmanship, and judo, which is a form of wrestling. In Japan, these practices, especially kendo, were explicitly linked to Japanese military training and worship of the emperor. In the United States, however, the clubs, while typically funded at least in part by the Japanese government, toned down or even eliminated the attention to the emperor and focused instead on physical, moral, and spiritual development.[16]

Another point of contact between at least some Nisei (as well as most Issei) and Japan was financial. For the Issei, who were categorically excluded from U.S. citizenship, Japan's militarism in the 1930s and its conflict with China led to an upsurge in nationalist feeling. Many Issei expressed their patriotism by making donations and sending care packages to various Japanese military relief organizations.[17] Indeed, until it began to become clear that Japan was on a collision course with the United States, the Issei were quite competitive amongst themselves about their charitable donations.[18] Japanese-language newspapers along the West Coast would print lists of the names of donors; the pressures to contribute, especially for businessmen trying to maintain a good name in the Issei community, were strong.[19] Although most Nisei wanted nothing to do with Japan's military conflicts, the "atmosphere of hyperpatriotism" did lead some "Nisei adolescents and young adults to participate monetarily in the competition for distinction as well."[20] An additional financial link from Japanese America to Japan was the practice of many Issei to maintain what were called "fixed deposits"—essentially certificates of deposit—in American branches of Japanese banks.[21] Sometimes they held these accounts in their own names; sometimes they opened them in the names of or in trust for their U.S.-citizen children.

Perhaps the most direct connection to Japan that some Nisei had was the time that they spent there before the war. Or course, many Nisei—we do not know how many—never stepped foot in Japan; their families were too poor, too busy, or too disconnected from Japan to plan a trip. Some Nisei, however, traveled to Japan, either once or more frequently, to visit relatives, especially grandparents. Typically, however, these trips did not generate feelings of cultural attachment so much as they did alienation. Most Nisei children spoke little Japanese and were used to the manners and customs of the United States; they often found that their ways clashed with those of their relatives.[22]

An additional number of Nisei spent considerably longer periods of time in Japan before the war because they were sent there by their parents for some or all of their education. This group, a subset of the Nisei, came to be known by the term "Kibei."[23] Estimates of the numbers of Kibei—and there are only rough estimates, as no comprehensive records exist—have ranged in the vicinity of 15 percent of school-age Nisei, or around 11,000 Kibei at the time of the Pearl Harbor attack.[24] The question of why certain Issei parents chose to send some of their children to Japan for part or all of their education is, sadly, quite underresearched. The uncertainty of most Issei about how long they would remain in the United States must have persuaded some of them that it would be helpful if their children were comfortable in both cultures. Some primary evidence suggests that their reasons were more practical even than that: most Issei lived close to the economic edge in retail or farming and needed the full-time working hands of both parents in order to survive. Sending a child to stay with family in Japan for some or all of his education freed the child's mother to work, and was less expensive than raising him in America.[25]

The experiences of the Kibei, both in Japan and, for those who returned, in the United States, varied widely.[26] Some Kibei were so comfortable in Japan that they remained there for good.[27] Some Kibei reported feeling like outsiders in Japan, never fully accepted because of their American birth and early upbringing.[28] Many felt again like outsiders when they returned to the United States, not fully American due to their Japanese schooling and their weaker English language skills. Because they spoke Japanese well, it was Kibei who formed the core of the squad of linguists who served in the Pacific with the U.S. Army's Military Intelligence Service (MIS).[29] In sum, it is impossible to speak of a single Kibei experience. The only thing the Kibei truly had in common was a greater familiarity with Japanese language and culture than other Nisei.

The assimilation of the Nisei into the American mainstream was thus a somewhat complex picture in the years leading up to Pearl Harbor. In language, in dress, in education, in culture, most Nisei lived largely American lives. Yet they lived those lives against a backdrop of pervasive anti-Asian and, as Japanese militarism built in the 1930s, specifically anti-Japanese prejudice along the West Coast.[30] That prejudice, and the resistance of many whites to the idea that a person of Japanese ancestry could ever really be an American, led some Nisei to declare their Americanism with an almost evangelistic zeal. In early 1941, Mike Masaoka, president of the JACL, penned and announced the organization's creed, which committed Japanese Americans to a kind of super-patriotism, a fervent hope to be "a better American in a greater America."[31] Many Nisei were uncomfortable with the extravagance of the JACL's pronouncements and expressed their identity more quietly. A small but unknowable number of Nisei—primarily though not exclusively Kibei whose experiences in Japan had been both extensive and favorable— undoubtedly identified at least as strongly with Japanese culture and traditions as with American, if not more so.

3:

PRESUMED LOYAL,
PRESUMED DISLOYAL

IN THE MONTHS just before and just after the Pearl Harbor attack, decision-makers at the highest levels of the federal government had a reasonably good grasp of the degree of assimilation and feelings of allegiance among the West Coast's Nisei. It was a matter that had been studied—perhaps not scientifically, but studied nonetheless. In the fall of 1941, John Franklin Carter, a Roosevelt confidante, undertook an intelligence study of the "Japanese situation" on the West Coast at the president's secret behest. Carter hired Curtis B. Munson, a Republican businessman, to serve as his chief investigator. Munson traveled to the West Coast early in October 1941 and met intensively with Japanese Americans and others who knew the Japanese American community. Between October and early November, Munson and Carter sent the president a stream of reports, all of which reported that the Nisei as a group (but excepting the Kibei) were overwhelmingly loyal to the United States.

Munson's final report even attempted to quantify Nisei loyalty. While he claimed, without foundation, that there were "still Japanese in the United States who w[ould] tie dynamite around their waist and make a human bomb out of themselves," these were the rare exception. Japanese Americans were "universally estimated from 90 to 98% loyal to the United States if the Japanese educated element of the Kibei is excluded," Munson asserted. "They are pathetically eager to show this loyalty." Carter agreed with Munson; in his covering memorandum to Munson's report, Carter stated that while a "few" "Japanese in the United States" were dangerous, "[f]or the most part the local Japanese are loyal to the United States or, at worst, hope that by remaining quiet they can avoid concentration camps or irresponsible mobs."[1]

These views were consistent with those of Lt. Cdr. Kenneth D. Ringle, an officer in the Office of Naval Intelligence (ONI) who had spent considerable time both in Japan and in Southern California doing investigative work about Japanese espionage and the Japanese American community. Late in January of 1942, Ringle reported that while it was possible that both aliens and citizens would act treacherously, the likely number inclined to do so was only 3 percent of the total number of American Nikkei. Ringle was of the view that the government ought to take affirmative steps to bolster Nisei loyalty by engaging them in the war effort.[2]

The FBI took a remarkably similar view. In November of 1940, the FBI capped off its investigations into security in Hawaii with a lengthy report that depicted the Nisei (and even some Issei) as loyal to the United States. While the FBI saw an "inner circle" of relatively recently arrived aliens as a high-risk group, the agency reported "much less sympathy for Japan among either 'the local born Japanese or the alien Japanese who have been residing in the Hawaiian Islands for the greater part of their life-time.' "[3] Concerned that the Nisei, "presently believed by some to be loyal to the United States," might be susceptible to anti-American propaganda from Japan, the FBI made a proposal not unlike Ringle's—that the government organize Nisei into patriotic organizations in order to cement their American identity and allegiance.[4]

These, then, were the views of the various investigators and agencies charged with the duty of assessing the loyalty of the Nisei before the Japanese attack on Pearl Harbor. The opinions were not entirely uniform, and they did not depict the Nisei as presenting no security risk whatsoever. They did, however, agree that a substantial, even overwhelming, percentage of the Nisei were loyal to the land of their birth, and they agreed that it would be wise for the government to take steps to bolster Nisei loyalty.

The Japanese attack on Pearl Harbor on December 7, 1941, did not change the basic views of any of these investigators. In the weeks following the attack, John Franklin Carter and Curtis Munson continued to insist that most Nisei were loyal and stepped up their plea that the government engage the Nisei in the war effort. Kenneth Ringle of ONI voiced similar views in a report late in January of 1942. And throughout the Roosevelt administration's internal debate about the possible wholesale removal of the Nisei from the West Coast in January and February of 1942, J. Edgar Hoover of the FBI maintained that no mass action was necessary or advisable.[5]

Unfortunately, these were not the views on Nisei loyalty that determined the outcome of that internal debate. The views that determined the outcome were the U.S. Army's, crucial units of which saw Nisei loyalty in a remarkably different light—the light of pervasive racial suspicion.[6]

The army organization that ordered the wholesale exclusion of the Nisei from the West Coast was the Western Defense Command (WDC), the service command responsible for the defense of the West Coast of the United States.

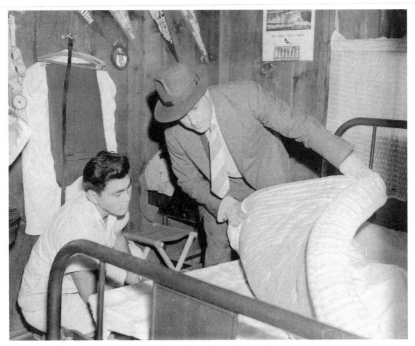

Not long after the Pearl Harbor attack, a law enforcement agent searches under a young Nisei's mattress at his home on Terminal Island, California. (From the Los Angeles Daily News Negatives [Collection 1387], Department of Special Collections, Charles E. Young Research Library, UCLA.)

President Roosevelt's Executive Order 9066, signed on February 19, 1942, conferred on Lt. Gen. John L. DeWitt, the WDC's commander, the power to remove any person from any military zone he might designate.[7] Within a month, DeWitt designated military zones encompassing the entire state of California, the western halves of Oregon and Washington, and the southern half of Arizona. When DeWitt proposed the exclusion of all American citizens of Japanese ancestry from those zones,[8] but not American citizens of Italian or German ancestry, he explained his focus on the Nisei in these terms: "In the war in which we are now engaged racial affinities are not severed by migration. *The Japanese race is an enemy race* and while many second and third generation Japanese born on United States soil, possessed of United States citizenship, have become 'Americanized,' *the racial strains are undiluted*. . . . It, therefore, follows that along the Pacific Coastal Frontier over 112,000 potential enemies, of Japanese extraction, are at large today."[9]

About a year later, when DeWitt filed a final report justifying the wholesale exclusion of the Nisei from the West Coast, he again spoke of Nisei loyalty in strictly racial terms. He explained that "the continued presence of a large, unassimilated, tightly knit and racial group, bound to an enemy nation by strong ties of race, culture, custom and religion along a frontier vulnerable to attack constituted a menace which had to be dealt with."[10] DeWitt made clear that the mass exclusion was necessary not because he had lacked time to determine who was loyal and who was not but because Japanese race and culture made it impossible to conclude that *any* American of Japanese ancestry really was loyal:

> Because of the ties of race, the intense feeling of filial piety and the strong bonds of common tradition, culture and customs, [the Japanese] population [on the West Coast] presented a tightly-knit racial group. . . . While it is believed that some were loyal, it was known that many were not. It was impossible to establish the identity of the loyal and the disloyal with any degree of safety. It was not there was insufficient time in which to make such a determination; it was simply a matter of facing the realities that a positive determination could not be made, that an exact separation of the "sheep from the goats" was unfeasible.[11]

It is hard to imagine a more bluntly racial indictment of the loyalty of Japanese Americans than DeWitt's.[12]

Seeing Japanese American loyalty through a thick racial lens was nothing new for the U.S. Army. In a basic way, DeWitt's analysis was an echo of the approach that the Hawaiian branch of Army Intelligence (G-2) had taken nine years earlier in a report titled "Estimate of the Situation—Japanese Population in Hawaii." According to that report, "[b]oth first- and second-generation Japanese in Hawaii . . . displayed Japanese 'racial traits' such as 'moral inferiority' to whites, fanaticism, duplicity, and arrogance." People of Japanese ancestry "resisted Americanization, while Japanese schools and churches inculcated their loyalty to the militarists in Japan." The report's author despaired that as Hawaii's ethnically Japanese population grew, "the territory would lose all its American character."[13]

Views like General DeWitt's did not disappear within the army after Japanese Americans were gone from the coast. In 1943, when Japanese Americans were being considered for release from their internment camps and for employment in plants engaged in war production, the army's Provost Marshal General's Office (PMGO) had the responsibility of training the men who would investigate their loyalty. In the training, the PMGO's expert on Japanese psychology explained to the investigator trainees that "this segment of our population is so completely disassociated from the way of life which is normally considered American that it can be profitably approached by the investigator only after considerable preparation and study of its peculiar culture and philosophy." That study would reveal to the trainees that they were "dealing with one member of a race which has on many occasions demonstrated its capacity for deceit. You can also be assured that far too great a number of the members of that race present in this country are admittedly, and in many cases, actively disloyal." The instructor explained that "in this class of cases, [U.S.] citizenship bears no relationship to the Subject's loyalty."[14]

This was a strong message indeed—that the American citizenship of the Nisei bore *no* relationship whatsoever to their loyalty. And the PMGO clung to that theory throughout the remainder of the war. When the PMGO's Japanese-American Branch filed its final report on its wartime work late in 1945, it continued to maintain that "[b]y Japanese tradition, customs and ethics, the family was so closely bound into one unit that loyalty and disloyalty was [sic] common to a family regardless of the citizenship of the individual members." It acknowledged that "[l]egally and constitutionally, a presumption of loyalty follows citizenship." But "among the Japanese," the PMGO's Japanese-American Branch insisted, "loyalty followed families."[15]

To be sure, the view of Japanese Americans as genetically untrustworthy and racially unassimilable was not unique to the American military. These sorts of views were in fact rather common in the United States in the early to mid-twentieth century. This was an era in which highly racialized extensions of Darwinian theory had captured broad segments of American society. Racial nativists had spent decades arguing for the racial superiority of certain categories of white people and the corresponding inferiority of people of African, Asian, and Southern and Eastern European descent. American scientists in the field of eugenics were exploring the claimed heritability of not only physical traits but also intelligence, mental illness, and proclivities to various sorts of disapproved behaviors. In this context, General DeWitt's assertion that the "Japanese race" was an "enemy race" was notable more for its succinctness than its aberrance.[16]

Whatever may have been the truth about Nisei loyalty, and whatever may have been the understanding of Nisei loyalty among investigators at the FBI and the ONI and among the president's confidential advisers, a very different view led to the mass exclusion of the Nisei from the West Coast. That view saw the Nisei as an unassimilable group of native-born foreigners, individuals whose "racial traits" and family bonds prevented them from forming true loyalty to the United States. As the Nisei were forced from their West Coast homes in the spring of 1942 and into government camps, they were a group of American citizens—indeed, the *only* group of American citizens—who were presumed disloyal.

THE CONSEQUENCES OF the army's presumption of dis-
loyalty were severe. The presumption led all of the Nisei in General DeWitt's
exclusion zone—more than 70,000 American citizens, of whom nearly
40,000 were over the age of eighteen—into so-called assembly centers.[1]
Without charges, without proof, without hearings, and with only a few days'
to a few weeks' notice, they were herded into makeshift barracks at racetracks
and fairgrounds in and near the major West Coast cities. There they spent the
summer of 1942 under the jurisdiction and control of the Wartime Civilian
Control Administration (WCCA), a largely civilian-staffed agency set up within the army's Western Defense Command (WDC).[2]

The matter did not end there. After just a few months, the presumption of
Nisei disloyalty soon dragged them deeper into detention. Over the course of
the summer of 1942, control of the evacuated people shifted from the WCCA
to the War Relocation Authority (WRA), a civilian agency wholly outside the
military that the Roosevelt administration had created in March of 1942 to
oversee the relocation of Japanese Americans.[3] Hoping to avoid a long-term
incarceration of the Nikkei, Milton Eisenhower, the WRA's first director,
proposed at a conference in Salt Lake City in April of 1942 that the Nikkei be
resettled from the assembly centers into open-gated agricultural communities or subsistence homesteads in the mountain west. The governors of the
mountain states, however, would have none of it. For example, Governor
Chase Clark of Idaho, admitting that he "didn't know which [Japanese
Americans] to trust and so therefore [didn't] trust any of them," demanded
at the Salt Lake City conference that the government keep any Japanese
people whom it shipped into Idaho behind barbed wire and under military
guard. The governor of Wyoming was blunter still: Eisenhower's plan, he
said, would lead to "Japs hanging from every pine tree" in the state; confinement was the only acceptable solution. Faced with this sort of opposition,
the WRA realized that it had no choice but to abandon its hope for Civilian
Conservation Corps–type camps and build camps for prolonged detention

under military guard.[4] Thus, by summer's end, the government scattered the Nisei (as well as their Issei parents) across ten permanent "relocation centers" in eastern California, Idaho, Wyoming, Colorado, Utah, Arizona, and Arkansas.[5]

To the Nisei, this must have looked like the end of the line. They were crammed into tarpaper barracks, behind barbed wire, and under armed military guard in some of the nation's most desolate and inclement locations. And all of this had come about because of a simple racial presumption that they were disloyal. But as it happened, the government was only beginning its consideration of Nisei loyalty, not ending it. No sooner had the Nisei set foot in the ten camps than complex pressures began to arise for both their release and their closer confinement.

Pressures for Freedom

The chief pressures for freedom were economic, military, and legal. The economic pressures were quite simple: the internees were now living near farms that had lots of crops (especially sugar beets) in the ground and not enough human hands to harvest them. This was a need that had emerged as early as May of 1942, when Japanese Americans were still in the WCCA assembly centers. Sugar beet producers, seeing the incarcerated Nisei as a huge pool of cheap labor, began lobbying the federal government intensively for help. When the White House got involved on the growers' behalf, WCCA and the WRA acceded to their demands and began issuing furloughs—first in small numbers from the assembly centers, and later, as the fall harvest approached, in large numbers from the relocation centers. By the end of 1942, about ten thousand people had left the assembly and relocation centers on temporary furloughs for agricultural work—without, it bears mentioning, any sort of security incident.[6] The irony here was stark: farmers in the very states that had demanded the incarceration of the supposedly untrustworthy and disloyal Nisei were now reaping the benefit of their labor.[7]

The military pressures on the presumption of Nisei disloyalty were a bit more subtle. On January 5, 1942, in a move that the most Nisei found quite insulting, the military shifted all American citizens of Japanese ancestry into the draft category for enemy aliens. Then, on June 17, 1942, the military declared all Nisei to be unacceptable for service in the armed forces, "except as may be authorized in special cases." In short order, however, it became apparent to the army's Military Intelligence Service (MIS) that the army would have trouble fighting Japan effectively without people who could speak some Japanese. Thus, beginning in mid-1942, the MIS quietly sent

Two Nisei women at the Amache Relocation Center in Colorado discuss potential employment with a representative of the WRA's Employment Division. (Courtesy of The Bancroft Library, University of California, Berkeley, 1967.014 v.9 AE-749.)

recruiting teams to the ten WRA relocation centers to enlist volunteers with strong Japanese language skills. Ironically, the most desirable internees were those for whom the military harbored the strongest presumption of disloyalty, the Kibei, who had gotten much of their education in Japan. By the end of 1942, 167 young men had quietly left the camps for training and service with the MIS.[8]

At around the same time, and at least as quietly, the military was internally debating the merits of a broader reopening of the military to Japanese Americans. Restoration of military service for the Nisei had been an article of faith for the Japanese American Citizens League (JACL) from the moment the military had suspended it. The JACL saw no quicker and more persuasive way to prove Nisei loyalty to a doubting public than the example of Nisei military sacrifice. By the fall of 1942, the JACL's lobbying efforts had garnered the support of top WRA officials and of Assistant Secretary of War

John J. McCloy, all of whom pushed hard to persuade others in the War Department to accept Japanese Americans back into the service. These efforts to reopen the military to Japanese Americans conflicted quite sharply with the presumption of disloyalty that had landed the Nisei in the camps in the first place—something that General DeWitt lost no time in pointing out to his superiors.[9]

The legal pressures on the presumption of disloyalty were the most subtle of all. Yet they also may have been the most powerful. After the disastrous Salt Lake City conference in April of 1942, at which the western governors had demanded the incarceration of the Nikkei, it became clear to WRA officials that they were going to have to implement and oversee a program not of assisted resettlement but of out-and-out detention. Stated more simply, they were to be jailers. This policy had important legal ramifications: it invited the incarcerated Nisei to file lawsuits against the WRA seeking their release through writs of habeas corpus.[10] And those lawsuits quickly came: one brought by Mary Asaba Ventura in April of 1942, one brought by Mistuye Endo in June of 1942, and one brought by Ernest and Toki Wakayama in August of 1942.[11]

Lawyers in the WRA's legal department immediately saw the risk that a successful habeas corpus challenge would torpedo the agency's work. As early as April 22, 1942—a moment before many of the Nikkei had even been ordered to leave their West Coast homes—a top WRA lawyer was already issuing a call within the agency for "the collection of facts that would be of value as evidence in litigation involving the constitutionality of detaining citizen Japanese."[12] Defeating a habeas challenge was a top WRA priority.

One way to accomplish that was to design its detention program in a way that would have the greatest chance of surviving judicial review. This was a luxury that WRA officials had because the agency was designing its program at the very same moment that its lawyers were worrying about defending it. And the lawyers' idea was to insist that the WRA's detention policies should include provisions that would permit many Nisei to leave WRA custody. "I cannot urge upon you too strongly the necessity for promulgating our furlough regulations on the most liberal basis," Assistant WRA Solicitor Maurice Walk wrote to Solicitor Philip M. Glick in July of 1942. "A wholesale detention" of the kind that WRA was contemplating, Walk argued, "would only be acceptable if promptly thereafter procedures were instituted for releasing [loyal and nondangerous internees] from custody." A furlough program—or a program permitting "leave," as the WRA ultimately came to call it—was, Walk argued, "essential . . . to gain judicial acceptance of our program."[13]

To be sure, many WRA officials wanted a furlough policy partly because they wished to minimize the harmful impact of the detention program on the Japanese American community. They were also concerned about creating a culture of government dependency in the Japanese American community. Abe Fortas, undersecretary of the interior, made this point bluntly when he explained in March of 1944 that the department did not want policies that would leave it with "another Indian problem on [its] hands."[14] But in a basic way, the WRA's furlough policies also reflected a cool, lawyerly calculation of the degree of freedom that might help persuade a court to uphold the WRA's detention program.

Pressures for Confinement

These pressures for freedom were not the only ones building in the fall of 1942. Balanced against them were powerful pressures for continued and even closer confinement of the Nisei. These came from the public, from politicians, and even from within the WRA itself.

Some of the political pressures came from the towns that neighbored the Japanese American relocation centers. For example, in May of 1943, the town councils of Cody and Powell, Wyoming, which sat just northeast and just southwest of the Heart Mountain Relocation Center, passed a joint resolution demanding that "the visiting of the Japanese in the Towns of Powell and Cody be held to an absolute minimum"—except insofar as their confinement would interfere with or discourage "those Japanese on temporary leave who are engaged in gainful employment essential to the war effort, and particularly necessary labor on ranches and farms."[15] As the historian Roger Daniels has noted, this attitude of Heart Mountain's neighbors toward the camp's residents translated to "work them when we need them, but don't give them any privileges."[16] This mistrustful and restricting stance toward the internees was common in all of the states that hosted relocation centers. It might seem odd that these communities would insist on conditions approaching lockdown at the camps when internee labor and internee resource consumption were buoying their economies.[17] But in the local debates about freedom of movement for the internees, racial suspicion of the disloyalty and danger of the internees generally prevailed.

Pressure to restrict rather than restore the liberty of the internees also came from the press and, perhaps not unrelatedly, from politicians. Poorly researched articles occasionally appeared in newspapers across the country, alleging that the WRA was mismanaging the centers and "coddling" and "pampering" the internees.[18] These articles invariably triggered outbursts of public anger at both the internees and the WRA. So too did news of violent disturbances and strikes at two of the WRA camps—the Poston Relocation Center in November of 1942 and at the Manzanar Relocation Center in early December of 1942. Although these incidents were the culmination of long-simmering tensions between the internees and the camp administrators, and indeed among the internees themselves, the nation's newspapers chose to depict them principally as outbursts of disloyalty and anti-Americanism. The conflict at Manzanar, which came to a head on December 6, 1943, was falsely described as a "celebration" of the anniversary of the Pearl Harbor attack.[19]

Predictably, these incidents and the incendiary press coverage led politicians into the fray. By September of 1943, two different congressional committees had concluded highly publicized investigations of the camps and the WRA.[20] The first of these, by a Senate military affairs subcommittee headed by Kentucky senator Albert B. ("Happy") Chandler, was at least modestly fair in its inquiries and conclusions; the second, a subcommittee of the House of Representatives Subcommittee on Un-American Activities headed by Representative Martin Dies of Texas, was rather more of a witch hunt.[21] Both committees, however, reached at least one common conclusion: the disloyal internees at the camps should be separated, or "segregated," from the rest of the population and interned separately.[22]

As it happened, segregation of the disloyal was an idea that had been circulating within the WRA and the military since the spring of 1942. Kenneth Ringle, the navy intelligence officer who had so closely studied the Japanese American community before the outbreak of war, was detailed to the WRA for a short time in mid-1942 to assist the agency in developing a plan for the uprooted Japanese Americans. In his report to the WRA of June 19, 1942, Ringle recommended the segregation of two groups of internees: those Issei who maintained strong ties with Japan and those Kibei who had studied for more than three years in Japan after reaching the age of thirteen.[23] The WRA went so far as to debate Ringle's proposal at an agency conference, but it concluded that Ringle's categorical treatment of Issei, Kibei, and Nisei was insufficiently sensitive to the range and complexity of their real views as individuals. The agency therefore tabled the subject of segregation for further study.[24]

This did not satisfy General DeWitt of the WDC, who responded by circulating an elaborate segregation proposal of his own. Sensitivity to the range and complexity of Nikkei loyalty was decidedly not a feature of De-Witt's proposal. He suggested a complete military lockdown of huge categories of Issei, Kibei, and Nisei, including any person "evaluated by the intelligence service as potentially dangerous." Segregated individuals were to be denied the privilege of sending or receiving communications to or from the outside world. And "suitable security measures" were to be in place to prevent what General DeWitt saw as "*probable* rioting and . . . bloodshed."[25] The WRA's top lawyer was horrified by DeWitt's segregation plan, opining that it "treated the evacuees as though they were so many blocks of wood." WRA director Dillon Myer agreed, and rejected it.[26]

That was not the end of the matter of segregation, however. While the WRA bristled at the suggestions that were coming from the military, what the WRA objected to was more their source than their substance. As it happened, in late 1942 and early 1943, WRA was deep in internal discussion about its own ideas for segregating and more closely confining some of the internees. Interestingly, however, the impetus to segregate came from the bottom up, rather than the top down. Dillon Myer was skeptical about the idea of separating out a subset of difficult internees from the general population; he believed that a better method for sifting the internee population was to try to get as many "good" internees as possible to *leave* the camps, so that they would "no longer be [WRA's] problem," rather than facing the complexities of forcing "bad" ones deeper into detention at special segregation camps.[27]

The staff of Myer's ten relocation centers, however, felt otherwise. They had camps the size of small cities to run, and internees they called "troublemakers," "problem boys," and "incorrigibles" made their lives difficult.[28] Some of these difficult cases were people with pro-Japanese sympathies, but many were just "agitators"—people whom administrators found "obstructive" to the smooth running of the camps.[29] They were, as Dillon Myer candidly admitted in September of 1943, "people who[ ] we consider trouble makers but whom . . . we don't have enough evidence to take into Civil Courts."[30] By mid-1943, the WRA's management realized that a formal program of segregation would allow the project directors to rid their camps of their troublemakers while at the same time emphasizing to the outside world that the internees whom the WRA was releasing from the relocation centers for jobs in the interior were truly trustworthy. For these reasons, the WRA acceded to the military's demand for a program of segregation, ultimately determining that the Tule Lake Relocation Center should be converted to use as a segregation center.[31]

Freedom, Confinement, and Loyalty

It should now be clear that the Japanese Americans in the WRA's relocation centers in late 1942 and early 1943 sat at the convergence point of many conflicting pressures toward both freedom and confinement. A broad presumption of Nisei disloyalty had landed them behind barbed wire in mid-1942. But some in the WRA, the military, and the public at large were pressing for the possibility of at least selective release, while others were demanding continued incarceration and selective segregation.

What all of these pressures had in common, however, was their vocabulary: all debate about freedom or confinement for the Nisei became a discussion about Nisei loyalty. As noted earlier, when General DeWitt ordered the exclusion of the Nisei from the West Coast in March of 1942, he had grounded his order on a presumption of Nisei disloyalty. This was also the view of Secretary of War Henry Stimson in May of 1943, more than a full year later. Writing to Dillon Myer about the worrisome "deterioration in evacuee morale" that the camps had recently seen, Stimson attributed the problem to rampant and spreading disloyalty. "This unsatisfactory development," Stimson wrote, "appears to be the result in large measure of the activities of a vicious well-organized, pro-Japanese minority group to be found at each relocation project. Through agitation and by violence, these groups gained control of many aspects of internal project administration, so much so that it became disadvantageous, and sometimes dangerous, to express loyalty to the United States." For Stimson, the internees fell into two groups—one that consisted of the "loyal," and another that consisted of "disloyal" "troublemakers" with "Japanese sympathies."[32]

Responding to Stimson, Myer objected to what he saw as Stimson's gross oversimplification of the situation in the camps. "I have known for some time," he wrote to Stimson in June of 1943, "that the Western Defense Command held [this] point of view on th[ese] questions . . . but I had not realized until I read your letter . . . that the point of view of the Western Defense Command on these questions appears to be settled War Department opinion." "The real cause of bad evacuee morale," Myer quite plausibly insisted, was not pro-Japanese agitation but "evacuation and all the losses, insecurity, and frustration it entailed, plus the continual 'drum drum' of certain harbingers of hate and fear whose expressions appear in the public press or are broadcast over the radio."[33] In light of these complex influences on Nisei attitudes, Myer appeared to argue, the military's single-minded focus on internee "disloyalty" did not capture the reality of the Nisei experience.

But even the WRA ultimately could not escape focusing on loyalty and disloyalty as the central determinants of Nisei freedom or confinement. This is clearly seen in an important exchange of letters between Scott Rowley, the project attorney at the Poston Relocation Center in Arizona, and Morton Glick, the WRA's solicitor in Washington, D.C., in mid-1944. Rowley wrote to Glick for clarification on the appropriate basis for denying an internee permission to leave Poston indefinitely for a job. Camp administrators at Poston could not agree with one another about what "loyalty" meant, whether a Nisei who preferred neither an American nor a Japanese victory in the war thereby declared himself "disloyal," or whether disloyalty was even an intelligible and appropriate standard for denying someone his freedom. Some administrators felt that disloyalty was too nebulous a concept to support an important decision about detention and that "probable danger to national security" could be the only valid basis for detaining an internee.[34]

The WRA solicitor's answer was telling. It was true, Glick admitted, that the most important concern was the risk that an internee posed to national security. But as a practical matter, loyalty and security risk reduced to the same thing: "Elusive though the actual concept of loyalty is," wrote Glick, "the essential core of its meaning, as we use it in talking about 'disloyal' and 'loyal' evacuees and as the public, I am sure, comprehends it, is the security factor—these persons are 'safe' or 'unsafe.'" Glick explained that an internee who showed "love for or belief in this country's institutions" and American "cultural assimilation" was entitled to "an inference of lack of potential danger." On the other hand, the opposite inference was due to an internee who showed "love for or belief in Japan's way of life" or "sympathy with her war aims, or strong disaffection toward the United States."[35]

To be sure, the WRA phrased its regulations for granting and denying furloughs to internees in broad language; the agency did not come out and say that loyalty was the linchpin of its policies. But this did not fool anyone— least of all Maurice Walk, the attorney who had been the WRA's first deputy solicitor. Walk was the youngest son of Lithuanian immigrants who came to the United States in 1893 to help build the World's Fair. After graduating from the University of Chicago Law School in 1921, he had served a five-year stint with the Foreign Service and then opened a corporate law practice in Chicago. Early in 1942, Walk had signed on as the WRA's deputy solicitor and had played a significant role in the agency's early work. By the end of 1942, however, Glick had decided to return to private practice but agreed to stay on as WRA solicitor Philip Glick's consultant on litigation.[36]

One of the most important tasks that Glick assigned to Walk was to draft the WRA's briefs supporting its detention policies in several cases before the

United States Supreme Court, including *Korematsu v. United States*[37] and *Ex parte Endo*.[38] But the task of building a legal theory for detaining allegedly disloyal citizens proved too much for Walk, and he resigned his consultant's position over the matter in September of 1943. "I am unable to collaborate in the defense of a policy of which I so strongly disapprove," Walk wrote in his letter of resignation. "The notions of 'segregation' and 'disloyalty' around which the [WRA's] program has been conceived," Walk maintained, "would, if allowed by the Courts, become the juristic formulation in terms of which future Fascist persecution of racial and political minorities will be justified." Walk argued that loyalty and disloyalty were not "terms of legal art at all" but "propaganda epithets, weapons of political eulogy and vituperation."[39]

Glick objected to Walk's strongly worded charges and initially declined to accept his resignation. He tried to persuade Walk that the WRA's basis for segregating internees was technically the risk they posed to national security rather than their disloyalty.[40] Walk, however, saw through Glick's defense. "The sworn testimony of the Project Directors [at the ten WRA camps] as to their actual procedure would show that they are segregating on their own finding of disloyalty pursuant to explicit instructions from the [WRA]." And so Walk reemphasized his desire to resign, saying that he wanted no part of "a doctrinal formulation of the executive power summarily to detain in terms of disloyalty" that "would be profoundly responsive to the fascist mentality of our times."[41]

Walk's rhetoric was perhaps a touch histrionic, but his vision was clear. Strong forces were pushing the interned Nisei toward both greater liberty and deeper confinement, and the WRA had allowed the military's simple-minded dialectic of loyalty and disloyalty to define and regulate those pressures.

THE LOYALTY
QUESTIONNAIRES OF 1943

BY THE END of 1942, these and other pressures on the internees began to tear at the surface of calm that lay over the WRA's relocation centers. In mid-November, internal tensions at the Poston Relocation Center in Arizona led to a widely publicized general strike. A few weeks later, the Manzanar Relocation Center in California erupted in demonstrations. In 1943, the government began to open vents to relieve these pressures. They were vents pointing in opposite directions—toward release from camp for some internees, and toward deeper confinement, and ultimately toward Japan, for others. The criterion of selection was the troubled concept of loyalty—and for that reason, the vents ended up building at least as much pressure as they relieved.

The first of the vents that began to open was the War Relocation Authority's furlough or "leave" program. As noted earlier, as early as the spring of 1942, the WRA had allowed a relatively small number of internees to leave camp on what came to be called "seasonal" leave in order to help local farmers with the fall harvest. On October 1, 1942, the WRA's first comprehensive regulations on the granting of leave took effect. These regulations envisioned three kinds of furloughs from camp: "short-term leave," which was to allow an internee to leave camp briefly to attend to personal affairs; "seasonal leave," which was to permit an internee to leave camp for short-duration agricultural work; and "indefinite leave," which was to permit an internee to leave camp in order to accept a permanent job offer in a community outside the West Coast where his presence was acceptable. Before granting any of these sorts of leave to an internee, the WRA initially asked the FBI to check its records for any "derogatory" information on the applicant. The FBI record check, however, took a very long time and was quite cumbersome, and as a result, very few internees took advantage of the leave procedures. By the end of 1942, internees had filed only 2,200 leave applications, camp administrators had granted only 250 of them, and only 193 of the successful internees had actually left camp. The leave process was floundering in a sea of administrative inefficiencies, as well as internee anxiety about what might greet them on the outside.[1]

Early in 1943, the WRA decided to press for what it called "all out" relocation—a strategy of vigorously pressing as many internees as possible to leave camp for the country's interior.[2] The agency developed several strategies to encourage internees to strike out on their own. It began setting up a network of "relocation offices" in cities throughout the country (except along the West Coast) to help internees find jobs and housing. It began offering cash grants to needy internees who were going out of the centers on indefinite leave.[3] And most importantly, it decided to insist that every internee fill out an "application for leave clearance." This was a four-page questionnaire that sought information that would allow the WRA to decide whether an internee was loyal enough to be trusted outside of camp. Every adult internee—Nisei and Issei—was expected to fill one out, regardless of whether he or she actually wished to leave camp for a new job and a new home away from the West Coast.

This last strategy for pressing internees to leave camp came about more or less by accident, as a consequence of a coincidental overlap of WRA and military policy in early 1943. It so happened that while the WRA was beginning to press for "all out" relocation, the army was opening up a second vent for internees, or at least for the subset of the internees who were Nisei men of military age. This vent was the option of Nisei military service.

Reopening the military to Japanese Americans had taken a lot of time and effort. As early as the middle of 1942, Assistant Secretary of War John McCloy, WRA director Dillon Myer, and the Japanese American Citizens League had all begun urging the army to return the Nisei to "1-A" status under the Selective Training and Service Act of 1940 and to reopen the draft. But General DeWitt at the Western Defense Command (WDC) did not like the idea of Nisei military service at all. He understood that the army could not possibly accept soldiers from the camps unless it first took visible steps to assure itself and the public that the soldiers were loyal Americans. He quickly understood that some sort of loyalty screening of the internees in the camps would be necessary—and this presented an exquisitely difficult problem for him. He had ordered the mass exclusion of Japanese Americans from the coast in the spring of 1942 on the basis that it was impossible to determine the loyalty of Japanese Americans. On the strength of this conviction of General DeWitt's, the War Department had uprooted everyone, and the government had spent many millions of dollars building and running assembly and relocation centers.

Now, less than a year later, the government was contemplating the very sort of screening that General DeWitt had maintained was impossible, and this angered and worried him and his staff. "I don't see how they can determine the loyalty of a Jap by interrogation . . . or investigation," DeWitt fumed in a telephone conversation with Allen Gullion, the army's provost marshal general. "There isn't such a thing as a loyal Japanese and it is just impossible to determine their loyalty by investigation—it just can't be done." Colonel Karl Bendetsen, an officer from the Provost Marshal General's Office (PMGO) who became one of DeWitt's top legal assistants and an architect of the plan to evict Japanese Americans from the West Coast in the spring of 1942, fretted about the public relations disaster that he saw looming for the WDC. He worried that if the military now took the position that the loyalty of Japanese Americans could be ascertained, the public would demand to know why the government had spent "80 million dollars to build relocation centers" rather than screening the Japanese American population in the spring of 1942. And he saw no way for the military to screen the internees without admitting that the WDC's "ideas on the Oriental ha[d] been all cock-eyed" and that "maybe he isn't inscrutable" after all.[4]

The WDC's opposition to Nisei military service did not block the project entirely, but it did force something of a compromise. Rather than reopening the draft and assigning Nisei draftees to units throughout the army, which is what the WRA wanted, the army agreed only to allow Japanese Americans to volunteer into the service, and it insisted that the Nisei would be permitted to serve in a segregated Nisei battalion. The army announced this decision on January 20, 1943, and began making plans to send recruitment teams to the ten WRA relocation centers in February. The personnel division hoped that the recruitment drive would net more than 3,500 volunteers out of about 10,000 eligible Nisei in the camps.[5]

To facilitate recruitment, the army decided to equip its recruitment teams with questionnaires probing the background and loyalty of Nisei of military age. But when administrators at the WRA learned that the army was planning to canvas the relocation centers for recruits, and to distribute loyalty questionnaires, they recognized that this presented a perfect opportunity to bolster the WRA's nascent "all out" relocation program. The WRA therefore asked that the military teams distribute loyalty questionnaires not just to draft-age men in the camps but to all adult internees. If all internees were screened for loyalty, WRA officials reasoned, it would be that much easier to engineer their departures on leave.[6]

Screening tens of thousands of internees for loyalty to the United States

A group of Nisei at the Amache Relocation Center in Colorado listen to an army officer's presentation about the loyalty questionnaires they were expected to complete in February of 1943. (Courtesy of The Bancroft Library, University of California, Berkeley, 1967.014 v.9 AE-749.)

was obviously a major undertaking, and it also reflected a major commitment to cooperation between the WRA and the military. That commitment to cooperation was most clearly embodied in a new interagency council that the War Department created late in January of 1943 when it announced the imminent loyalty investigations of all internees in the centers. The January 20 directive, issued by the Adjutant General's Office in the War Department, announced that "[a] plan ha[d] been formulated whereby the War Department w[ould], upon request of the War Relocation Authority, assist in determining the loyalty of American citizens of Japanese ancestry under [WRA] jurisdiction." Under that plan, "[a] Joint Board . . . , composed of a representative of the Federal Bureau of Investigation, Office of Naval Intelligence, War Relocation Authority, Assistant Chief of Staff, G-2, War Department General Staff, and The Provost Marshal General w[ould] be created." This Japanese American Joint Board (JAJB) would have two main responsibilities: it would make recommendations to the WRA "concerning the release of . . . individuals from relocation centers on indefinite leave," and it would "state whether the Joint Board ha[d] any objection to the employment in plants and facilities important to the war effort of any of those American citizens of Japanese ancestry who [were] released by the War Relocation Authority pursuant to its recommendation."[7]

Once the WRA and the military joined forces to bring about the mass loyalty screening of all adult internees, the process moved forward with stunning speed. A mere two weeks after the January 20, 1943, directive, teams of military personnel fanned out to the ten WRA relocation centers to start the process, which came to be known as "registration."[8] They went equipped with two very similar questionnaires—the "DSS-304A" for draft-age Nisei and the "WRA-126" for female Nisei and all Issei. The forms were, in all important respects, identical. In addition to seeking basic biographical information about the internees, the questionnaires asked them to report on whether they had relatives in Japan, the extent of any education in Japan, whether and when they had taken trips to Japan, what sorts of organizations (Japanese and non-Japanese) they affiliated with, whether they held dual citizenship, and the like.[9]

Those questions were, for the most part, uncontroversial. Two others, however, were anything but uncontroversial. Question 27 on the forms asked the internee, if he was a draft-age Nisei, whether he was "willing to serve in the armed forces of the United States on combat duty, wherever ordered." Question 28, in its initial format, asked all internees (including the Issei) whether they would "swear unqualified allegiance to the United States of America and forswear any form of allegiance or obedience to the Japanese emperor, or any other foreign government, power or organization." When outraged Issei internees pointed out that Question 28 was asking them effectively to render themselves stateless, the WRA changed the language of Question 28 for the Issei to inquire whether they would "swear to abide by the laws of the United States and to take no action which would in any way interfere with the war effort of the United States."[10]

The anxiety, confusion, and anger that these questions unleashed in the internees have been extensively documented in the literature.[11] Many internees feared that by making them fill out a form called an "application for leave clearance," the WRA was planning to force them out on their own whether they were able to fend for themselves or not. Many of the young Nisei men believed, not unreasonably, that Question 27 was a trick—an underhanded way to get them to volunteer into the army without realizing they were doing so. The question was especially worrisome and confusing to fathers of young children and to sons of elderly or infirm Issei parents; many of these Nisei believed that they had good reason not to have to serve, and feared that the question was tricking them into waiving their objections. The head of one recruitment team reported bluntly to the Office of the Assistant Secretary of War in mid-February that "little information [could] be gained from the answer to question #27, regardless of what that answer may be," because the Nisei were so "confused in their own minds" that the recruiters could not "explain the question to them in such a manner as to secure a sound answer."[12]

Question 28 was no less angering and distressing. Many Issei were so unsettled by the original phrasing of the question that they could not bring themselves to trust that the amended language meant what the government said it meant. And worst of all, many Nisei were outraged by Question 28's clear insinuation that they had ever had an allegiance to the Japanese emperor that they could "forswear" or renounce.[13]

Both the military and the WRA had rushed headlong into the registration program, with the military expecting some 3,500 volunteers and the WRA expecting a flood of certifiably loyal internees rushing out of the camps. But by any measure, the registration program was a disaster. First, rather than dissipating tensions in the camps, the registration program fanned them. The reaction was the most severe at the Tule Lake Relocation Center, where huge sections of the camp dug in their heels and refused to fill out the registration forms. The standoff at Tule Lake grew so intense in one block of barracks that camp administrators called in military policemen to arrest and jail several dozen young resisters.[14] Resistance and noncompliance were less widespread at most of the other camps but were still far greater than anything either the military or the WRA had expected. Every WRA camp "was the scene of many mass meetings among evacuees, of impassioned speeches by evacuees stirred by one issue or another which registration raised."[15]

Second, from the standpoint of military recruitment, registration was a failure as well. Only 805 young men volunteered at the ten WRA camps. More than a quarter of these volunteers came from a single camp, the Minidoka Relocation Center, where registration had gone comparatively smoothly. At the Heart Mountain Relocation Center, home at the time of registration to nearly 11,000 internees, only thirty-eight men signed up for military service.[16]

Third, the registration process was accompanied and followed by an explosion of internee requests for repatriation to Japan (in the case of Issei) and expatriation to Japan (in the case of Nisei). In January of 1943, the month before registration, only fifty-two internees asked for repatriation or expatriation. In February, however, the number shot up by a factor of *nineteen* to 987 people. The number stayed at around that level in March, and then

Page 4 of George Ochikubo's "registration" form, submitted February 18, 1943. Questions 27 and 28 appear toward the bottom of the form. (National Archives [College Park, Maryland], Record Group 60, File 146-42-107, series 1. Courtesy of National Archives.)

climbed again in April to 1,514 internees—almost thirty times the number who had sought repatriation or expatriation to Japan during the month before registration was announced and begun.[17] In those three months, a total of 3 percent of the entire population of the WRA camps filed requests to be removed to Japan.

But most devastating of all were the internees' responses to Question 28, which directly asked the Nisei to forswear allegiance to Japan and pledge loyalty to the United States. Of the 74,588 Nisei who filled out the questionnaire, 6,733, or 9 percent, said "no." Another 2,083, or nearly 3 percent, gave a qualified answer rather than a simple "yes." In other words, when asked to forswear allegiance to Japan and swear loyalty to the United States, 12 percent of the Nisei refused to do so unambiguously. Among male Nisei, the number of outright "no" answers was stunningly high: almost 22 percent of male Nisei answered Question 28 with an unambiguous "no."[18]

The officials in the War Department and the War Relocation Authority who had thrown together the registration program were disheartened by what one of Assistant Secretary of War John J. McCloy's top assistants called "the high mortality of loyalty"[19] that the program had brought about. Those officials had hoped that registration would throw open two vents of freedom for the Nisei—through relocation and military service. Paradoxically, however, the chief effect of registration was to speed the opening of a very different sort of vent in the camps: the vent of segregation. The disturbances at Poston and Manzanar late in 1942 and the opposition to registration that grew at most of the camps in February and March of 1943 gave renewed force to the arguments of those who were pressing for segregation of the disloyal. And registration itself supplied them with hard evidence supporting their position, in the form of thousands of questionnaires with the loyalty question marked "no."[20] By July of 1943, the WRA had settled upon and begun planning a program to siphon those identified as disloyal out of each of the camps and shift them to closer confinement at the Tule Lake Segregation Center.[21]

PROCESSING LOYALTY AT THE
JAPANESE AMERICAN JOINT BOARD

ALL OF THE pressures on Nisei loyalty, freedom, and segregation came to a head in the spring and summer of 1943, as the War Relocation Authority (WRA) and the War Department tried to deal with the unanticipated and disturbing results of their registration program. In a basic way, the two departments had tried to marry their loyalty screening efforts in January of 1943, when they agreed that they would undertake registration jointly and coordinate the processing of registration's results through the intradepartmental Japanese American Joint Board (JAJB). At first there had been great optimism: writing to the attorney general in early February of 1943, Assistant Secretary of War John J. McCloy predicted that the JAJB's work "w[ould] take [not] much more than the equivalent of a day's time per week" of its staff's time, and that "the whole job w[ould] probably be accomplished within three or four months."[1] It soon became clear, however, that the honeymoon for the WRA and the military would be short. The JAJB quickly became a vehicle not so much of cooperation for the WRA and the military but of estrangement. Its work bogged down in wrangling, complexity, confusion, and delay. And its task lasted not three or four months but sixteen.

The JAJB's Purposes and Members

The January 20, 1943, directive that created the JAJB was specific about the two roles that the JAJB was to play. The Board was to

(1) transmit the investigation report and copies of the [loyalty] questionnaires to the War Relocation Authority, together with its recommendation concerning the release of subject individuals from relocation centers on indefinite leave; and
(2) . . . state whether the Joint Board has any objection to the employment in plants and facilities important to the war effort of any of those American citizens of the Japanese ancestry who are released by the War Relocation Authority pursuant to its recommendation.[2]

In other words, the JAJB was to advise the WRA about granting indefinite leave to internees, and was to pass judgment on whether released internees could take jobs in war industries. However, the JAJB stopped performing the second function in October of 1943 when that responsibility was transferred to the Provost Marshal General's Office (PMGO).[3]

This transfer of responsibility was in some respects illusory, because the PMGO was already playing an enormous role in determining who was eligible for war plant work. Indeed, the PMGO had great influence over the JAJB's processing of all cases, because the PMGO—specifically its "Japanese-American Branch"—was the agency tasked with the administrative duty of compiling and processing the investigative record on every internee whose case came before the Board for any reason.[4]

The PMGO also held one of the voting seats on the Joint Board itself. The other voting members of the Board, at least initially, were the WRA, the Office of Naval Intelligence (ONI), the Office of the Assistant Chief of Staff of the Army's G-2 (Intelligence) Division, the FBI, and the War Department General Staff. Coordinating the JAJB's work—chairing its meetings and handling other like tasks—was a representative from the Office of the Assistant Secretary of War. Each represented entity had a single vote on the Board.[5]

This lineup did not last long, however. In early May of 1943, just two months into the JAJB's work, the FBI's representative, Frederick G. Tillman, told McCloy that his boss at the FBI thought the JAJB's work was taking up too much time and that he would not be attending future meetings or participating in the Board's deliberations. McCloy wanted the FBI to stay on the Board and therefore appealed directly to J. Edgar Hoover. Tillman had "proved to be a very valuable member of the Board," McCloy wrote, and the time commitment was never more than a half-day a week. The assistant secretary of war put it bluntly to Hoover: "The Board needs [Tillman's] services."[6]

But Hoover wanted no part of the JAJB. Without even bothering to mention the rationale that Tillman had offered about being too busy, Hoover simply told McCloy that he "regret[ted] that [he was] unable at this time to continue the assignment of a Bureau representative to the Japanese-American Joint Board." Hoover was also distressed by McCloy's suggestion that Tillman had played a valuable role in the JAJB's early work; this was not a story that Hoover wanted circulating. He took the opportunity to clear up McCloy's supposed misimpression: "I must point out that the function of the Bureau's representative in serving on the Board has been not to participate in the deliberations and findings of the Board but to serve in the capacity of a liaison officer between the [FBI] and the Board." It appears that Hoover did not trust the JAJB, and did not want the FBI's name on a domestic security project that he could not control.[7] Hoover would allow his agency only to be publicly designated as "maintaining a liaison" with the Board and would confine its future participation to the ministerial task of providing requested information from its files.[8]

With the FBI gone, the WRA became the JAJB's lone civilian representative on a decision-making body heavily skewed toward the military. This did not create an easy situation for the WRA's representative, and the stress took its toll. Board service became an assignment that WRA officials resisted, and two of them resigned during the Board's short life.[9]

The JAJB's Sources of Information

Faced with the task of screening some 40,000 citizens for loyalty to the United States, the JAJB immediately confronted a problem of information. The only way to make any sort of judgment about a person's loyalty was to gather as much data as possible about his background, activities, personal contacts, group memberships, views, and beliefs. Yet the JAJB had no investigative staff of its own, and one of its primary investigative members, the FBI, quit the Board after just two months. While the FBI did continue to perform record checks on specified internees at the JAJB's request even after it departed the Board, this minimal screening was hardly enough to support a finding of loyalty or disloyalty. If the JAJB was to do its job, it needed masses of information that the FBI could not provide.

For these purposes, the Board turned to two investigative offices within the military. One was the Japanese-American Branch of the PMGO. This unit, which came into being shortly after the January 20, 1943, announcement of the registration program, had a staff of seven officers, all of whom had just finished heading registration teams in the ten WRA relocation centers; twenty-three sergeant investigators, of whom nine had been on registration teams; and twenty-three civilian employees.[10] It was no accident that the personnel of the PMGO's Japanese-American Branch included so many recent members of registration teams; the internees' registration questionnaires were the primary source of information that the Japanese-American Branch gathered and collated. For every internee whose case came before the JAJB, either for indefinite leave clearance or for permission to work in a plant or factory important to the war effort, a sergeant investigator poured over that internee's answers to the questions on his registration form and converted them to marks on a preformatted checklist.[11] In certain cases that were deemed to require field investigation, the PMGO's Japanese-American Branch added information to the internee's file that field investigators in the various Army Service Commands around the country turned up.

The other investigative office on which the JAJB relied was the Civil Affairs Division of General John DeWitt's Western Defense Command. That office had the ambitious mission of "reconstruct[ing], insofar as feasible, . . . the pre–Pearl Harbor activities of West Coast Japanese which would have an important bearing on their attitude toward the United States in the event of war with Japan." To this end, it generated lists of every person of Japanese ancestry who had arrived from Japan by ship between 1930 and 1941, every person mentioned in the Japanese American press before the war as having any connection with a Japanese business, athletic, military, or cultural organization in the United States, every Japanese organization mentioned in a variety of books, magazines, and directories concerning Japanese life in America, and every deposit of money by a person in the United States into a fixed-term account in an American branch of a Japanese bank. Put together, these lists produced a catalogue of more than 250,000 items involving around 50,000 people of Japanese ancestry.[12]

At the outset of the JAJB's work, neither the Board nor the Japanese-American Branch of the PMGO knew that the Western Defense Command had such a resource. But the Japanese-American Branch reported that "[a]s the program developed it became more and more evident . . . that [the Civil Affairs Division of the Western Defense Command] was one of the most important sources of information as to the loyalty and activities of West Coast Japanese."[13] According to the Final Report of the PMGO's Japanese-American Branch, what it found most attractive about the WDC's records were their conclusiveness: "The information . . . was taken from the printed record compiled by [the] Japanese themselves," the Japanese-American Branch observed, and was therefore "irrefutable."[14]

This concern for "irrefutable" evidence might lead a casual observer to conclude that the military's investigations of Japanese Americans were objective and neutral inquiries. This was not so. In fact, these investigations took place in an atmosphere of intense racial suspicion. Training sessions for field investigators in the Army Service Commands included the following sorts of advice:

Because of the inscrutability of the Japanese, their reticence, clannishness and other Oriental traits, they very rarely take white people into their confidence. As a matter of fact many have been taught to look down upon white people and have learned that anything not Japanese is to be despised. This is a form of "inverted inferiority complex." The result of the foregoing is that references, neighbors, employers and acquaintances are not considered as good a source of information in the Japanese case as in the average case. The speaker has personally interviewed many Caucasians who spent as much as thirty years in associating with Japanese and who admitted "You can never get to know those people."

Membership in any Shinto sect is absolutely fatal to [a] subject's loyalty.

Citizenship is a Western concept. In the minds of the Japanese there is the belief that once a Jap always a Jap.

Frequent trips to Japan indicate pro-Japanese tendencies in the family. Two trips should be viewed with suspicion and three or more trips may be considered grounds for stamping a subject as disloyal.

The main purpose of [Japanese language schools in the United States] was to inculcate in the young Japanese a knowledge and love for Japanese customs, traditions and ideology and maintain them as a distinct racial group to prevent their assimilation into the American society.

Note . . . employment in Alaska fishing canneries and in fishing colonies on Terminal Island off the West Coast. Many of these "fishermen" were actually Reserve Officers in the Japanese Army who are believed to have been engaged in checking soundings and obtaining other available information for the Japanese Navy.

[W]hile the Japanese are generally shifty, tricky, and evasive, it is not difficult to trip them up. It must be remembered that rarely can an agent gain the subject's confidence as often happens in the case of a German. The Japanese traditionally do not take white people into their confidence with the result that it might be helpful at times to adopt a bullying attitude and create the impression that you know more about them than you actually do, that there are official records covering all their activities and that they may as well be absolutely truthful about everything.[15]

In other words, at every turn the military investigators in the Service Commands were trained to take the dimmest possible view of Japanese American loyalty and the most paranoid possible interpretation of Japanese cultural association.

Attitudes of this sort directly infected the WDC's Civil Affairs Division and the PMGO's Japanese-American Branch as well. In a speech describing the Civil Affairs Division's investigative work, Lt. Col. Claude B. Washburne, the division's officer-in-charge, framed the issue before his office this way: "Considering the environment in which most of these Nisei grew up and the pressures which have been exerted upon them, who among them can be trusted as loyal to the country of their birth—the United States—and who are probably loyal to the land of their parents and grandparents—Japan—or at least not loyal to the United States? That is THE important question and [the] question which if wrongly answered and dealt with may be fraught with danger to the wartime security of the United States."[16] It is important to notice Washburne's subtle framing of his office's inquiry: it was to determine whether, given the purported pro-Japanese "pressures" under which all Nisei were raised, any particular Nisei was "at least not loyal" to the United States. And this was no neutral inquiry. "Look at the historical background," Washburne continued, "look at the Japanese language schools, look at the pro-Japanese clubs, pro-Japanese religions, the financial, the blood, the cultural ties with Japan. It is hard, very hard, for a citizen borne [sic] of Japanese parents in this country, particularly on the West Coast, to feel loyal to the United States of America. . . . It is easy, on the other hand, for him to feel that he is at heart Japanese and not American even although [sic] he has never seen Japan."[17] A similar perception shaded the work of the PMGO's Japanese-American Branch, whose chief officer lamented that "[o]ne of the greatest barriers to a smooth operating security program was the fact that our own constitution extended certain protection to American-born citizens who are not morally entitled to that benefit." "[A]mong the Japanese," he maintained, "loyalty followed families," not citizenship.[18]

Organizing and Processing the Data

If the JAJB was to succeed at its task of determining the loyalty of some 40,000 Japanese Americans, it would need more than masses of information. Unless the Board was willing to commit years to its task, its members could not read each one of the 40,000 files from cover to cover and then gather to discuss and vote on each one. The Board needed a method of boiling that information down into some sort of user-friendly format.

For this purpose, the army turned to a statistician named Calvert L. Dedrick. Dedrick, the chief of the Census Bureau's Statistical Research Division, had been "loaned" to the War Department by the Census Bureau in February of 1942, "to assist [the] Western Defense Command first in alien

One of the summary forms on a loyalty case that the Provost Marshal General's Office prepared for the Japanese American Joint Board. This form for George Ochikubo is dated November 17, 1943. (National Archives [College Park, Maryland], Record Group 60, File 146-42-107, series 1. Courtesy of National Archives.)

registration and subsequently in the detailed planning of the forced evacuation of the Japanese Americans."[19] When it became clear that the army/WRA registration program of early 1943 would generate a huge volume of personal data on tens of thousands of internees, the army decided to reassign Dedrick to the Office of the Assistant Secretary of War, from where he could oversee PMGO's organization and analysis of the data.[20]

Dedrick did not approach his task from the position of objectivity that one might expect from a scientist. In a memorandum he prepared on June 10, 1943, when the JAJB was just gearing up its loyalty review process, Dedrick described "the Japanese" as "our 'enemy within the gates,'" a "racial group [that] has not been assimilated by our nation." "Because of the known disloyalty of many Japanese, American-born as well as alien," Dedrick asserted, "the entry of this group into industrial pursuits presents a real threat to the personnel security of the United States."[21]

Dedrick did not maintain, of course, that *all* Japanese Americans were disloyal. His challenge was to devise a formula that would permit the JAJB quickly to sift the loyal from the disloyal, and to do so, to the greatest extent possible, on the basis of criteria that large numbers of Nisei shared. Dedrick's dilemma was, at bottom, the same as the one that confronts any school admissions officer or any hiring official at a large company: how to devise selection criteria that maximize the numbers of applicants approved or disapproved automatically, and to keep to a minimum the number of applicants who require the more time-consuming task of individualized review. Whereas Assistant Secretary of War McCloy had predicted in February of 1943 that the task would take just a few months, Dedrick was more realistic: in June, he informed McCloy's office that "[t]here appears to be no possibility of accomplishing this [task] in less than from six to nine months."[22]

Dedrick's first plan was a point system. Investigators in the PMGO's Japanese-American Branch would go through each internee's registration questionnaire and assign "plus" and "minus" point values to the internee's answers to each of its numbered questions according to a predetermined schedule. A reproduction of significant portions of the schedule helps communicate its mechanical, oversimplified, and intensely mistrustful approach:

Ques. 7.	a. If registered in Communist Party.	2-Minus
	b. If registered voter.	1-Plus
Ques. 8.	a. If spouse is citizen of Japan.	1-Minus
	b. If spouse is a Nisei.	1-Plus

Ques. 11.	a.	If one or more relatives in U.S. Military Service voluntarily.	1-Plus
	b.	If father is interned.	3-Minus
Ques. 12.	a.	If subject has one or more of the following in Japan: wife, children, parents, brothers, or sisters.	3-Minus
Ques. 13	b.	If subject attended school in Japanese territory six months or more, for each 2 years or part thereof.	1-Minus
	d.	If subject attended Japanese Language School more than 3 years in this country.	2-Minus
	f.	If subject received entire education from schools in U.S.	3-Plus
Ques. 14.	a.	If subject has travelled to Japan 3 or more times.	Reject
	d.	If subject has travelled to Japan once.	1-Minus
	e.	If subject has travelled to Japan twice.	3-Minus
	f.	If subject has never travelled to Japan.	1-Plus
Ques. 15.	d.	If subject was employed as Japanese Language school instructor.	3-Minus
	f.	If subject was fisherman, licensed or amateur radio operator, hotel owner or operator, steamship line, Merchant-Marine.	2-Minus
	g.	If subject was employed by reputable American business doing business only in U.S.	2-Plus
Ques. 16.	a.	If subject is Shintoist.	Reject
	b.	If subject is Buddhist.	1-Minus
	c.	If subject is Christian.	2-Plus
Ques. 17.	a.	If subject is member of Kyudo, Jyudo, Kendo or other Japanese National Club or other Japanese named organization.	Refer[23]
	c.	If subject is member of Japanese-American Citizens League.	1-Plus
	d.	If member of Boy Scouts of America, Y.M.C.A., Y.W.C.A. or other recognized American Clubs.	2-Plus
	e.	If member of K of C,[24] Masons, Rotarian or other American fraternal society.	2-Plus
Ques. 18.	a.	If subject reads, writes and speaks Japanese good [sic].	2-Minus
	b.	If subject reads and/or writes Japanese fair, or good.	1-Minus
Ques. 19.	a.	If subject is an instructor in Japanese hobbies or sports. (Jyudo, Kyudo, and Kendo)	2-Minus

	b. If subject is an instructor in American sport or hobby.	2-Plus
	c. If licensed or amateur radio operator.[25]	2-Minus
Ques. 23.	a. If subject has made substantial contribution to organizations connected with Japanese Army, Navy or kindred agencies.	Reject
	b. If a contribution were made to any organization containing a Japanese name.	Refer
	c. If contributions were made to American organizations prior to Pearl Harbor.	2-Plus
Ques. 24	a. For each Japanese or Japanese-American periodical, trade journal or magazine.	1-Minus
Ques. 25	a. If subject's birth was or is recorded with Japanese Consulate and cancellation has been made or is pending.	3-Plus
Ques. 26	a. If subject himself has ever applied for repatriation.	Reject[26]

Perhaps the most remarkable feature of this point system, beyond its rigidity and simple-mindedness, is its perverse focus on a handful of outward markers of supposed disloyalty. It must be remembered that the PMGO's investigation was entirely on paper: it included no personal contact at all with the investigated internees. Moreover, Dr. Dedrick shared the view of the WDC's Civil Affairs Division that nothing was to be gained from interviewing the sorts of "informants who are most useful in ordinary cases," such as "[t]he person's relatives and close friends[,] neighbors and employers[,] and former employers, ministers, and business associates, if Japanese." Japanese informants simply could not be trusted. Thus, the PMGO was left attaching great significance to identifiably "Japanese" activities and skills: reading a Japanese-American newspaper, attending Japanese language school, joining a club with a Japanese name, speaking Japanese, learning martial arts. This meant that the screening system was likeliest to identify as treacherous those people who, in the years leading up to the war, had lived most openly and least treacherously. If Japan had recruited spies among the Nisei before the war, it surely would have encouraged them to minimize rather than maximize the public's perception of their connections with Japan. Yet Dr. Dedrick's point system principally indicted those who behaved least like spies.

The point system was also remarkably stacked against the ordinary Nisei. Consider a hypothetical farm worker in his early twenties who got his education through high school in the United States, traveled to Japan once as a child to visit relatives, attended four years of Japanese school in the United

States while in elementary and junior high school, had a sister in Japan and a brother in the U.S. Army, read the English-language *Rafu Shimpo* newspaper, attended a Buddhist church, and was a registered voter. That young man would have a *negative* loyalty score.[27] He might have won an award for oratory in high school for the most moving rendition of the Gettysburg Address, and might have resolved after his childhood trip to Japan that he never wished to go back. None of that would matter. His loyalty score would be negative.

The point system was short-lived. For reasons that the historical record does not disclose, Dr. Dedrick announced just five weeks into the JAJB's work that "after careful analysis, grading questionnaires by the point system had proved unworkable."[28] He replaced it with a new system designed not to score individual cases but to group them for mass processing. PMGO staff members would convert an internee's answers to the key questions on the registration questionnaire into check marks on a PMGO-devised summary sheet.[29] The summary sheet would not produce a numerical score but would allow PMGO staff to place the internee into one of three color-coded categories. One category was "white." A white case was that of an internee who, in the PMGO's opinion, deserved two things: (1) automatic Joint Board approval for release on indefinite leave and (2) immediate, provisional approval for work in an industry important to the war effort, pending a record check by the WDC's Civil Affairs Division. At the other end of the spectrum was the "black" category. This category was, as one might expect, for internees whom the PMGO believed to deserve automatic rejection, both for release on indefinite leave and for war plant work.[30]

The middle category, a catch-all for those cases that were neither white nor black, might have been expected to be called the "grey" category. But in a move that may have hinted at a racial consciousness animating the program, Dedrick called the middle category "brown."[31] At various points, when even subtler color gradations were needed, staffers often referred to cases of questionable loyalty as "tan" cases, "light brown" cases, and "dark brown"[32] cases—all on a spectrum stretching from black to white.

The key to this new system was the method for placing cases into one or another of the categories. Dedrick's approach was to sift from the mass of data on the registration questionnaires certain pairs or multiples of factors that tended—at least in Dedrick's view—to correlate both with one another and with loyalty or disloyalty. Seeking approval of this approach in a conversation with Capt. John M. Hall of Assistant Secretary of War McCloy's office, Dedrick offered pairings such as "Buddhist and [Japanese] language school in the U.S." or "one trip to Japan and Buddhist." People with these attributes, Dedrick argued, were predictably "all right." Captain Hall agreed that these paired attributes "simply [went] together like ham and eggs," and he approved of Dedrick's new method.[33]

Turning Dedrick's color-coding approach from an idea to a functioning system was, however, a challenge. Through the months of May and June of 1943, the Joint Board wrangled over which aspects of a Japanese American life were "white" and which were "black." At first, it took a rather minimalist approach. The white category was to consist of those internees whose files contained either no "derogatory" information at all, or just one of the following features:

(1) attendance for any number of years at a Japanese language school run by a Christian church;

(2) attendance for less than ten years at any other Japanese language school, unless the attendance post-dated high school graduation;

(3) one trip of six months or less to Japan; or

(4) membership in or affiliation with a Buddhist church.[34]

Meanwhile, "black" cases were those in which the internee either

(1) answered "no" to the loyalty question (Question 28) on the registration questionnaire,

(2) requested repatriation or expatriation to Japan,

(3) had worked on a Japanese naval vessel, or

(4) had *gunji kyoren* military training in Japan.[35]

Notably, Robert Frase, the WRA's representative on the JAJB, argued that none of these should count as a disqualifying criterion except the first one. Even as to a "no" answer on Question 28, the WRA representative insisted that the many internees who had gone back and changed their answers from "no" to an unqualified "yes" did not deserve automatic condemnation. The rest of the Board, however, could not be persuaded. It insisted that an internee's change from "no" to "yes" on Question 28, just as his cancellation of a repatriation or expatriation request, was insignificant unless he could present "special circumstances indicating basic undeviating loyalty to the United States."[36]

All cases that had derogatory information other than the items on these two lists were to go in the intermediate "brown" category. But it soon became clear that this would be quite a large number of cases, and a backlog began to build. Late in May 1943, in order to trim this growing backlog, the

Board significantly expanded the white category to include a number of additional factors that would not be seen as detracting from an internee's loyalty. These included residence in Japan under the age of six, the present residence of sisters (but not brothers) in Japan, an internee's stated preference to work in the still-closed exclusion zone of California, an unexplained time interval in the internee's personal history of not more than one year, minor inconsistencies in the information supplied on the registration form, and a few other features.[37] The JAJB also recognized a number of "ham-and-eggs" combinations of these criteria (such as being Buddhist, living in Japan while younger than six, and having sisters in Japan) that would qualify a case as "white." However, the Board tempered these expansions of the white category by adopting an interpretive rule that in any case presenting conflicting derogatory and nonderogatory information on the same point, "the more derogatory [w]ould determine the classification."[38] In other words, a case with information supporting either a white or a brown classification would be brown. A case with information supporting either a brown or a black classification would be black.

Having clarified the content of the white category, the Board then turned its attention to the black category. At its meeting on June 3, 1943, the Board added three additional factors that would turn a case black:

1. Where individual was an officer, agent or member of an active subversive organization or association.
2. For males, ten years or more residence in Japan after the age of 6 unless individual has a spouse of American birth and American born child or children.
3. Three or more trips to Japan after the age of 6, except in the case of seamen.[39]

The WRA representative objected to two of these disqualifying criteria, agreeing only that leadership or membership in an active subversive organization ought to merit a black classification. His objections, however, again fell on deaf ears.[40]

With the white and black categories settled, the JAJB finally turned in August of 1943 to its thorniest problem: how to handle the cases in its catch-all brown category? These were cases that, on an initial screening in the Japanese-American Branch of the PMGO, had earned neither automatic approval nor automatic disapproval by the Joint Board. Under JAJB policy, the Japanese-American Branch had been sending these brown cases to the WDC's Civil Affairs Division at the Presidio in San Francisco for further investigation. As explained earlier, this meant a canvassing of the huge compendium of references to the prewar religious, financial, travel, and cultural activities of the West Coast's ethnically Japanese population that the Civil Affairs Division had compiled. Notably, though, the investigation did not focus solely on the internee whose case was referred for investigation. Proceeding on the basis of the strong conviction that loyalty had nothing to do with citizenship but instead "ran uniform within the family,"[41] the Civil Affairs Division also checked its files for information on the referred internee's father.[42] And with 250,000 pieces of information on some 50,000 people of Japanese ancestry, the Civil Affairs Division managed to produce new derogatory information in an astonishingly high percentage of the cases referred to it—between one-half and two-thirds.[43]

Naturally, this created quite a backlog for the JAJB, and if Board review meant individual consideration for each "brown" file, the screening work might outlast the war itself. The Board therefore broke the brown category into two subgroups: "those having minor derogatory information" and "those having major derogatory information."[44] The cases with minor derogatory information would be treated as if they were white—that is, they would be automatically approved without individual consideration. The cases with major derogatory information would be reviewed individually.

The method for sifting the "minor" and "major" cases in the brown category reflected a shift from Dedrick's original "ham-and-eggs" approach to what might have been termed a "Chinese menu" approach. The PMGO's Japanese-American Branch compiled two lists of derogatory factors, an "a" list and a "b" list. On the "a" list were "major factors" such as "immediate relative interned," "father and/or brother in Japan," "seriously objectionable occupation," "undisclosed foreign investments in Japan of $250 or over," and "residence in Japan after the age of six for more than ten years though married to citizen wife with citizen children."[45] The "b" list included minor factors such as "mother and/or sister in Japan," "objectionable occupation," "parent's investment in Japan of $1000 or more," "disclosed assets in Japan of $250 or over," and "residence in Japan from five to nine years inclusive over the age of six though married to citizen wife with citizen children."[46] A case would qualify as a "major" case requiring individual review if it had at least two features from just the "a" list, or one feature from the "a" list and two features from the "b" list, or four features from just the "b" list.[47]

With its full methodology finally in place by the end of August 1943, the JAJB, meeting twice a week through the end of October and once a week thereafter, processed cases until May 12, 1944, when it was dissolved.[48] The final tally of its rulings did not sketch a particularly encouraging picture of Nisei loyalty. In fifteen months, the JAJB handled the cases of a total of 38,449 Nisei internees and made adverse findings in 12,404 of them—nearly one-third of the cases it heard.[49]

This description of the Board's tenure and work is, in one sense, misleading. To outsiders it may have looked as though the JAJB cooperated for fifteen months to produce final loyalty determinations in the cases of nearly 40,000 interned Nisei. Those on the inside of the JAJB's work, however, knew otherwise. As a cooperative enterprise, the Board really lasted only a few months, and by the time it formally dissolved in May of 1944, its constituent agencies had long since stopped treating its conclusions as final.

A fissure between the WRA and the other voting members of the JAJB opened early in the Board's life. The point of disagreement was how the JAJB would word its announcement of an adverse finding on an internee's loyalty. The Board's initial plan was to announce that it was "recommend[ing] against the granting of indefinite leave at this time."[50] To the WRA, this language—especially the word "against"—was unacceptably negative, and by early April of 1943, just five weeks into the Board's life, disagreement over the language developed into what an assistant to Assistant Secretary of War John McCloy called "something of a battle."[51] To the WRA, the wording was crucial because it would have a grave impact on the agency's ability to manage the camps. "[B]efore the summer is over," WRA director Dillon Myer explained to Capt. John Hall of the Assistant Secretary of War's Office on April 9, 1943, "we are going to be pressured for manpower to the place that we probably won't want to keep all these 'no' answers on the inside."[52] In other words, Myer understood that there were powerful forces pushing for at least some form of liberty for the internees, and he did not want the WRA's leave program to be constrained by clearly worded negative loyalty findings by the JAJB. By the same token, the PMGO, which was responsible for security in the nation's war plants and industries, very much wanted a strong, "positive" declaration of disloyalty[53]—precisely in order to keep those Nisei who failed the JAJB's screening process out of factories doing war work. And the other members of the Board "felt very strongly that the Joint Board would not be living up to its functions and responsibilities if it merely gave favorable recommendations in deserving cases and no recommendation in undeserving cases,"[54] which was what the WRA preferred.

After a delicate process of negotiation between the WRA and a representative of the Assistant Secretary of War's Office, the members of the JAJB settled on language acceptable to all. In cases where the JAJB made an adverse finding, it would state that "[i]t c[ould] not recommend indefinite leave at this time."[55] This language was suitably ambiguous: as Captain Hall said, it was "a set of words that w[ouldn't] put [WRA] in too much of a bad position" but that "for the sake of the integrity of the Board . . . [was] able to blow both ways."[56]

This agreement on the language of a JAJB denial temporarily restored peace to relations on the Board. The War Relocation Authority, however, soon began pressing the Board for a degree of speed that the Board's military members, the PMGO's Japanese-American Branch, and the WDC's Civil Affairs Division either could not or would not attain. The WRA, it will be recalled, saw the loyalty questionnaires and the JAJB approval process as a device for implementing the "all out" relocation program that WRA had come to support by early 1943. Not only was the WRA itself eager to trumpet to the nation the JAJB's endorsement of the internees who would be leaving the camps, but the internees themselves saw an endorsement from the JAJB —particularly a clearance for war plant work—as a "superior" form of clearance to that issued by the WRA alone.[57] The WRA therefore urged that *all* cases in the white category—even the whitest of the white—be sent for a WDC record check, so that the Joint Board would be in a position to recommend not merely in favor of indefinite leave but also in favor of war plant work. "I'm very much interested in that group of white cases getting some restrictions off and getting some clearance so that they'll feel like they're citizens of the U.S.," Dillon Myer explained to Captain Hall in early May of 1943.[58]

To statistician Calvert Dedrick, however, the WRA's proposal seemed an enormous waste of time. The point of creating the "white" category had been to avoid as many individualized investigations as possible in cases of obvious and unmistakable loyalty to the United States. Yet here the WRA was seeking more, rather than fewer, investigations in those sorts of cases. In addition, Dedrick saw no purpose to securing a resource-consuming record check on those internees who had little or no interest in actually doing war plant work.[59] Working behind the scenes, Dedrick—a War Department employee, not a voting member of the JAJB—lined up the votes on the Board to defeat the WRA's request for WDC record checks in all white cases.[60] On May 6, 1943, the Board voted to seek a WDC record check only for those white cases in which the internee presented a "reasonable possibility . . . of employment in plants and facilities important to the war effort."[61]

Even with this limitation, the processing of the "white" cases—especially those in which an internee wished to take work in a war plant—moved slowly. By the end of June 1943, more than 1,000 such cases had been sent out for investigation, but by the end of July 1943, only 86 had been approved.[62] At the JAJB's June 29 meeting, the WRA representative pleaded with others on the Board to remedy the situation. He explained that "[o]pportunities for the employment of [Nisei] in vital war plants ha[d] developed in increasing numbers and the WRA [was] naturally anxious to take advantage of these openings as they present[ed] themselves."[63] He asked the Joint Board to authorize the WRA to place internees in war plants provisionally, subject to eventual Board review when investigation was complete. The military members of the Board, however, said "no" to this WRA proposal; they did not trust the WRA to make these decisions even provisionally. Instead, they insisted that the military security officers in the various army service commands around the country make any provisional approvals for war plant work.[64] This did little to speed up the process, and little to foster good feeling between the WRA and the military members of the Joint Board. On July 13, 1943, a frustrated Dillon Myer told the JAJB that the idea of seeking provisional approval from military security officers around the country was just not working and that the WRA would therefore just abandon, for the time being, its efforts to place workers in war plants.[65]

What Dillon Myer did not say, but became apparent soon thereafter, was that the WRA was quietly disengaging from the work of the JAJB. Once the Joint Board agreed to express its disapproval by announcing that it could merely "not recommend in favor of indefinite leave at this time," and once the WRA realized that the Joint Board would be slower and stingier with its indefinite leave and war plant approvals than suited the WRA's needs, the agency quietly walked away from the Joint Board's positions on indefinite leave.[66] It did not do this formally: as a formal matter, it remained a part of the JAJB and continued to send its representative to the Board's biweekly meetings. Informally, however, the WRA began disregarding adverse findings by the JAJB in great numbers.

This practice came out into the open at the JAJB's meeting on November 30, 1943. Captain James Hughes of the Office of the Assistant Secretary of War asked Robert Thurber, the WRA's representative, for an accounting of the numbers of internees whom the WRA had released in the teeth of an adverse finding by the Joint Board. Thurber explained that of the roughly 10,000 cases the JAJB had declined to recommend in favor of indefinite leave, the WRA had, through its own internal processes, segregated around 6,000 to the Tule Lake Segregation Center. (Most of these were internees who had answered Question 28 on the registration questionnaire with an unequivocal "no.") Of the remaining 4,000, Thurber explained, the WRA had granted indefinite leave to 3,200, or 80 percent. Captain Hughes responded that he could not believe "that 4 out of 5 were let out," and told Thurber that he "could not understand why there would be such a difference of opinion between the . . . [JAJB] & WRA." Thurber explained that part of the difference stemmed from the WRA's decision to hold individualized hearings in its leave and segregation processes. Still, the military members of the Joint Board found it "shocking" that the WRA was reaching opposite conclusions on loyalty in such a large number of cases.[67]

Part of what may have made this realization so shocking to the military members of the Joint Board was that the release of an internee on indefinite leave was irrevocable. By midsummer 1943, the PMGO began to realize that the WRA was releasing some internees on indefinite leave before the JAJB had time to make a recommendation, and that as a result, there were Nisei at liberty in places throughout the country about whom the Joint Board had concerns about disloyalty. WRA director Dillon Myer asked Attorney General Francis Biddle what could be done about these internees: could the FBI pick them up and return them to WRA detention on the strength of an adverse determination on indefinite leave by the JAJB? The attorney general's answer was blunt. "I know of no legal authority to arrest and intern Japanese-American citizens now residing outside of the evacuated military areas," he told Myer. "Therefore, I could not instruct the Federal Bureau of Investigation to apprehend and to return to relocation centers the individuals [already released by the WRA] after they have been released." In other words, once the WRA released an internee on indefinite leave, he or she was free.[68]

The military members of the Joint Board learned of this at their meeting on November 4, 1943, when "[i]t was pointed out . . . that the effect of this letter [from the attorney general] was virtually to nullify unfavorable action by the Board after an individual had been released."[69] In other words, if it was not yet clear to the military members of the JAJB, it became clear on November 4, 1943, that the WRA had the power to disregard the JAJB's conclusions, and there was nothing the JAJB or any other agency could do about it.

But the revelation that the WRA was allowing thousands of disapproved internees to leave the camps on indefinite leave was also undoubtedly "shocking" to the military members of the JAJB because they also knew that some of those released internees were managing to land jobs in vital war plants. As early as August 24, 1943, it was noted at a JAJB meeting that although "[v]ery few individuals ha[d] been released [from relocation centers] for war plant employment, . . . they [were] get[ting] indefinite leave and migrat[ing] to the big cities and get[ting] into war jobs" with the WRA's help and with "complete disregard to the . . . [JAJB's] clearance [process]."[70] Some military members of the JAJB worried that even though the Board had had no hand in approving these former internees for work in war plants, the Board might nonetheless "be held responsible for these cases" if things did not turn out well.[71]

Nisei workers in sensitive war plants without JAJB approval were a matter of especially grave concern for the PMGO, because war plant security was one of the PMGO's raisons d'être. By October of 1943, the PMGO had had enough. A directive dated October 14, 1943, announced that all future applications from Nisei for approval to work in war plants would be investigated by the relevant regional army service command and that the PMGO—not the JAJB—would have final authority to approve or disapprove all applications. The JAJB would retain authority over only those internees whose applications predated the October 14 directive.[72] As a technical matter, the impact of this shift was not enormous: the PMGO's Japanese-American Branch had been shouldering most of the labor on the war plant cases while the JAJB had formal decision-making authority. Perhaps the most significant impact was symbolic: the most notable thing about the shift was that the War Relocation Authority lost even the modicum of influence on war plant approvals that its single JAJB vote had represented.

With the October 14 directive in place, the separation between the WRA and the PMGO became, in practice, complete. The effort to marry their efforts under the auspices of the JAJB had come to naught. They were to have cooperated on indefinite leave and war plant approvals. Yet in the matter of indefinite leave from relocation centers, the WRA retained, and exercised, independent final authority; in the matter of war plant approval, the PMGO had independent final authority. The WRA and the PMGO remained under the common roof of the JAJB through May of 1944, when the JAJB was dissolved, but the agencies were more going through the motions of cooperation than actually collaborating.

At times the collapse of collaboration on the JAJB risked public exposure in potentially mortifying ways. The most poignant illustration of this came early in 1944, when the Board considered the idea of publicizing a story about the good work that Nisei workers were doing in war plants. At the Board's meeting on March 2, 1944, Capt. John Hall read aloud an excerpt from a confidential intelligence summary produced by the army's Fifth Ser-

Ikuro Wada, granted indefinite leave by the War Relocation Authority from the Poston Relocation Center in Arizona, at his produce-packing job in Denver, Colorado. On Wada's left is Dillon S. Myer, director of the WRA. On Wada's right is the owner of the produce-packing plant. (Courtesy of The Bancroft Library, University of California, Berkeley, 1967.014 v. 35 EB-740.)

vice Command. Hall reported that during the month of January 1944, the Cleveland Steel Products Company in Cleveland, Ohio, had employed eighteen former internees between the ages of eighteen and twenty-two on its production line. The company's experience had been superb: the Nisei "were always constantly at their work and the absenteeism in the factory was reduced to a minimum." In addition, the company "ha[d] caught up to production schedule," and the Nisei's outstanding work habits had "stimulate[d] the white people to real production." Everyone on the JAJB agreed that "this would be a good article to print in the paper" and that no lesser a figure than Interior Secretary Harold Ickes should issue the release.[73]

Only one person at the meeting expressed any reservation about the plan, and that was Capt. Clarence Harbert of the PMGO. Harbert suggested that before publicizing this story about Nisei contributions at war plants, it might be a good idea to make sure that all of the Nisei workers at the Cleveland Steel Products Company had actually been cleared for war plant work by the JAJB.[74] The Fifth Service Command launched an investigation of the situation at Cleveland Steel Products and learned that only *four* of the eighteen Nisei employees had been cleared by the JAJB for war plant employment. In addition, investigators learned that in the eyes of their white co-workers, the Nisei had been *too* conscientious, and the whites had been griping about it. The result of all of this was that Nisei productivity had actually declined: the company's owner reported that the Nisei were no longer "producing as much as they [were] capable of because of labor difficulties and complaints from the Caucasians that their rate of production [was] too high."[75]

Captain Harbert therefore advised that "any attempt to publicize the employment of persons of Japanese ancestry at the Cleveland Steel Products Company, is not only very unwise but could very easily result in a dangerous kick-back."[76] Not only would publicity reveal that Nisei workers were in sensitive war plants without any sort of Joint Board clearance, but "any glory given to the Japanese element could easily result in further and more complicated labor difficulties" among "the Caucasian employees of the firm."[77] The Provost Marshall General's Office followed Harbert's advice, recommending to the Office of the Assistant Secretary of War that the War Department should give no publicity at all to the story of the hardworking Nisei at the Cleveland Steel Products Company. And to add insult to injury, after further investigation of the individual cases, the PMGO also ordered that two of the conscientious Nisei steelworkers be fired for security reasons.[78]

The rift between the WRA and the military members of the JAJB led not only to potentially embarrassing public disharmony but also to angry re-crimination. So dour were the military's views of the War Relocation Authority that evidence of vituperation surfaces even in the JAJB's official written minutes. In the minutes of the meeting of July 29, 1943, in the midst of agenda items concerning ordinary Joint Board business, the following item appears: "4. *Criticism of* WRA *by the Joint Board.* The Joint Board was in complete agreement with Mr. Holland [of the WRA] that it was not a proper function of the Joint Board to criticize WRA operations, except insofar as they related to the activities of the Joint Board."[79] The minutes do not reflect what the military members of the Board had been caught saying, or to whom, but it must have been extreme in order to earn a mention at a JAJB meeting, let alone inclusion in the official record of the Joint Board's proceedings.

Once the Joint Board's work was done, neither the War Relocation Authority nor the PMGO shied away from publicly criticizing the other. The WRA, for its part, was at least modestly circumspect in its public statements. In a report on the WRA's relations with other government agencies that WRA director Dillon Myer wrote in 1946, he said that on "matters affecting restraints" on Japanese Americans, War Department officials were "generally arbitrary."[80] Similarly, in its final report, the WRA argued that while the Office of the Assistant Secretary of War played a constructive role on the JAJB, "some other staff members of the War Department and of the Western Defense Command . . . succeeded in distorting the functions of the Board rather badly."[81] In a private interview in January of 1945, Myer was considerably more caustic, fuming that the PMGO's entire approach was "unnecessary and . . . gumming up the works," a silly system of "running IBM cards through machines and totaling arbitrarily such weighted factors as education in Japan, 'No No' answers, repatriation requests, FBI reports," and the like. Myer told his interviewer that he thought this "canned" system, with its "big room full of cards," was "nonsense."[82]

The Japanese-American Branch of the PMGO, by contrast, was anything but circumspect in its final assessment of the WRA. The WRA, complained the Japanese-American Branch in its final report, "was staffed largely with trained social workers who could not become war minded even temporarily." The WRA was, in the Japanese-American Branch's view, "a civilian agency whose personnel and exponents of civil liberties have read only that portion of our constitution dealing with the Bill of Rights," and who had left "the wartime powers provided in other sections of that document . . . either . . . ignored or unscanned." "With plenty of moral and political support from higher authority and pacifist and non-war-winning groups in our country," the WRA had "winked at War Department regulations and deliberately placed Japanese in employment and positions contrary to the provisions of specific regulations and when the War Department sought to take appropriate action, pleaded the constitutional guarantees to citizens." The WRA never "volunteer[ed] to assume one iota of the security burden"[83] shouldered by the War Department and "was non-cooperative in any program created by security regulations." "It had," alleged the Japanese-American Branch, "breached its responsibilities of reasonable cooperation and fair dealing."[84]

In the WRA's work with the JAJB, groused the PMGO's Japanese-American Branch, the civilian agency "was permitted to pass responsibility to the Board for the release of all persons favorably recommended, but was permitted to completely ignore any adverse recommendations by the Board based upon derogatory information as to [an internee's] loyalty." Most damagingly of all, the Japanese-American Branch alleged, the WRA had managed to "force" the military personnel on the JAJB into "acced[ing] to the demands of WRA"—"concessions" that "resulted in compromises as to the loyalty of individuals."[85] This was harsh criticism indeed.

Loyalty and Disloyalty According to the JAJB

According to the PMGO, WRA pressure led the JAJB to compromise national security by approving the release and employment of Nisei who were not loyal to the United States. This is a view that hindsight allows us to test. If the PMGO was right, and the JAJB was too lax, it would stand to reason that at least a few dangerous Nisei would have slipped out of the camps and into the nation's war plants. Yet there was not a single reported incident of industrial sabotage by a Japanese American anywhere in the United States during World War II. Indeed, with the exception of one instance in which three Nisei sisters helped two German war prisoners escape from their Colorado POW camp,[86] there was not a single reported incident of *any* sort of sabotage or subversion by a released Japanese American internee anywhere in the United States during or after World War II.

As a logical matter, this whistle-clean record could be taken as proof of absolute precision in the JAJB's screening methods. Perhaps the camps held scores of Nisei saboteurs, and the JAJB got things exactly right, frustrating the plans of every single one of them by forbidding them access to war plants. Perhaps every single one, or the majority, or even just a healthy minority of the more than 12,000 Nisei for whom the Joint Board entered adverse loyalty findings really were spies and saboteurs, and the Board judiciously recommended against their release. In practice, though, this seems quite unlikely. The template that Calvert Dedrick designed for the Board was so wooden, so skewed toward the sorts of outward signals of Japanese cultural affiliation that any true subversive would avoid, and so ridiculously oversimplified that the system simply could not have worked that accurately. The fairer inference is that the JAJB very often got things wrong.

A look at a few of the human lives touched by the Joint Board's errors supports this inference.[87]

Harry Iba

Harry Hayao Iba was born in Los Angeles to Issei parents on November 11, 1915.[88] His family was Buddhist. He never traveled to Japan in his childhood and did not hold dual citizenship. He never attended a Japanese afterschool program, and described his spoken Japanese as "fair." He could write and read the language only poorly. He graduated from high school in

1934 and went to work in the family nursery business. He had a brother in the U.S. Army and a brother in medical school in Boston whose tuition he helped pay.

He subscribed to the *Los Angeles Times*, the *Examiner*, *Reader's Digest*, *Time*, *Life*, *Sunset*, and *Popular Mechanics*. He liked to play football, ping-pong, and outdoor sports. He collected camellia plants. On his registration form, he said that he would serve in the U.S. armed forces if drafted and answered "yes" to Question 28, which asked about his willingness to forswear allegiance to the emperor of Japan or other foreign powers. His attorney, landlord, and neighbors in Los Angeles—all of them white—wrote glowing reference letters for him. His lawyer said he was "as loyal to America as any Japanese could be"—an "honest, intelligent, respectable, law abiding citizen." "He is extremely honest and his word means much," said his former landlord, adding that he was "a credit to our neighborhood." He was "100% American," said family friend Larry Keary, certain to "pass every test for loyalty and sincerity." To his landlord, he and his family were "excellent tenants and good neighbors."

On his registration form, he indicated that he had no account in foreign banks and no investments in foreign countries. He also wrote that in 1937, when he was twenty-two, he traveled to Japan with "a group of boys for personal reasons" on the ship *Taiyo Maru*. At a WRA leave clearance hearing at the Amache Relocation Center, he explained that the trip was a sightseeing trip with his judo club. He was also told at the hearing that a record search had turned up an account in his name at the Los Angeles Sumitomo Bank in the amount of 591 yen (about $147), a joint account with his mother at the same bank in the amount of 11,090 yen (about $2,977), and a trust account in his name, with his mother as trustee, in the amount of 1,669 yen (about $417). This surprised Iba; he said that he "didn't know anything about it unless my family deposited this money in to me when I was a small tot." "You know how mothers are," Iba said, "you know how she saves it for you, then if you get hard up it comes up some place. She won't tell you until you need it."

At its meeting on August 19, 1943, over the dissent of the WRA representative, the JAJB recommended indefinite confinement for Harry Iba.[89]

Hiroshi Hishiki

Hiroshi Hishiki was born in Los Angeles to Issei parents on April 17, 1918.[90] He did not hold dual citizenship. His father, a manufacturer, had arrived from Japan in 1902, his mother in 1914. Hishiki was a Protestant and a member of St. Mary's Church, the Brotherhood of St. Andrews, and the YMCA. He received all of his education in the United States, graduating from UCLA in 1940 with ROTC training and a major in business administration. He registered to vote in 1941 as a Democrat. He worked in his father's handkerchief manufacturing business and, by the time of his family's exclusion from the West Coast in 1942, was running the business because his father was ill. He enjoyed photography, basketball, and tennis and subscribed to the Los Angeles Times, Life, Reader's Digest, and Newsweek.

Hishiki traveled with his parents to Japan in 1932 to visit his grandparents and great-aunts and great-uncles. He attended Japanese language school in the United States for nine years as a child and spoke the language well enough to work as a teacher at the Los Angeles Nippon Institute, a Japanese language school. His salary was $6 per month. He explained at his WRA leave clearance hearing that he taught once a week, on Saturdays, and that teaching gave him the chance to maintain his own language skills. The school's principal, a Mr. Yoshizumi, was an Issei who had been in the Japanese army in the past and who was interned as an enemy alien some months after the attack on Pearl Harbor. On December 8, 1941, when the U.S. government froze the bank accounts of all Issei and Japanese organizations in the United States, Hishiki became the treasurer of the Nippon Institute's Alumni Association and occasionally withdrew small subsistence payments for Mr. Yoshizumi. Over the months following Pearl Harbor, these payments amounted to between $200 and $300 out of the $2,000 in the alumni account.

On his registration questionnaire, Hishiki avowed his loyalty to the United States on Question 28. On Question 27, which asked whether he would agree to serve in the armed forces of the United States, he wrote "no, unless social conditions change to satisfaction or unless drafted." At his leave clearance hearing, he explained that as an only son, he "had parents that were ill, and relatives that had been interned," and he believed that "if [he] were drafted there would be no one to take care of them in case something happened." This was what he meant by "social conditions": he could not envision himself in the service unless he knew his family would be cared for. Asked whether he would have any objection to going into the service if he were drafted, he replied, "If I were drafted, it would have to be." He said he preferred not to fight the Japanese army because "there is a certain amount of mixed feeling when you are fighting your own blood," but "if there were no choice," he would serve. When asked whom he would like to see win the war, Hishiki replied, "Naturally this country," because "I was born in this country, have been to Japan and I know what it is like and I still feel that my place is over here."

At its meeting on August 19, 1943, the JAJB recommended indefinite confinement for Hiroshi Hishiki.[91] The WRA representative dissented.

Dorothy Ito

Dorothy Ito was born on January 20, 1909, to Issei parents in Betteravia, California.[92] She was not a dual citizen. Her family, which included a sister and seven brothers, was Buddhist. She neither traveled to Japan nor attended a Japanese after-school program in the United States, so she could neither read nor write Japanese. Her spoken Japanese was poor. She liked to read the *Los Angeles Times*, *Reader's Digest*, *Life*, *Look*, and *Ladies' Home Journal*. She was unmarried and never registered to vote. One of her brothers was in the U.S. Army, having joined before the Japanese attack on Pearl Harbor. She answered "yes" to both Questions 27 and 28 on her registration form.

Ito's father was interned after Pearl Harbor because of involvement in several Japanese organizations in the late 1930s, but Ito knew nothing of his activities because she had left home in 1936. Ito's mother was stricken with brain cancer in the late 1930s and was an invalid in critical condition by the time of the evacuation of the Japanese from the West Coast in the spring of 1942. It was Ito's job to provide her mother with round-the-clock care. In April of 1942, Ito's mother was moved to the Sisters' Hospital in Santa Maria, California, and Ito moved in to the hospital to care for her.

Because Ito feared that her mother would not survive evacuation, she sought to keep her in the hospital in California as long as she could. By the end of 1942, however, the government insisted that she and her invalid mother had to leave the Western Defense Command. Because her brother was in the army, Ito "made a lot of requests that [her family receive] a little consideration about . . . being pushed around here and there." She even pressed her brother in the army to ask his commanding officer to help them.

But all of her requests were in vain. In January of 1943, Ito was forced to take her critically ill mother to the Gila River Relocation Center in Arizona. She asked that the government defray the costs of the move, but the government did not. She had to pay for the move out of her own pocket. As late arrivals at Gila River, Ito and her mother found themselves without many basic necessities. Ito spent her first six months at Gila River without even receiving a basic clothing allowance.

The hospital at Gila River was not set up to accommodate patients for long-term care, so Ito had to care for her mother by herself in their camp barrack. The hospital would care for Ito's mother only during acute episodes, and when her mother stabilized, the hospital would return her to her barrack.

On January 21, 1944, the Office of Naval Intelligence (ONI) reported to the War Relocation Authority that "[t]here [were] indications that the subject had attempted to discourage [her brother] from doing his [military] duty as a loyal citizen of this country." The ONI also reported an allegation that Ito "had . . . expressed strong animosity against the United States Government and also a strong personal contempt and dislike of one Dr. Sleath, the supervisor of the hospital at the Gila River Relocation Center." The first allegation appears to be someone's uncharitable interpretation of the pressure that Ito placed on her soldier brother to get the help that Ito felt the government owed a military family. And after a leave clearance hearing, a WRA official concluded that the second allegation of an "outburst" at the Gila River Hospital was "adequately explained" as "an emotional reaction resulting from [Ito's] mother's invalid condition, and the cares placed on her."

The JAJB did not agree. At its meeting on February 2, 1944, it ruled that Dorothy Ito should remain in confinement.[93]

The stories of Harry Iba, Hiroshi Hishiki, and Dorothy Ito put a human face on the JAJB's adjudications of the loyalty and disloyalty of Japanese Americans. But it is important to remember that the JAJB's review process was not about human stories. The Board had neither the time nor the interest to consider the life stories of the individuals before it, more than half of whom it evaluated on the basis of nothing more than their answers on a registration questionnaire.[94] The cases were "white" cases or "brown" cases or "black" cases, and if they were brown, then what mattered was which pairs of "ham-and-eggs" factors they revealed, or which configuration of items from the "Chinese menu" of Japanese American loyalty they presented. What mattered were Calvert Dedrick's templates—mechanical devices that made an internee's perceived cultural identification with Japan—or that of his male relatives—into a proxy for disloyalty and danger to national security.

PROCESSING LOYALTY AT THE
PROVOST MARSHAL GENERAL'S OFFICE

BETWEEN JANUARY AND mid-October of 1943, the Provost Marshal General's Office was forced to abide by the Japanese American Joint Board's findings on the suitability of Nisei internees for work in war-related industries. After mid-October of 1943, however, the PMGO was freed of the JAJB's control and assumed sole responsibility for these decisions. The PMGO, left to its own devices, generally took an even dimmer and more suspicious view of Nisei loyalty than did the Joint Board.

It should come as no surprise that the PMGO took a generally jaundiced view of Nisei loyalty. Suspicion of the Nisei floated in the air at the PMGO like smoke in a tavern. Consider the views of Capt. Stanley Arnold, the officer who headed the PMGO's Japanese-American Branch. Arnold was openly scornful of the idea that Nisei citizenship meant anything. "By Japanese tradition, custom and ethics," Arnold maintained, "the family was so closely bound into one unit that loyalty and disloyalty was [sic] common to a family regardless of the citizenship of individual members." The fact of Nisei citizenship was regrettable for Arnold because citizenship conferred rights on Japanese Americans to which they were not "morally entitled"—rights that presented "great barriers to a smooth[-]operating security program." In Arnold's view at war's end, the war effort would have been much better served if all Nisei workers had been categorically excluded from all work in war plants. And in the postwar period, Arnold maintained, the country would be best served by a system of publicly shaming and forcibly expelling "the disloyal" among the Nisei. The "effort to treat all Japanese in the same class should immediately cease," he argued late in 1945, and "the disloyal should be so designated publicly" so as to place the loyal in a better light. "Voluntary or involuntary expatriation and deportation of all pro-Japanese elements"—aliens and citizens alike—would "remove an evil influence" from postwar America.[1]

In a military hierarchy headed by an officer with these views, it would have taken a miracle for staff members to see Nisei applicants for war plant work in anything but the darkest light. And that is just how they saw them. Consider, for example, the case of Yukio Ikegami, a Los Angeles–born Nisei who was nineteen years old in 1943 when his case came before the JAJB. Ikegami had never left the United States, but his sister was in Japan. He never attended a Japanese after-school program, spoke Japanese poorly, had no foreign investments, and liked football and stamp collecting. His high school principal in California said that Ikegami was "very American in every way"; the teacher of his American history and government class wrote that he was "a true American [who] would fight and die for his country." On his registration form, he indicated that he was willing to serve in the armed forces and to forswear loyalty to any foreign power.[2]

The Joint Board approved Ikegami for work in a war plant.[3] But the PMGO representative dissented. These were the PMGO's reasons:

> It will be noted that the Subject's father was a director of Nokai, which is a Japanese agricultural association. While there is no stigma attached to this association in and of itself, it had many members within it who may be classified as disloyal. It is believed that the Subject's father showed his hand as being one of the disloyal members, when he campaigned for the Japanese war relief fund in 1937.

> It will also be noted that the Subject has a sister who, although American born, is a student in Japan at the present time. This is also indicative of the fact that the father of both of these children still regards Japan as being his homeland and the country to which he owes his loyalty. Under these circumstances it is believed that the Subject, as the only male child, would be under great influence from his parent.[4]

In other words, the PMGO had nothing incriminating on Ikegami at all, and nothing incriminating on the agricultural organization of which Ikegami's father was a member. It believed, however, that some members of that organization were disloyal and that Ikegami's father might be one of them. Because it suspected that Ikegami's father was loyal to Japan, it inferred that Ikegami was too. After all, for the PMGO, loyalty was strictly a family affair.

Or consider the case of Sho Horibe, another nineteen-year-old Nisei who had never traveled outside the United States. Horibe, a Christian, was educated entirely in the United States and held only American citizenship. He had four years in a Japanese after-school program but spoke the language only poorly. He had no close relatives in Japan, and his father had not been interned as an enemy alien after Pearl Harbor. He answered "yes" to both the loyalty and the military service questions on his registration questionnaire. He enjoyed American sports and liked to fly model airplanes. His references all regarded him as a loyal American.[5]

The JAJB voted to approve Horibe for work in a war plant, but again the PMGO representative dissented:

> [W]hereas the Subject is regarded as loyal by his school mates and school teachers, his home influence has been just the contrary. His mother refused to deny allegiance to the Emperor and to swear allegiance to the United States. His father has more than $2600 in Japan. Both of these are indications that the Subject's mother and father hope to return to Japan some day and that their foremost interest is in Japan and not in the United States. It would be only natural that they would try to sway their only male child in the same way. It is also logical to assume that the Subject, being but a boy of eighteen, would be influenced by what his mother and father, both pro-Japanese, would tell him. Under such circumstances it is believed the Subject's loyalty should be questioned.[6]

Again, the PMGO's assessment of Horibe's loyalty began and ended with an assertion about the loyalty of Horibe's parents. And even that assertion was absurdly sketchy: Horibe's mother was suspect because she refused to make herself stateless. Horibe's father was suspect because over the years he had made forty-eight small fixed deposits in a Japanese bank in the United States totaling $2,600.

It is not only with the benefit of hindsight that we can see the extreme negativity of the PMGO's approach. It was evident even at the time, and even to others in the military. In October of 1943, a War Relocation Authority (WRA) official telephoned Capt. John Hall of the Office of the Assistant Secretary of War to complain that the PMGO was abruptly removing large numbers of Nisei workers from their jobs in war plants, often without even offering an explanation. Captain Hall conceded that the Provost Marshall General's Office was taking an overly hard stand in war plant cases. "I have been a little bit concerned about it for some time," said Hall, "because it's obvious to me that the PMGO, a different part of [it] than the part that fools around with the JAJB[,] has been applying fairly rigorous standards, acting on paper reports."[7]

Captain Hall was concerned that in adjudicating war plant removals, the PMGO was adopting a tough approach out of concerns for strategy rather than concerns for truth. Any employee removed from a war plant job had a right to appeal his removal to the Industrial Employment Review Board

(IERB), an independent appellate panel of three reviewing officers under the aegis of the PMGO. The IERB investigated each removal to make sure that it was supported by "substantial evidence."[8] What "worrie[d Captain Hall] a little bit," he explained, was that "the PMGO[,] when they come to a decision to remove[,] they are . . . anxious to see that the[y] are not [overturned] every time"[9] and that the "decision they make which is an important and vital decision in the life of the individual does not appear to be arbitrary and without basis."[10] Captain Hall observed that as a result, when the PMGO "decides to remove a guy[,] they paint that case about as black as they can and they draw the wildest kind of pictures."[11] Captain Hall illustrated his point with an example: "[I]f the father has been to Japan recently they argue like this: 'The father was in Japan in 1939 and this shows a strong and close affiliation with the Japanese. The fact that this son lived with his father indicates that he came under this strong Japanese influence and it must be concluded that there is reason to question his loyalty to the U.S.' "[12]

Captain Hall was exactly right. The PMGO's strategic "blackening" of Nisei's profiles in war plant cases is apparent, even ubiquitous, in the surviving records of its adjudications. In addition to its dissenting votes on war plant approvals by the JAJB, its scorched-earth strategy also dominates the surviving records of the independent war plant adjudications it performed in the period after October of 1943, when it assumed sole responsibility for those cases.[13] For example, the PMGO removed Isamu Kamibayashi from a job as a laborer at the International Harvester Company's Chicago Tractor Works because he was a Buddhist who had attended a Japanese after-school program from 1930 to 1939 and who had answered Question 28 on the registration questionnaire "No, unless we have equal rights as people outside." "By reason of [Kamibayashi's] qualified negative answer to the loyalty question . . . , his loyalty to the United States is open to serious question," said the PMGO.[14]

Noboru Mitsuoka was a trainee inspector at International Harvester whom the PMGO removed in March of 1945. He had a brother in the U.S. Army, was a Buddhist and a member of the Young Men's Buddhist Association, attended a Japanese after-school program for ten years, and asked for expatriation to Japan in March of 1944 along with his Issei parents and several of his siblings on account of "poor treatment he received while on seasonal leave from the relocation center." He later withdrew the request for expatriation, but the PMGO did not find him sincere. "In view of [his] family background and the pro-Japanese activities of his father and older brother," said the PMGO, "it seems difficult to believe that his request for expatriation was based solely on the poor treatment which he received outside the relocation center." The expatriation request, according to the PMGO, was actually "an election to declare his loyalty to the Japanese Emperor[,] and his subsequent withdrawal of this request does not in any way lessen the serious doubt it created as to his loyalty to the United States."[15]

Tashi Hori was yet another International Harvester inspector removed by the PMGO early in 1945. Hori attended Japanese language school from ages five to twenty and was active in the Young Men's Buddhist Association. His Issei father was a leader in Japanese agricultural associations and was briefly interned as an enemy alien after Pearl Harbor. On Hori's registration questionnaire, he initially answered Question 27 concerning military service with a "no," and Question 28, concerning loyalty, in the following way:

INASMUCH AS there is extreme demand and necessity for farmers, and
INASMUCH AS I was a farmer until the time of evacuation, and
INASMUCH AS "the farmers are the backbone of the country," and
INASMUCH AS the farmers are classified equally as essential as soldiers, and
INASMUCH AS the government announced the use of Japanese as farm laborers, and
INASMUCH AS the government is encouraging "white" Americans to the farms, and
INASMUCH AS the WRA and War Department states that they shall aid the loyal Japanese,

If the government guarantees me 100% with written statement to place me on the farming position almost equivalent or exact standing as prior to evacuation, or at least as a farm laborer, at a satisfactory location, I shall answer Question #28 YES.

If the government will not place me on a farm, I must answer NO, because, otherwise, I must voluntarily continue to believe that the PAST, PRESENT, AND FUTURE sentiment of the American public, government, and any other influence has been, is, and will be entirely prejudiced against any human with Japanese facial characteristic regardless of citizenship or loyalty to the extent that we cannot lead a normal life.

Some time after giving this astonishing answer to Question 28, Hori changed his answers on both Questions 27 and 28 to a simple "yes."

The PMGO was not much interested in the subtleties of Hori's initial answer to Question 28. "The influence of Subject's pro-Japanese father," said the PMGO, "is reflected in the answers of Subject . . . to the loyalty question and a serious doubt arises as to Subject's loyalty to the United States."[16] And that was the end of the matter. For the PMGO, it all came down, as always, to the supposed influence of family. The notion that an American citizen might react angrily but not subversively to the injustices of evacuation and internment was simply foreign to the PMGO's approach.

PROCESSING LOYALTY AT THE
WAR RELOCATION AUTHORITY

BY COMPARISON TO the Provost Marshal General's Office, the War Relocation Authority's approach to adjudicating Nisei loyalty was positively progressive. On every potential indicator of disloyalty, the WRA dug deeper into the real lives of the Nisei than did the PMGO, and showed less willingness to indulge attenuated inferences of subversion and deception.[1] This is not to say, however, that the WRA's adjudications ultimately captured the truth about Nisei loyalty and disloyalty, because like the PMGO, the WRA had its own agendas to pursue, and its loyalty assessments ultimately came to serve them.

If there was one score on which the WRA distinguished itself from the PMGO in assessing loyalty, it was the impact on the Nisei of their eviction from the West Coast, their prolonged detention in the relocation centers, and the controversial registration process of early 1943. For the PMGO, a "no" answer to Question 28 on the registration questionnaire, or even an equivocal answer, placed an internee into the "black" category and was categorically disqualifying for both indefinite leave and war plant work. This was true even if an internee later changed his mind and asked to switch his answer to "yes." The PMGO viewed any request for expatriation that a Nisei filed in the same way; it was automatically disqualifying.[2]

To its credit, the WRA saw that these matters were not so simple. The WRA well understood, for example, that the registration questionnaires in early 1943 stirred up such complex feelings among the internees about their experiences that a "no" answer to Question 28 meant little about an internee's loyalty. In an internal WRA memorandum of April 23, 1943, the chief of the Community Analysis Section confirmed to the chief of the Community Management Section that "[t]he basic issue which created discussion and dissension at the [relocation] centers over registration was that of civil rights[,]not loyalty." "Since civil rights was the main issue on the projects in relation to registration," the official insisted, "no repressive measures should be taken against persons who, through their objections to registration, were attempting to defend their civil rights," including "a number of people who answered 'No' or gave qualified answers to Question 28." Pointing a barb at those in the War Department who were quick to damn every Nisei who answered Question 28 in the negative, the WRA official noted that "[i]t is Machiavellian to thrust self-respecting citizens into concentration camp conditions and then call them disloyal for protesting this treatment by refusing to pledge allegiance in this situation, and then turn about and say to the public that this proves we were right in detaining these people, they were largely subversive in the first place."[3] That "Machiavellian" position was precisely the one taken by the PMGO, but WRA officials understood the situation more deeply and compassionately.

The WRA was similarly thoughtful about internees' requests for expatriation to Japan, which the WRA understood often to have little to do with loyalty. In a letter to a War Department official in July of 1944, WRA director Dillon Myer explained that many expatriation requests filed after the reinstatement of the military draft in January of 1944 reflected a desire to avoid military service rather than genuine affection toward Japan. He emphasized, however, that experience had taught the WRA that "in many cases even prior to the reinstitution of Selective Service, requests for expatriation [were] not motivated by pro-Japanese or anti-American attitudes." Some had been "motivated by a fear of forced relocation and a desire to insure continued residence in a [relocation] center." Many expatriation requests from young people "were the result of parental or group pressure" rather than true confessions of disloyalty. Thus, Myer concluded, the WRA "believe[d] that it would be a mistake to assume that a request for [ex]patriation" was a reliable indicator of disloyalty.[4]

The WRA did not merely preach this policy of understanding; to a great extent, the agency also practiced it. In its leave clearance and segregation hearings, the WRA did not treat either a "no" answer to Question 28 or a request for expatriation as conclusive evidence of disloyalty. Rather, for each internee who answered "no" to Question 28, or qualified his answer in some way, or asked for repatriation, the WRA held a hearing at the internee's relocation center, at which the internee was given the opportunity to change or explain his negative answer or expatriation request.[5] Only in those cases where the internee adhered to the expatriation request or to "an unsatisfactory answer to the loyalty question" did the WRA deny leave clearance without regard to anything else in the internee's record. It was only in these cases, the WRA's solicitor explained in mid-1944, that the agency was comfortable that the internee "appreciated the significance and consequences of his action and was not merely acting out of temporary anger or bitterness," and was "definitely deciding upon allegiance to Japan."[6] Of course, the WRA's approach to Question 28 and expatriation requests did end up condemning Japanese Americans whose anger at exclusion and prolonged detention never cooled enough to lead them to change their negative answers or withdraw their expatriation requests. In this sense, the WRA's approach to ferreting out disloyalty was undoubtedly overinclusive. By comparison to the PMGO's methods, however, the WRA's showed considerable sensitivity to the actual situation of the Nisei.

So did the WRA's methods for adjudicating loyalty in leave clearance cases that did not involve negative answers to Question 28 or expatriation requests. Like the PMGO, the WRA developed a point system for evaluating leave clearance applications. By comparison to the PMGO's, however, the WRA point system weighted features of Japanese cultural association far less negatively and features of an "American" lifestyle far more positively. Some excerpts from the point chart show this quite clearly:

	Weight	
	Positive	Negative
Question 7		
1. Registered voter	7[7]	
Question 8		
2. Married, and spouse is Japanese alien		
3. Married and spouse is not of Japanese race	3	
Question 11		
1. Sons or brother in U.S. military or government service	3	
2. Collateral relatives in U.S. military or government service	1	
Question 12		
1. Parents living and in Japan		1
3. Brothers, sisters, in Japan		1
4. Married and spouse now in Japan		2
5. Parent, sons, or brothers in Japanese military or government service		3
Question 13		
1. Attended American high school	1	
2. Graduate of American high school	2	
5. Attended elementary school in Japan		1
6. Attended middle school in Japan		2

	Weight	
	Positive	Negative
7. Attended college in Japan		3
8. Military college in Japanese school		2
9. Attendance at Japanese language school in U.S. for more than two years		1
Question 14		
1. Traveled twice to Japan since 1935		2
2. Traveled three or more times to Japan since 1935		3
4. Total duration of trips to Japan (after 10 years of age)		
Less than 1 year		
1–3 years		1
3–5 years		2
More than 5 years		3
Question 15		
5. Employment by an American-Caucasian firm or individual except canneries, fisheries, or other Japanese gang labor employers	2	
6. Occupation—Japanese language school instructor		3
Question 16		
1. Christian	1	
2. Buddhist priests		2
3. Shinto Priests (Tenriko sect)		3
4. Shinto Priests (Dai Jingu shrine)		Deny
Question 19		
1. Japanese sports instructor		2
Question 23		
1. Small contributor to Japanese patriotic or military organizations		1
2. Substantial contributor to same		3
Question 25		
1. Application to cancel registration of birth with Japanese government	3	
Question 26		
1. Application for expatriation to Japan		
Subsequent application for cancellation		2
No subsequent application for cancellation		Deny[8]

To be sure, there are points of agreement between the WRA's point system and the one that the PMGO initially used in its work for the JAJB. Both systems generally agreed on the significance of Nisei employment. Both systems assigned identical values to being an instructor of Japanese sports and to seeking to cancel Japanese birth registration.

In most respects, however, the WRA system took a more generous and sensitive view. On several points the WRA showed itself a bit out of step with its time: its point system had no special punishment for Communists; it awarded only one point for Christianity rather than two; it did not see Buddhism as meriting any negative points at all; it was willing to distinguish among different sects of Shinto rather than lumping them all together; and it awarded three points to a Nisei for being in a racially mixed marriage. The WRA's system did not subtract points for marriage to an alien, which the PMGO's did. The WRA's system also attached much greater significance to a Nisei's having a brother in the U.S. military; it awarded three points for this, whereas the PMGO's awarded but one. Even more notably, the WRA was willing to award points to a Nisei whose sibling was in *any* sort of government service, while the PMGO rewarded only *military* service.

In addition, the WRA took a markedly less suspicious approach to a Nisei's contacts with Japan than did the PMGO. It deducted fewer points than the PMGO for a Nisei's having family members in Japan, and was far more tolerant of prewar travel to Japan. The WRA did deduct three points from a Nisei who was a "substantial" donor to a Japanese organization, but the PMGO rejected substantial donors outright. Finally, the WRA was willing to forgive a Nisei who had requested expatriation if he relented and withdrew the request; the PMGO simply rejected him.

Perhaps the easiest way to see the difference between the WRA's point system and the PMGO's is to reconsider the hypothetical case, discussed in Chapter 6, of a Nisei farm worker in his early twenties who got his education through high school in the United States, traveled to Japan once as a child to visit relatives, attended four years of Japanese school in the United States while in elementary and junior high school, had a sister in Japan and a brother in the U.S. Army, read the English-language *Rafu Shimpo* newspaper, attended a Buddhist church, and was a registered voter. Under the military's system, this hypothetical Nisei ended up with a loyalty score of negative two. Under the WRA's system, he would receive a score of *positive six*.[9] While the surviving records do not indicate the score that either the PMGO or the WRA used as a cut-off for indefinite leave, the difference in results between the two systems on the same, rather average hypothetical case is striking.

A Japanese American family leaves the Topaz Relocation Center in Utah, January 3, 1945. (Courtesy of The Bancroft Library, University of California, Berkeley, 1967.014 v. 78 H-592.)

Thus, by comparison to the PMGO's, the WRA's deliberations on Nisei loyalty and disloyalty were quite enlightened. This did not mean, however, that the WRA's determinations achieved anything like a gold standard of accuracy. The WRA did not rule on Nisei loyalty in the abstract; it made its decisions in the context of two politically charged programs—one of leave clearance, which visibly scattered internees across the country, and the other of segregation, which drove them into a highly visible internal exile at Tule Lake. Public perception of the success of both programs was crucial to the WRA's survival.

It must be remembered that for the WRA, questions of Nisei freedom and confinement, loyalty and disloyalty, were intimately bound up in the agency's efforts to fend off legal challenges to its very existence. In the agency's very earliest days, as internees began filing habeas corpus petitions, its lawyers were already urging WRA staff to scour the camps for evidence specifically of Nisei disloyalty. "The keystone of our defense in any litigation," one top lawyer told WRA staff, "will be the proof of facts showing disloyalty or possibility of disloyalty among the Japanese to an extent justifying the special precaution of detention."[10] This was no evenhanded inquiry into the truth of Nisei loyalty that the lawyer had in mind. It was a quest for the "dirt."[11]

Thus, in a perverse way, the survival of the WRA's entire program depended on a premise of broad Nisei disloyalty. This was undoubtedly part of what explained the WRA's willingness to accept unchanged "no" or equivocal answers to Question 28 on the registration questionnaire and nonwithdrawn expatriation requests as categorical evidence of disloyalty warranting segregation. WRA officials knew full well that exclusion and internment had crushed the spirits of many Japanese Americans and that the registration process had left the internees even more disaffected than they had been before it.[12] As Dillon Myer, the WRA director, said to Assistant Secretary of War John J. McCloy in June of 1943, "[t]he real cause of bad evacuee morale is evacuation and all the losses, insecurity, and frustration it entailed, plus the continual 'drum drum' of certain harbingers of hate and fear whose expressions appear in the public press or are broadcast over the radio."[13] WRA officials "knew that registration had . . . sorted people, but not in terms of loyalty to the United States and to Japan."[14] An anthropologist on the staff of the WRA's Community Analysis Section at the Manzanar Relocation Center recommended to the agency's top staff "that the answers to the so-called loyalty question, question 28, be thrown in the waste basket where they belong."[15] But in the end, the agency privileged those answers by treating them as conclusive evidence that an internee was disloyal and needed segregating.

The WRA needed evidence of disloyalty not only to bolster the legality of its policy of detention but also to insure the success of its policy of relocation. Dillon Myer made this equally clear in his June 1943 letter to John J. McCloy. "Our real problem," wrote Myer, "both in maintaining morale in the centers and in securing the relocation of evacuees[,] arises . . . from the public attitude often expressed that no Japanese can be trusted, from the point of view which engenders restrictive and discriminatory legislation, which seeks to deprive Japanese-Americans of their citizenship, and to class all of them as enemies no matter what their individual records may be." Relocation would only work if white Americans were willing to accept the notion that a Japanese American could actually be a loyal citizen. Segregation of the disloyal was just a means to that end, a public method of stigmatizing some so as to cleanse others. "If it will help to secure acceptance of the relocation program," Myer told McCloy, "we are willing to accept the consequences of segregation in the centers."[16]

Finally, it is important to remember that WRA decision-makers saw internee loyalty through the distorting lens of camp control. Every camp had its lot of "troublemakers," "problem boys," "agitators," and "incorrigibles" who, in one way or another, obstructed the camp's smooth operation. These people were not disloyal, nor were they criminals; they were simply thorns in the side of the WRA. The segregation process—ostensibly a method of gauging loyalty to the United States and resulting risk to national security—became a device for managing difficult internees by incarcerating them at Tule Lake.

The case of Heart Mountain internee Kiyoshi Okamoto is an excellent example of this abuse of the WRA loyalty screening process. Okamoto was a Hawaii-born Nisei with a background in chemistry, engineering, and horticulture. By the time of his exclusion and detention in the spring of 1942, he was fifty-four years old, but he had never traveled to Japan or participated in any significant Japanese cultural organizations or activities. He was a bachelor, a loner, and something of an eccentric, listing color photography, mineralogy, and "desert philosophy" as hobbies on his registration questionnaire. And he gave louder voice to the pains of exclusion and detention than did most internees.

Soon after arriving at the Heart Mountain Relocation Center in the fall of 1942, Okamoto began complaining about the deprivation of Japanese Americans' civil liberties and about what he saw as the mismanagement of the camp. Evacuation, bad food, substandard health care, denial of due process, overcrowding, inadequate wages, deprivation of property, corruption and chaos in the camp's cooperative canteen—all of these, and more, were the subject of lengthy and sometimes acerbic petitions and letters that Okamoto sent to every official from Heart Mountain's project director all the way up to the president of the United States. In the spring of 1944, however, Okamoto found an issue that attracted a wide and supportive audience: the military draft. Along with a few other older Nisei, Okamoto organized a "Fair Play Committee" at Heart Mountain that argued for the restoration of civil liberties as a precondition to Nisei compliance with the draft. The movement had stunning success, leading almost ninety young men to resist the draft before the government shut it down.[17]

Even though Okamoto's draft resistance movement at Heart Mountain was overtly loyal, welcoming only those internees who had answered "yes" to the loyalty question on the registration questionnaire, the camp's director quickly invoked the leave clearance mechanism to get Okamoto out of camp and under segregation at Tule Lake in order to break the back of the draft resistance. After a leave clearance hearing at Heart Mountain, his examiners wrote that Okamoto's was a "case of an American citizen who is disgruntled about evacuation"; he was "not necessarily disloyal," they said, "but his case [was] questionable." "It seems bad not to grant leave clearance to a man who has never been to Japan and who is a citizen," the examiners wrote, but "giving leave clearance would jeopardize the standing of [the WRA's] relocation [program]" by reflecting poorly on other internees.[18]

Guy Robertson, the director of the Heart Mountain camp, was less equivocal. "Kiyoshi Okamoto is very voluble and bitter in his denunciation of the United States government for evacuation," he wrote to Dillon Myer. "Because of his bitterness toward our Government and his outspoken contempt and derision for the administration that evacuated him," Robertson opined, "he should not be permitted to relocate in our society as . . . our institutions, his own safety and the safety and security of other evacuees who have relocated would be jeopardized if he were given indefinite leave." Not only should he be denied permission to relocate, Robertson urged, but he should also be forbidden from "remain[ing] in a center with loyal evacuees as his preachments are likely to have some effect on the loyalty and judgment" of other internees. Okamoto was nothing but a "crackpot with a strong loyalty to Japan" who should be denied leave clearance and segregated.[19] Robertson got his way; in late March of 1944, Okamoto was shipped to Tule Lake on the strength of Robertson's findings that "the issuance of leave . . . would interfere with the war program or otherwise endanger the public peace and safety and that [Okamoto's] loyalties do not lie with the United States."[20] Robertson sent Okamoto off with a letter to the director of Tule Lake that called Okamoto "an agitator and an irreconcilable . . . without scruples," a "troublemaker . . . [who] should be placed some place [sic] where he cannot agitate."[21]

For the most part, the self-serving distortions in the WRA's loyalty determinations operated beneath the surface of the leave clearance and segregation programs, only occasionally appearing in interoffice letters and memoranda, as they did in Kiyoshi Okamoto's case. But in one very telling document, they burst into the open. At most of the WRA camps, the leave clearance and segregation decisions were unstructured; a center staff member or a panel of staff members interviewed the internee and then wrote up a memorandum recommending leave or segregation and briefly stating reasons. At Gila River in Arizona, however, the review process was considerably more structured: each staff member who sat in on a leave clearance or segregation hearing filled out a comprehensive evaluation form. It is a stunning document. For each of five broad categories ("personal appearance," "attitude during hearing," "answers [to interviewers' questions]," "social attitude," and a category about loyalty), the form offered the interviewer long checklists of adjectives that potentially described the internee's performance. For example, for "attitude during hearing," the interviewer could underline any of "eager," "pleasant," "cooperative," "talkative," "reticent," "uncooperative," "sullen," "nervous," "tense," "relaxed," "sincere," "vacillating," "alert," "lackadaisical," and "cynical." At the end of the form, the interviewer could recommend either "leave clearance," "rehearing," or "segregation."

For the category assessing the internee's loyalty, one might have expected two black-and-white alternatives: "loyal" and "disloyal." In fact, however, the form provided fourteen shades of gray. An interviewer could choose among the following: "loyal to U.S.," "a-loyal" (which meant "without apparent loyalty for any country"), "straddling," "disloyal to U.S.," "loyal to Japan," "interested in democratic principles," "knows meaning of democracy," "interested only in 'his rights,'" "family centered," "interested in 'getting out,'" "influenced by friends," "interested in helping to win the war," "influenced by educational opportunities," or "interested in peace and harmony." And most interestingly of all, the form's penultimate section required the interviewer to underline one of the following statements:

> I consider the issuance of leave for the applicant:
> Very advantageous and helpful to the war effort.
> Advantageous and safe for national security.
> Not particularly advantageous but not dangerous for
>   national security.
> Not advantageous or advisable for public relations.
> Not advantageous and dangerous to national security.[22]

This Gila River form tears the cover off the WRA's leave clearance and segregation mechanism. It provides a glimpse of the real factors that drove the process—a dizzying menu of internee attitudes, only a few of which were directly related to loyalty and disloyalty, coupled with a frank calculation of whether release or confinement would be more "advantageous" to the WRA and, presumably, the country. The distinction that the form drew between a release that was "not advantageous . . . for public relations" and a release that was "dangerous to national security" is especially chilling. This amounted to an invitation to recommend the indefinite jailing of an American citizen in order to burnish the public image of a government agency.[23] Such an invitation did not reflect anything like a balanced inquiry into the loyalty of Japanese Americans. It reflected just politics.

PROCESSING LOYALTY AT THE
WESTERN DEFENSE COMMAND

FROM EARLY 1943 through the middle of 1944, loyalty ad-judications were the business mostly of the Provost Marshal General's Office and the War Relocation Authority. The staff of the Western Defense Command, particularly its Civil Affairs Division, played just a supporting role, gathering and collating information about the prewar activities of the West Coast's Japanese Americans for the use of the other agencies. As the war began to draw to a close, however, things shifted. With the Japanese American Joint Board dissolved and the WRA's segregation program complete, the PMGO's and the WRA's adjudications moved to the background, while the WDC stepped into the spotlight. In 1944 and 1945, it created and then administered yet another system for sifting Japanese Americans, this time to determine who was loyal enough to be allowed to return to the West Coast.

It is a mistake, however, to think of the WDC's loyalty program as a single system. It was, in fact, multiple systems—or perhaps a single system with multiple faces. There was the system that the WDC fancied for itself, a screening mechanism that was at least as suspicious of Nisei loyalty as any program that had gone before but that the WDC never actually used. There was the system that circumstances forced the WDC actually to use—a screening mechanism that was milder, but in some ways even more arbitrary, than the JAJB's, the PMGO's, and the WRA's loyalty screening programs. And then there was the system that the WDC defended (and dissembled about) in federal court—a mechanism of absolute and unguided discretion that it wanted a court to validate for the benefit of military commanders in future conflicts.

The one thing that the WDC's three systems had in common with those that preceded them was their disconnection from the lives and loyalties of the people they purported to judge. As with the earlier programs, the WDC's systems reflected far more about that agency's preconceptions and needs than it did about the loyalty of Japanese Americans.

The Genesis of the Large-Scale Individual Exclusion Program

In 1943 and 1944, when the JAJB, the WRA, and the PMGO were adjudicating Japanese American loyalty, Japanese Americans were excluded en masse from the West Coast. President Roosevelt's Executive Order 9066 remained in effect, as did the various proclamations of mass exclusion that Gen. John DeWitt issued in the spring of 1942 pursuant to the authority of the president's executive order. By September of 1944, a handful of Nisei—just thirty-seven—had been granted individual permits to return to California, Oregon, and Washington. As a group, however, the Nisei remained excluded.[1]

Just a few months later, in December of 1944, the government announced that mass exclusion would end and be replaced by a narrower and more targeted system of individual exclusion. As a group, the Nisei would be permitted to leave the camps and return to the Coast; certain individuals whom the military saw as especially dangerous would continue to be excluded. The WDC would be responsible for identifying these individuals and ordering their exclusion. In other words, this military organization would be responsible for undertaking in early 1945 what its former commander, General DeWitt, had said was impossible three years earlier: separating "the sheep from the goats."[2]

The deliberations that led to this huge change in policy had been lengthy, tortured, driven by the resolve of a handful of government officials, and utterly dominated by politics. These deliberations are important in their own right because they clearly demonstrate how political rather than military considerations dominated the end of the program of mass exclusion of Japanese Americans, just as they had so strongly influenced that program at its inception. But the deliberations also provide a crucial narrative backdrop for the three different and shifting systems of loyalty adjudication that the WDC formulated, used, and defended in court.

Debate about ending the mass exclusion of Japanese Americans began in March of 1943, almost a year and three-quarters before it came to fruition, when Dillon Myer, the director of the WRA, raised the idea with Secretary of War Henry Stimson. At that time, the WRA was struggling to stem the crisis of internee morale that the notorious Questions 27 and 28 of the loyalty questionnaires had precipitated. Myer argued in a letter to Stimson that ending the mass exclusion of Japanese Americans from the West Coast would raise the internees' spirits and bolster their loyalty. He proposed two alternative plans—one quick and one slow—that would reintroduce Japanese Americans to the coastal region from which they had been excluded.[3]

Stimson let two months lapse before even taking the trouble to respond to Myer's proposal. On May 10, 1943, he replied to Myer by letter, dismissing out of hand the idea of ending mass exclusion. The solution to the problem of declining internee morale, Stimson said, was to segregate the disloyal internees from the loyal, cutting off their nefarious influence. There was no sense in even talking about an end of the mass exclusion of Japanese Americans from the West Coast until the WRA segregated the bad from the good.[4] Stimson's response took the idea of ending mass exclusion off the table at least until segregation was complete.

In July of 1943, the U.S. Senate passed a resolution calling for the segregation of the loyal from the disloyal and requesting a report from the administration on how it planned to continue operating the Japanese American camps and supervising the movements of the internees. The task of preparing that report fell to James Byrnes, the director of the Office of War Mobilization; he issued a report to the Senate on the progress of the segregation program on September 14, 1943. Accompanying his report was a letter of transmittal signed by President Roosevelt himself, and that letter included language that revived the debate about ending mass exclusion:

> We shall restore to the loyal evacuees the right to return to the evacuated areas as soon as the military situation will make such restoration feasible. Americans of Japanese ancestry, like those of many other ancestries, have shown that they can, and want to, accept our institutions and work loyally with the rest of us, making their own valuable contribution to the national health and well-being. In vindication of the very ideals for which we are fighting this war it is important to us to maintain a high standard of fair, considerate, and equal treatment for the people of this minority as of all other minorities.[5]

Historian Greg Robinson notes that Roosevelt did not draft this message himself and that the historical record does not reveal how the passage about "restor[ing] . . . the right to return to the evacuated areas" made its way into his letter. Robinson suspects that the passage may have been designed to respond to the racial unrest that had spread across the country during the summer of 1943.[6] Whatever its origin, though, this language would end up forcing the military to respond to the WRA's demands for an end to mass exclusion more constructively than Henry Stimson had done late in the spring.

The change did not happen immediately, though; the WDC was committed to the policy of mass exclusion and would not give up on it easily, even if the commander in chief was talking publicly about ending it. On

September 15, 1943, General DeWitt was promoted to a position at the Army and Navy Staff College in Washington, D.C., and Gen. Delos C. Emmons replaced him as the commanding officer of the WDC. Eventually this personnel shift would lead to greater receptiveness to the idea of ending mass exclusion. General Emmons arrived at the Presidio after nearly two years as the army's commander at Pearl Harbor, where he had adopted a more humane and measured approach to Hawaii's Japanese Americans than John DeWitt had ever shown to the Japanese Americans of the West Coast.

But Emmons's initial position on ending mass exclusion was categorical and negative. On the day of his appointment—the same day that the president's letter promising the restoration of the right of loyal internees to return to the West Coast was made public—Emmons sent Assistant Secretary of War John McCloy a message about what he planned to say on the subject at the moment he took command a few days later: "The reasons which prompted General DeWitt to direct and complete the evacuation from the Pacific Coast were impelled by military necessity and internal security," wrote Emmons, and "[t]he conditions which then existed have not materially changed." So long as the coast was "in danger from Japanese action[,] no person of Japanese ancestry will be permitted to return to the evacuated areas except upon the express approval of the War Department." His position was clear and strict, but he was not content to leave anything to the imagination; he concluded his proposed message with these strong words: "As far as I personally am concerned the policy which has been inaugurated, developed and maintained in the Western Defense Command with respect to the evacuated areas will be continued and there will be no relaxation of current restrictions unless and until the military situation changes."[7] Plainly, General Emmons had little use for the idea of ending mass exclusion.

McCloy was uncomfortable with the starkness of Emmons's proposed statement. Replying the same day, he told Emmons that he did "not think that [one could] say without challenge that '[c]onditions which then existed have not materially changed for the better.' " McCloy advised Emmons that it would be much better "to be frank in stating the change" that "[t]he military situation which then existed has materially improved," but to note that because "the possibility of enemy action" within the WDC "remains real," "[t]he general policies which have been inaugurated, developed, and maintained in the WDC with respect to persons of Japanese descent will be continued."[8]

In early October of 1943, Dillon Myer pressed McCloy for an end to the mass exclusion of Japanese Americans from the West Coast. Meeting with

McCloy at his office in the War Department, Myer noted that the WRA had largely accomplished the task of segregating the disloyal internees at Tule Lake, thereby satisfying Secretary of War Stimson's condition precedent to planning an end to exclusion. He also reminded McCloy that two lawsuits were pending—Fred Korematsu's appeal of his conviction for resisting evacuation and a habeas corpus petition brought by Mitsuye Endo that challenged continued WRA detention—either of which threatened "a very chaotic situation" if decided adversely to the government.[9] It was time, Myer argued, for the War Department and the WRA to put their heads together and cooperate in bringing mass exclusion to an orderly end.[10]

McCloy decided to pass along Myer's suggestions to General Emmons at the Presidio for comment. But recognizing that Emmons would not likely be a receptive audience, McCloy did some arguing on Myer's behalf. In a letter transmitting Myer's written suggestions, McCloy did all he could to persuade Emmons to take the matter of ending mass exclusion seriously. He reminded Emmons of President Roosevelt's words in his September 14 letter, quoting them verbatim, and then said, "I suppose that we might as well face the fact that before the end of the war, the day will come when we cannot in honesty say that the exclusion of all Japanese is still essential." Indeed, he continued, "if the question of whether or not to evacuate arose now, instead of soon after Pearl Harbor, the decision would be against mass evacuation." While this fact was "not determinative of the question of whether any of them should now be let back," it was "something to keep in mind."

McCloy also tried to appeal to Emmons's sense of fairness. He noted that the JAJB had already recommended in favor of employment in sensitive war industries for some 400 released internees, and that these cleared internees nonetheless remained personae non grata on the West Coast. "It is pretty difficult to say," he argued, "that a man who has been found eligible for war industry cannot with safety be permitted to return to the West Coast." McCloy also played on Emmons's heartstrings a bit. He noted that the rules of mass exclusion allowed a Nisei woman married to a white man to enter the exclusion zone if she had dependent children but barred her if she was childless. "Perhaps this was a sound policy to start off with," McCloy said, "but the necessity for such an arbitrary separation of families has long since passed." And McCloy told the sad story of the half-Japanese wife of a Nisei soldier and their "two three-quarter blood children," whose application to return to Seattle so that they could live with the children's white grandmother had been turned down. "Such action is entirely unnecessary from a security point of view," the assistant secretary of war urged, "and it is certainly a hell of a way to treat an American soldier's family."[11]

Still Emmons was unmoved. He wrote to McCloy on November 10, 1943, that he had no interest in partnering with Dillon Myer and the WRA on a project of returning the excluded Japanese Americans to the West Coast. "I recommend that the War Department . . . [should] not enter into any joint policies or agreements reference the return of the Japanese to the West Coast," Emmons advised, "but that we do retain a veto power" over any plans the WRA might develop. Emmons conceded to McCloy that the ice beneath the WDC's refusal to consider ending mass exclusion was thinning. He noted that ten days earlier, the West Coast had "ceased to be classified as a theater of operations." That military change, coupled with the president's language about ending exclusion in his September letter to the Senate, "leaves us in a very weak legal position." But he would not budge in his opposition to ending mass exclusion, and his reasons were mostly political. He reported "a tremendous amount of anti-Japanese feeling on the West Coast," with "the politicians riding along at full speed." These factors made it "very good policy . . . to let this feeling subside before any considerable number of Japanese are returned to the Coast." He was "quite sure," he told the assistant secretary of war, "that if we ram down the [western governors'] throats any plan to return Japanese to the Western States, such political opposition would be aroused as to nullify even a perfectly sound plan."[12]

As Emmons dug in his heels at the WDC, events conspired against Myer and McCloy in their efforts to push the idea of ending mass exclusion. In early November, violent protests erupted at the Tule Lake Segregation Center. The military marched in troops, rolled in tanks, and took over the camp, running it under martial law until mid-January 1944. The riot and the clampdown were major national news stories, with most of the coverage depicting the Tule Lake segregees as rabidly disloyal and the WRA as ineffectual in controlling them. In such a climate, talk of ending the mass exclusion of Japanese Americans from the coast was impossible. Instead, talk shifted to the idea of ending the WRA's control of the camps. By the time the dust of the Tule Lake riots finally settled in the late winter of 1944, President Roosevelt had ended the WRA's tenure as a freestanding agency and placed it under the supervision of the Department of the Interior and its tenacious and irascible chief, Harold Ickes.[13]

Ickes was at least as eager to see the end of mass exclusion as Myer and McCloy. Starting in February of 1944, he and Abe Fortas, his undersecretary of the interior, began pressing McCloy to return the War Department's attention to an early end to mass exclusion. McCloy was again receptive to the idea—receptive enough to suggest to his boss, War Secretary Henry Stimson, that he raise the subject at a cabinet meeting in mid-March of 1944. McCloy went so far as to draft comments for Stimson to deliver at the meeting, comments arguing that the government would risk "another American Indian problem" if it continued to exclude Japanese Americans from the coast beyond the moment when military necessity no longer required it. Ending exclusion would be "a political football" because of "violent objections [of] a very articulate group of people on the West Coast, particularly the Californians, and a large portion of the press," but the government nonetheless had the responsibility to oversee an orderly, peaceful return and to support the former internees in resettlement.

Stimson, however, did not deliver McCloy's remarks at the March cabinet meeting.[14] He undoubtedly understood that outside the office of his assistant secretary of war, there was little support in the military for ending mass exclusion. This is something that McCloy himself learned directly in the weeks after the cabinet meeting: one by one, the navy and the army's various units commented on McCloy's draft comments for Stimson, and every single one of them weighed in against the idea of returning Japanese Americans to the West Coast. McCloy, however, had a trick up his sleeve, in the person of the enormously influential Gen. George C. Marshall, the War Department's chief of staff. On May 8, 1944, the assistant secretary appealed to Marshall for his opinion on whether the mass exclusion of Japanese Americans remained militarily necessary.

Marshall replied promptly. He placed no stock at all in the concerns for sabotage and espionage that continued to surface in War Department discussions. Rather, he saw only one slim military objection to ending mass exclusion, namely that acts of anti-Japanese violence by white civilians on the West Coast might endanger the well-being of American prisoners of war in Japanese captivity. "There are, of course, strong political reasons why the Japanese should not be returned to the West Coast before next November"—here he referred to the upcoming presidential election—"but these do not concern the Army except to the degree that consequent reactions might cause embarrassing incidents." This was good news for McCloy, who had already gotten the assurance of California's attorney general that so long as the military was willing to attest to the loyalty of the returning ex-internees, state and local police would be able to handle any disturbances that occurred. With the support of the War Department's chief of staff, McCloy finally had what he needed to overcome the objections and hesitations that continued to plague other military decision-makers.[15]

On May 26, 1944, War Secretary Stimson finally decided the time was right to broach the subject of ending mass exclusion in a cabinet meeting. His approach was restrained; he stated that the War Department no longer believed it had a military rationale for barring Japanese Americans from the coast, but he echoed General Marshall's concerns that anti-Japanese violence in California might endanger American war prisoners, and urged the president to move cautiously. Attorney General Francis Biddle seconded Stimson's cautious support for ending exclusion, noting that because a Supreme Court ruling on exclusion and internment were still months away, the matter of ending exclusion could safely wait until after the November election without any fear of pressure from the courts. Only Interior Secretary Harold Ickes voiced full-throated support for immediately opening the camps and allowing Japanese Americans to return to their homes.[16]

In response, President Roosevelt equivocated. He stated that he agreed with Ickes "in principle" but thought it wiser gradually to scatter the internees across the country than to "dump" them on California. He asked Ickes to have the Interior Department study the possibility of stepping up efforts to relocate Japanese Americans outside the exclusion zone. To Ickes, however, this was no solution at all; the continuing coastal exclusion made it virtually impossible to persuade communities in the interior that Japanese Americans were loyal and trustworthy. He therefore followed up his presentation at the cabinet meeting with a sharply worded letter to the president reiterating his arguments for ending mass exclusion. Memorably, if rather provocatively, Ickes told Roosevelt that continuing to warehouse Japanese Americans in the camps would be "a blot upon the history of this country."[17]

The president was not moved. On June 12, 1944, he responded to Ickes' exhortations, writing that "the more I think of this problem of suddenly ending the orders excluding Japanese Americans from the West Coast[,] the more I think it would be a mistake to do anything drastic or sudden." "For the sake of internal quiet," wrote the president, Ickes should investigate, "with great discretion, how many Japanese families would be acceptable to public opinion" on the West Coast, and "seek[ ] to extend greatly the distribution of" Japanese Americans elsewhere in the United States—"one or two families to each county as a start."[18]

Any doubt that Roosevelt had politics chief in mind in reaching his decision to keep Japanese Americans out of the West Coast vanished the following day, June 13, 1944. On that day, John McCloy, not yet knowing of the president's decision of the previous day, went to the White House to meet with the president to discuss the terms of a plan for returning Japanese Americans to the West Coast that WDC commander Delos Emmons had finally put together. He was startled to find the president in the company of his top political, rather than military, advisers. Later that day, McCloy told Emmons over the telephone what had happened:

> I just came from the President a little while ago—keep this to yourself—he put thumbs down on this scheme [of rescinding mass exclusion and readmitting large numbers of Japanese Americans to the West Coast]. He wants to reinvigorate the distribution in the rest of the country and it is all right, he said, to introduce some very gradually as a relaxation of the general program into California but to do it on a very gradual basis and nothing like the scheme we have in mind. He was surrounded at that moment by his political advisors and they were harping hard that this would stir up the boys in California[,] and California, I guess, is an important state.[19]

Japanese Americans would stay off the West Coast and behind barbed wire for many more months in order to avoid antagonizing white California voters in the November election.

The matter might have rested there if it had not been for another change in personnel at the WDC. Later in June of 1944, Delos Emmons was reassigned to the army air force, and Maj. Gen. Charles H. Bonesteel replaced him. Unlike Emmons, who had come to the WDC from the command of the Hawaiian Department, Bonesteel brought little familiarity with Japanese Americans to the job. He was a Nebraskan by birth and came to the WDC after two years at the helm of the Iceland Base Command in the Atlantic theater. With this background, he might have been expected to defer to the expertise of others on matters relating to Japanese Americans, and to continue his predecessor's policies as Emmons had announced he would do when he took control from DeWitt. But Bonesteel quickly defied any such expectations.

On June 27, 1944, John McCloy wrote Bonesteel a letter summarizing what had transpired at the highest levels of government on the question of ending the mass exclusion of Japanese Americans just before he arrived. McCloy told the new WDC commander that the president had rejected Emmons's plan for ending mass exclusion and that Bonesteel's job was now to prepare a secret plan for the sharply limited return of small numbers of

Maj. Gen. Charles H. Bonesteel, the new Western Defense Commander, at his desk at the Presidio late in June of 1944. (Courtesy of The Bancroft Library, University of California, Berkeley, 1959.010 —NEG, Part 2, Box 97, [77830.10].)

internees. Bonesteel's response was stunning. On July 3, 1944, he replied to the assistant secretary of war in a letter with the following opening words: "My study of the existing situation leads me to a belief that the great improvement in the military situation on the West Coast indicates that there is no longer a military necessity for the mass exclusion of the Japanese from the West Coast as a whole." "There is still a definite necessity for the exclusion of certain individuals," Bonesteel allowed, but continued mass exclusion was groundless. The general maintained that he was "[t]aking the President's memorandum as a basic directive," but in truth he was simply disavowing any military basis for the president's decision to maintain mass exclusion.[20]

In a telephone conversation the following week, the reason for Bonesteel's flirtation with disobedience became clear. Bonesteel started the conversation by digging in his heels. "I have studied this thing pretty carefully now," he told McCloy on July 18, and he "d[id]n't find anything to change the basic recommendation" in his July 3 letter. "You should know," McCloy responded, "that I had a talk with 'the top' " about ending mass exclusion, and that "there was a feeling that at least this summer we shouldn't rescind across the board." Instead, "the very top level" thought that "a sort of general infiltration of appropriate citizens of Japanese ancestry might be all right." But Bonesteel would not be deterred. "There are a lot of angles to that, you know," he said.[21]

The angle that concerned him most was litigation: Bonesteel was the defendant in a lawsuit. In the middle of July 1944, the civil rights lawyer A. L. Wirin had filed suit on behalf of several internees in a Los Angeles court, seeking an order restraining General Bonesteel from enforcing the WDC's mass exclusion order against them.[22] And while those at "the top" might wish to ignore the question of returning Japanese Americans to the coast until after the election, General Bonesteel did not enjoy this luxury. He had to deal with "this . . . suit w[hich] the Civil Liberties outfit has brought against us." McCloy agreed with Bonesteel that the injunction suit against him was "a tough baby" that he would "hate to think of . . . getting into court."[23] A few days later, after conferring with Justice Department lawyers, McCloy instructed Bonesteel to "take whatever dilatory tactics we can" in the lawsuit to "tie the thing through" until after the fall election.

This strategy of courtroom delay did not entirely satisfy Bonesteel. Later that same day, he wrote to McCloy, warning him that significant danger lay in "allow[ing] matters to drift until action is forced." The danger was that an adverse court decision would both cause a "loss of prestige" to the military and leave a precedent "on the . . . books which might be used to thwart or curtail the authority of a military commander in some future emergency." Bonesteel thought it far wiser to take "prior positive action" to preempt an adverse court decision. And if that prior action required any sort of mass screening of former internees to determine who could return to the coast and who could not, Bonesteel explained, the WDC was woefully ill-prepared. He reported that he had found "no written statement which sets up a yard stick against which an individual Japanese may be measured to determine whether or not he is a person whose exclusion should be continued." Bonesteel told McCloy that he would set up a policy that would "provide a definite standard against which individual cases can be measured," so that it would be ready "when and if it is decided to change present exclusion policies."[24]

Bonesteel continued to argue for affirmative steps to end mass exclusion later in July when he met one-on-one with the commander in chief during a presidential visit to San Diego. Roosevelt pressed on Bonesteel his opinion that the whole problem of the excluded Japanese Americans could be solved by scattering the internees across the rest of the country, one or two families per county. But Bonesteel, in a letter to McCloy about his meeting with the president, said that he found Roosevelt's position unrealistic. The scattering plan might work if the Japanese themselves were willing to be scattered, Bonesteel conceded, but "the great majority of the Japanese will insist on going back to the areas from which they were originally removed." And this was "more than a question of obstinacy" on the part of the internees; the president's scattering plan would leave them "isolated from their own people" and would deprive them of "the religious, social and cultural contacts . . . which the Japanese particularly treasure." Bonesteel also noted that Japanese Americans had economic reasons for wanting to return to their prewar communities: a Japanese dentist or merchant, he predicted, would "have great difficulty in establishing himself in a white community." Thus, despite the president's preferences, the WDC commander told McCloy that the War Department needed to recognize that "a major portion of the excludees will wish to return to their original homes[,] and that if they are not returned[,] a very large number of them will bring legal action to accomplish it."[25]

Through the late summer and into the fall, Bonesteel kept up the drumbeat for "positive action" on the exclusion issue. The centerpiece of his efforts was a lengthy memorandum that he wrote for War Department chief of staff George Marshall on August 8, 1944. In this revealing document, Bonesteel first argued that the military situation in the Pacific had progressed to a point of such Allied strength that any lingering risk of sabotage or espionage along the coast would be at most of "secondary nature." Because the WDC commander could imagine no pro-Japanese espionage or sabotage that might "seriously change the final outcome of the war," he told Marshall that "there no longer exists adequate military or legal reason justifying the continuance of the mass exclusion of Japanese from the [WDC's] prohibited areas."

The WDC commander noted, however, that the excluded Japanese American population included a "very large number" of people who "may be expected to commit acts of sabotage and who are potential spies" and whom the army should therefore continue to exclude on an individual basis. Bonesteel boasted that "[t]he policy which defines the type of individual who is to be excluded has now been formulated"; it targeted "leaders of Japanese groups of strong nationalistic tendencies," people who had "definitely opposed the war effort," people who had renounced their American citizenship, people who had made "considerable contributions to the Japanese war effort," and people who had "organized propaganda campaigns to support the Japanese government as against our own." Of these, Bonesteel predicted, there would be "many thousands" who would need to be excluded "until the war with Japan is concluded."

Bonesteel advised Marshall that any plan to return large numbers of Japanese Americans to the coast would pose political, if not military, risks. "Large numbers of Americans in the West Coast states" opposed their return because of "economic considerations" and "hatred of the Japanese," and this would lead to "unrest, disturbances, . . . some physical violence," and maybe even "race riots." In addition, authorities would have trouble finding housing for the returning internees, because "[d]wellings formerly occupied by the Japanese are now being used . . . to house Negroes, Mexicans, and other war workers." Finally, Bonesteel reported bluntly that certain "militant" newspapers and organizations still wished to secure the permanent exclusion of the Japanese from the coast "as part of a campaign of long standing to eliminate them from economic competition." These factors, argued Bonesteel, counseled caution and care in reopening the coast to Japanese Americans but would not justify a decision to continue mass exclusion.

Bonesteel wrapped up his letter to the chief of staff with several proposals. In order to create an efficient loyalty screening system, he asked that all government files on Japanese Americans—particularly those maintained by the Provost Marshal General in Washington, D.C.—be moved to the WDC's headquarters at the Presidio. He recommended the screening of the "more than 100,000 individual cases" of Japanese Americans then subject to mass exclusion in order to generate a list of those who should continue to be excluded on an individual basis, and recommended the creation of an appeal board to hear challenges to that screening. And he called for "a meeting . . . at some time in the near future in Washington, where representatives of all agencies concerned can be brought together for the purpose of working out detailed plans for the accomplishment of the program."[26]

Bonesteel had said he favored "positive action" on the question of ending mass exclusion, and his August 8 memorandum to the chief of staff was a call to arms. But it went unheeded, presumably because it was so much at odds with the president's wish to avoid the whole issue until after the November election. Six weeks later, with no reply to his August 8 memorandum in hand, Bonesteel wrote to John McCloy to reiterate has arguments. "The more one goes into this question the more apparent it becomes that there are some Japanese American citizens who are definitely loyal to the Japanese government," he wrote. "On the other hand there are many thousands of loyal Japanese" whose numbers and exemplary military service "combined with the improved military situation provide ample basis for the conclusion that mass exclusion is no longer justified." With so many loyal and so many disloyal Japanese Americans in the camps, Bonesteel again pressed for "the establishment of a system which will treat them as individuals and not as a mass." He ended by ratcheting up his rhetoric another notch: "If the situation is allowed to drift until a legal judgment is secured which nullifies the exclusion or results in an uncontrolled flow of Japanese Americans to the West Coast[,] the result may well be disastrous."[27]

Another month passed; still General Bonesteel got no response. And so he tried again, in a letter to McCloy on October 25, 1944. "The situation with reference to the Japanese-American exclusion has reached a point where there appear to be several matters which can be best solved by personal contact," Bonesteel wrote, calling for a "personal conference" at McCloy's office in Washington as soon as possible. He reported that "much of the activity of the WDC during the past few months" had focused on setting up a system for shifting from mass to individual exclusion, but he had no approval to carry it forward, and his several-month-old request for the transfer of intelligence files from the PMGO in Washington to the WDC's Civil Affairs Division at the Presidio had still not been honored. Obviously tired of writing memoranda that just got ignored, Bonesteel decided that the only way to break the logjam was to show up at McCloy's doorstep and insist that the War Department shift from mass to individual exclusion.[28]

This letter finally broke the War Department's silence. McCloy responded diplomatically on October 31, 1944. "I will be glad to have you . . . come at any time to discuss these problems," he said, "but from what I can judge to be the sense of those who will have the ultimate decision on most of these questions, there is a disposition not to crowd action too closely upon the heels of the election" on November 7, 1944. Because "many of the considerations will have to be dealt with on high political rather than military levels," McCloy said he was "inclined to think we shall have a greater opportunity for constructive plans at a date somewhat later than November 6th."[29]

McCloy's political instincts were correct. On November 7, 1944, Franklin Roosevelt was elected to an unprecedented fourth term in office as president, and his party gained four California seats in the House of Representatives. Three days later, at his first postelection cabinet meeting on Friday, November 10, 1944, the president agreed to bring the mass exclusion of Japanese Americans to an end and asked the secretary of war to send him a plan to achieve that goal.[30]

On Monday morning, November 13, 1944, representatives of the War Department, the WRA, the Justice Department, and the WDC gathered in

Washington to begin planning the shift from mass to individual exclusion. Even with the months of WDC planning that General Bonesteel had overseen, the changeover from mass to individual exclusion promised to be a logistical nightmare. Some of the likely individual excludees were under segregation at Tule Lake; some were still in the other nine WRA relocation centers; some had been granted leave clearance by the WRA and were at liberty in various places all over the country (except, of course, the West Coast); and nobody had the faintest idea where some of them were. Moreover, the planners were laboring under time pressure; by early December, Justice and War Department officials were exquisitely aware that an adverse Supreme Court decision in Mitsuye Endo's habeas corpus challenge to continued WRA confinement was just days or weeks away, and they wanted to blunt the impact of such a ruling by announcing an end to mass exclusion before the Supreme Court ordered it.[31]

By mid-December, negotiators for the War Department and the Departments of Justice and Interior had worked out the contours of a plan for the president's final approval. War Secretary Stimson encapsulated that plan in a memorandum that he had hand-delivered to the White House on December 13. The plan envisioned that the "Department of the Interior [would] put into effect a program based on a gradual and orderly return to the West Coast and a vigorous continuation of the efforts to relocate persons of Japanese descent throughout the entire United States." The commanding general of the WDC would be prepared to announce "the termination . . . of mass exclusion of persons of Japanese descent and the designation of those whose present status of exclusion is to be maintained"—individuals "against whom information is available showing their pro-Japanese attitude." These individual excludees would be entitled to a hearing at which they would be permitted to introduce evidence. And, Stimson reported, "it is expected that less than ten thousand persons will be excluded in this manner."[32]

The next day, December 14, President Roosevelt let it be known that he did not object to the plan. On December 17, the WDC—not General Bonesteel, who on December 10 had been reassigned to other duty, but Gen. Henry Pratt, the new WDC commander—publicly announced the plan, just a day before the Supreme Court unanimously decided, in Ex parte Endo, that the WRA could no longer continue to keep loyal internees behind barbed wire.

The rescission of mass exclusion and the commencement of the broad program of individual exclusion came into effect on January 2, 1945, just days after the War Department and the Departments of Interior and Justice nailed down a final agreement fixing more precise terms for the shift in policy than they had managed to reach in the mid-December rush to beat the Supreme Court's *Endo* decision. That agreement, formalized on December 29, 1944, specified that the WDC would provide the WRA with the names of the people who would continue to be subject to individual exclusion, and it required the WDC to establish "approximately 10 review boards of 3 officers each to review" all of those individual cases.[33]

This agreement among the Departments of War, Interior, and Justice also specified that the commanding general of the WDC would find continued exclusion to be necessary for only "about 10,000 persons."[34] The historical record does not reflect how these agencies settled on this arbitrary number of 10,000 likely excludees. But this ceiling would end up having a huge impact on the method that the WDC would be forced to use in deciding who was loyal enough to return to the West Coast and who was not.

Fantasy: The Individual Exclusion System the WDC Wanted

As the pressure to end mass exclusion began to mount in the spring of 1944—before President Roosevelt decided to postpone the discussion until after the election—the WDC was in no position to handle large numbers of individual requests from Japanese Americans to return to the West Coast. It had a little-known process in place that allowed Japanese Americans to apply for individual exemption from mass exclusion. But it did not advertise the process to the internees in the camps, and it would have been utterly overwhelmed if it had done so. The process required an applicant to request an application form from the WDC's Civil Affairs Division (CAD), fill it out with extensive personal information, and then return it to the CAD for processing. The CAD would request intelligence information on the applicant from every conceivable military and civilian source all over the country. With this information eventually in hand, the CAD would organize the applicant's file and evaluate his record. The evaluation was entirely standardless; the CAD passed judgment simply on whether the applicant was "predominantly American" or "predominantly Japanese," and made a corresponding recommendation to the WDC's commanding general. The commander's decision was final and unappealable.[35]

Because so few Japanese Americans applied for exemption under this system, the WDC did not use it much. By even as late as August of 1944, the commanding general of the WDC had granted only 700 applications for exemption.[36] But in May of 1944, the CAD realized that it would need to begin thinking about what might happen if large numbers of Japanese Americans were to begin to apply for exemption from mass exclusion, or if the program of mass exclusion were to come to an end. On May 25, 1944, Victor W. Nielsen, the chief of the research branch of the CAD, alerted the CAD's officer-in-charge, Lt. Col. Claude Washburne, that because the process then in place was so lengthy and cumbersome, "it [would] be necessary to create a procedure which is quicker and more fluid." Nielsen did not foresee enormous numbers of applicants for several reasons: "the largest 'Little Tokyos'" on the West Coast had been "completely overrun by Negroes" who could not be evicted to make room for the returning internees; the internees knew they would encounter "hatred by the civilian population on the Pacific Coast"; whole families would be deterred from applying if just one of their members was refused; and many of the internees would not "see any secure economic future for themselves" on the coast. Still, Nielsen argued, the WDC and the CAD needed to be prepared.[37]

Nielsen proposed a new review board not unlike the JAJB, with voting representatives from a variety of civilian and military agencies, charged with the responsibility of evaluating the significance of some of the most prominent of the factors that the JAJB, the WRA, and the PMGO had deemed relevant to the loyalty or disloyalty of a Japanese American: membership in "any one of 3,500 Japanese organizations"; ownership of fixed yen deposits in Japan; relationship to a suspicious family member; the pendency of a request for expatriation; negative or ambiguous statements about loyalty; dual citizenship; education in or trips to Japan; decoration or recognition by the Japanese government; attendance at a Japanese language after-school program in the United States; and contribution to the Japanese war effort. To streamline the process, Nielsen suggested that this new board consider Japanese Americans not individually but as family units.[38]

By mid-June, Nielsen's idea had made its way up the chain of command to the WDC commander, Gen. Delos Emmons. In a telephone conversation with Assistant War Secretary John McCloy on June 12, 1944, Emmons made the case that the loyalty screening system that the WDC wanted to develop would be a simple and generally forgiving affair, "a burden to nobody[,] but a big help." "We don't propose and never did propose to do anything more than examine the intelligence records that have been accumulated from many sources including the WRA except in rare cases," Emmons assured McCloy. "We are not going to have these Japs make out a lot of forms and appear before this board[;] we are just going over the things and then clear them by family before this [new review] board." He predicted that there would be only "one or two cases perhaps out of every 100 or 150 that we will want to make a further investigation of."[39]

The staff of the Civil Affairs Division, however, had other ideas. Claude Washburne, who as the CAD's officer-in-charge played the most important role in designing and implementing the WDC's screening systems, laid out the case in early July for the most comprehensive and suspicious screening system that any government agency had devised since Pearl Harbor. His overarching view—which he expressed just a few days after the WDC's commander, Charles Bonesteel, wrote to the assistant secretary of war about the "greatly improved military situation on the West Coast"—was that the standard for identifying who was safe to return to the coast ought to be just as high as the standard for determining who ought to be allowed access to classified military information. "The basic consideration is the loyalty of the person," Washburne maintained, and while "the range of loyalty may run from 100% allegiance to the United States to 100% allegiance to Japan, with all gradations in between," the "basic test" was "whether the person predominantly owes his allegiance to Japan."[40]

But in Washburne's view, this was not an easy thing to discern in a person of Japanese ancestry. In fact, Washburne maintained, "[d]ue to the religious and nationalistic concepts of the Japanese philosophy, it is impossible to judge the individual by his own activities alone." Rather, the real focus needed to be on "the head of [the] Japanese family[, who] controls all of the family members to a very high degree." It was "not unreasonable to assume" that Japanese Americans would "do anything demanded by the[ir] parents" —a decidedly worrisome tendency, given that the "bulk" of the parents themselves lived by "their philosophy . . . that they will do anything requested in the name of the Emperor."[41]

The CAD's officer-in-charge then presented a five-page, single-spaced list of "some of the principal factors to be considered in the determination of loyalty of persons of Japanese ancestry." But the list was not simply "some" of those factors; it contained and elaborated on *every single factor* that any prior loyalty adjudication mechanism had examined, and then some. Beyond the usual considerations, it included such items as "[p]articipation in Emperor Birthday Celebrations," "[p]articipation in any program for the Japanization of American born Japanese," "any activities that would raise any suspicion that the individual's loyalty may be purchased," "the possession or dissemination of Japanese propaganda . . . phonograph records," and "the possession of . . . short wave radios." As complete as the list was, Washburne conceded that it was ultimately of limited usefulness because "there is no possible rigid set of standards or formula that can be created." The variables and the "variations within the variables" were nearly endless, with the result that "the final decision must be one of considered judgment by an individual . . . who ha[s] decided . . . that the preponderance of the evidence should be that the individual is predominantly Japanese rather than American."[42]

In several respects, Washburne's proposed approach to loyalty screening was tougher on Japanese Americans than anything that had gone before. Family connections and social hierarchy were, for Washburne, not merely relevant but controlling factors. Japanese children were puppets, and their parents the puppeteers; at a wider level, Japanese *parents* were puppets, and the *emperor* the puppeteer. Washburne's list of indicators of disloyalty was long and detailed, but he flagged nothing about a Japanese American's life or interests that tended to *disprove* his disloyalty, or, more positively, to prove his *loyalty*. The degree of loyalty that a Japanese American needed to display in order to win the simple privilege of returning to his home on the West Coast was astonishingly high—the same as he would have needed if applying for access to classified government secrets. And a mere "preponderance of the evidence" was enough to tip the scales toward disloyalty. If, in the view of a military screener, the evidence made it slightly likelier than not that an American citizen of Japanese ancestry owed his predominant allegiance to Japan, that citizen would continue to be excluded from the West Coast.

This CAD proposal was breathtakingly skeptical of the idea of Japanese American loyalty. With its loose preponderance-of-the-evidence threshold, its indulgence of guilt by association and familial rather than individual culpability, and its attachment of suspicion to virtually every aspect of Japanese cultural and economic life, the system came very close to capturing Gen. John DeWitt's atavistic view that "there [wa]sn't such a thing as a loyal Japanese." More stunning still was the timing of the CAD's reprise of this hypersuspicious approach to loyalty. Lieutenant Colonel Washburne circulated the CAD proposal in July of 1944, when Japanese Americans were fighting and dying for the United States on European battlefields and working in sensitive war industries—and months after the highest military and civilian officials in the War Department had recognized that Japan's military fortunes were crumbling beyond repair and that no military basis remained for the mass exclusion of Japanese Americans from the coast. The CAD's proposal reflected nothing at all about the reality of the military situation or the actual lives and loyalties of Japanese Americans. It reflected nothing more than the fantasy—or nightmare—that had haunted the halls of the WDC since the war began.

It is impossible to know whether the CAD's approach to loyalty screening would have met with the approval of General Emmons; by the time the WDC put the finishing touches on its proposed screening process in late July, Emmons was gone. And General Bonesteel, who replaced Emmons and brought to the job a stronger determination to end mass exclusion, thought Washburne's CAD plan pushed a bit too far. On August 8, 1944, Bonesteel gave his approval to a "statement of policy" for the evaluation of Japanese exclusion cases—the written "yard stick" for measuring the loyalty of Japanese Americans that he had been surprised not to find at the WDC when he assumed command. Compared to the system that the CAD had envisioned, Bonesteel's August 8 policy statement cast a somewhat narrower net. At the outset, it set an evidentiary bar that was at least arguably higher than the CAD's preferred "preponderance" standard: "The important consideration is that there shall be *material evidence* which indicates that the individual being considered is dangerous to military security"; without "material evidence," the person would be "classed as not dangerous."[43] The statement did not define the word "material," but in common parlance that word implies a degree of real importance that a bare "preponderance" of the evidence seems to lack.

The policy statement then listed eighteen "examples of the type of individuals" who should continue to be excluded. In the main, they tracked the sorts of activities and attributes that had also been Lieutenant Colonel Washburne's concern; naturally, they isolated "individuals who ha[d] directly or indirectly expressed a desire, since Pearl Harbor, to renounce their American citizenship or to assume Japanese citizenship" and "individuals who ha[d] refused without qualification to serve in the American Armed Forces." But in notable ways the tone and phrasing of many of the categories differed from the CAD's. The statement mentioned "individuals who [had] assumed *leadership*" of "pro-Japanese societies" and of those religious groups "whose teachings [were] highly nationalistic in character." It called for exclusion of those who had "made contributions to the Japanese war effort," had "had residence in Japan," and had "sponsored, directed, or given financial support to Japanese Language Schools"—but only if they had done these things "*to a marked degree.*" (Mere attendance at a Japanese language school was not sufficient to trigger scrutiny.) It required exclusion of those who "ha[d] opposed the war effort or urged others to oppose the war effort" but was careful to note that "[t]he mere objection to the removal of the Japanese from the West Coast" would not count as disqualifying opposition to the war effort.[44]

The policy statement did continue the tradition of judging Japanese

Americans on the basis of their family ties but called for exclusion only of those who were "members of a family *strongly dominated* by a member who is suspect." Finally, the policy statement included a catch-all category that permitted the exclusion of a Japanese American as to whom no single factor was serious enough to warrant condemnation but "whose record when all categories are considered cumulatively" presented a red flag.[45]

This draft approach to loyalty screening showed some effort at moderation. Its target was not the rank-and-file Nisei but certain of the leaders and the "doers" of that generation—people who had somehow distinguished themselves through markedly pro-Japanese conduct. It recognized the idea that parental domination might be lesser in some families than in others. And it took the surprisingly sympathetic position that a Japanese American's complaints about exclusion and internment were not in themselves evidence of disloyalty.

As the WDC continued to circulate, debate, and refine this proposed statement of policy for individual exclusion in the late summer of 1944, the trend toward moderation continued. On September 8, General Bonesteel adopted a revised version of the policy statement that scuttled what had long been a crucial criterion of disloyalty: the notion of family guilt. It entirely eliminated "members[hip] of a family strongly dominated by a member who is suspect" as a basis for exclusion. Under this version of the policy statement, a Japanese American would be judged on the basis only of *his own* conduct and history, not that of his parents or his siblings.[46]

Yet at the same time as the WDC was scaling back its proposed criteria for gauging Japanese American disloyalty, it was also ramping up a new plan to compile and process vast amounts of intelligence data about the entire Japanese American population in the United States. Under the plan, WDC technicians would key every known piece of biographical information onto IBM punch cards for every Japanese American in the United States—age, sex, citizenship, last known address, residency in a relocation center, and so on. This biographical information would take up half the card; the other half would be reserved for codes reflecting every piece of derogatory intelligence information about the person that was to be found in the files of every military and civilian investigative agency in the country. A processing machine would then allow the WDC to sort Japanese Americans' punch cards for any type of biographical data and any type of derogatory intelligence information. This punch-card system was to be the "total information awareness" program of its day—a massive, mechanized system for keeping tabs on an entire American ethnic group.[47] If, for example, the WDC wanted a list of all Buddhist Nisei from Los Angeles who belonged to the Japanese American Citizens League and competed in judo, the system was designed to produce that list.

Reality: The Loyalty Screening System the WDC Actually Used

None of these grandiose plans would come to fruition—neither the punch-card project, nor Lieutenant Colonel Washburne's pie-in-the-sky loyalty screening system, nor the somewhat leaner policy statements on loyalty screening that the WDC adopted in August and September of 1944. As the presidential election approached and then passed, and it became clear that the government would need a loyalty screening system that it could actually implement in many thousands of cases, all of these plans collapsed under their own weight, to be replaced by a far more slender system that found disloyalty in manageable, if utterly arbitrary, numbers.

Most of the pressures on the WDC's plans for loyalty screening were logistical, not conceptual. For example, the WDC wanted all available intelligence information about a Nisei's pre–Pearl Harbor life before making a decision about his continued exclusion from the coast. Much of the information it needed was in the files of the FBI and the Office of Naval Intelligence, but because of short wartime staffing, these agencies often took up to three months to produce the information that the WDC wanted. This was a prohibitively lengthy time lag.[48]

A somewhat related, but even more difficult, problem was the number of people whom the screening system would label "disloyal." In early December of 1944, as War, Interior, and Justice Department officials haggled over the terms and timing of the switch from mass to individual exclusion, the WDC did a test run of its loyalty screening system in order to see how it would function. The tested screening standards were similar not to Washburne's wild proposal of July 1944 but to the milder ones in the WDC's Proposed Policy Statement of early September. And the test run of these more moderate criteria projected findings of disloyalty in *30,000 cases.*[49]

While this staggering number of excludees may not have displeased WDC officials in the abstract, it was completely out of step with the number of expected excludees that top War, Justice, and Interior Department officials were discussing and sharing with the president. In formally proposing the end of mass exclusion to the president on December 13, Secretary of War Henry Stimson predicted "less than ten thousand" individual excludees, and the tripartite agreement among the War, Justice, and Interior Departments of December 29, 1944, confirmed that number. Yet the WDC was preparing a screening system that would net *three times too many* "disloyal" Japanese Americans.

Given these pressures, the WDC had no choice but to chop away at its screening system so that it would produce the arbitrarily agreed-upon number of 10,000 individual excludees. The chopping was as rough as it was· capricious. First, the WDC decided to declare that no woman could be individually excluded from the coast, regardless of her backgrounds or beliefs.[50] An officer of the PMGO who spent time at the Presidio studying the WDC's screening system in January of 1945 was skeptical about this move; he argued that "some women are of strong and independent character and may be dangerous," that "many" Nisei women were "sentimentally loyal to Japan," and that "while women may not be inclined to physical sabotage[,] they have been known to violate confidences and act as aids to men."[51] Yet he acknowledged that the wholesale exemption of women from the individual exclusion process was necessary, "a practical means of eliminating approximately 50% of the population from consideration."[52]

Next, the WDC exempted from eligibility for individual exclusion all children under the age of fourteen, all members of the U.S. armed forces, all parents of children serving in the armed forces if the parents had approved of their children's service, and all people holding an honorable discharge from the U.S. Army.[53] Here, too, the observer from the PMGO worried that these exemptions were too broad: some Nisei soldiers were of less-than-certain loyalty, he argued, and no parent deserved a presumption of loyalty simply for allowing his son to be drafted.[54] Still, the WDC had to slash the number of excludees to 10,000, and these categorical exemptions helped it reach that goal.

But they only helped; they did not do enough. The WDC therefore had to do something even more radical: it had to pare down its list of criteria for disloyalty. It chose to draw a line in time, at the moment of the Pearl Harbor attack. With narrow exceptions, the only conduct and statements on which the WDC would rely in deciding whether to exclude a Japanese American from the West Coast would be those occurring *after* Pearl Harbor: a "no" answer to Question 28 on the 1943 loyalty questionnaire, a demand for expatriation to Japan, or a renunciation of citizenship. Pre–Pearl Harbor conduct could trigger individual exclusion only if it amounted to "leadership" of certain religious and Japanese nationalist organizations.[55]

This was a paradigm shift in the American military's assessment of the loyalty of Japanese Americans. Gone were virtually all of the old chestnuts of Nisei disloyalty: education and travel in Japan, dual citizenship, suspect family ties, membership in religious and cultural organizations, and ownership of fixed deposits in Japanese banks.[56] The change came with misgivings and regret; WDC officials understood that the new standards were "at wide variance with the established policies of the Intelligence and Security agencies." They were still of the view that "many acts prior to Pearl Harbor were obviously important"; they felt that in a perfect world, the simple fact that "those acts could not be repeated after Pearl Harbor, due to the fact that the Japanese were in custody in the Assembly Centers and Relocation Projects" would not mean that those acts "should . . . be ignored" by loyalty screeners. But the WDC was not operating in its own ideal world; it was operating in the world of reality, a political world that required it to set up a system as "a matter of expediency," with a nervous eye to what the courts might eventually be persuaded to uphold.[57]

The overhaul of the WDC's screening system late in 1944 was neither logical nor pretty, but it produced the right numbers, which is mostly what it was designed to do. Using its new criteria, the WDC served almost exactly 10,000 adult male Nisei with individual exclusion orders in January of 1945. Their families were, at that point, finally free to return home to the West Coast. They, on the other hand, remained under military orders to keep out.

The punch cards were boxed up and forgotten, well before WDC typists even had the chance to begin keying in "derogatory" intelligence information on the nation's Japanese American population.

DEFENDING (AND DISTORTING)
LOYALTY ADJUDICATION IN COURT

WHILE THE WESTERN Defense Command's loyalty screen-
ing system shared a great deal with those that had gone before it, especially that
of the Provost Marshall General's Office, it was unique in one respect. It was the
only system to be tested in court. In July of 1944, George Ochikubo, a Nisei dentist behind the barbed wire of the War Relocation Authority's Topaz Relocation
Center in central Utah, filed a lawsuit challenging his continued exclusion from
the West Coast under Gen. John DeWitt's mass exclusion orders of 1942.
Because the government responded to the lawsuit by initiating individual exclusion proceedings against Ochikubo, his legal claims ended up focusing on the
screening system that the WDC used to determine which individual Japanese
Americans to exclude, rather than on the mass exclusion orders of 1942.

The federal district court's decision in Ochikubo's case ended up turning
on a different legal issue than the merits of the WDC's screening system. The
court therefore said nothing about that system's lawfulness. Nonetheless,
the story of Ochikubo's legal challenge to the WDC's loyalty screening system, and of the government's response to that legal challenge, is important
and revealing. For the most part, the story reveals the WDC's loyalty screening
system to have been marred by the same sorts of flaws that marred earlier
systems, but to an even more serious degree. Screening officials examined the
lives of the Nisei through thick lenses of fear, melodrama, and caricature. The
judgments of government officials—including government lawyers—had
nearly everything to do with the needs and objectives of the government, and
nearly nothing to do with the loyalties of the Nisei before them. But the story
of the Ochikubo lawsuit also revealed something disturbing and new: a willingness of some officials to equivocate about the government's program in order
to protect it, even to the point of misrepresenting it under oath.

The Plaintiff: George Ochikubo

George Akira Ochikubo was born in Oakland, California, on January 8,
1911, the oldest child and only son of an Issei farmer and his wife who came

to the United States shortly after the turn of the century.[1] His father registered young George's birth with the Japanese government in order to qualify him for Japanese as well as American citizenship, but in 1924, his father applied to cancel his Japanese citizenship, and the Japanese government approved that application.

Ochikubo never visited Japan and knew no Japanese relatives (other than his parents). His family, although nominally Buddhist, was not religious, and Ochikubo grew up with no real sense of religious identification and without regularly attending any house of worship.

Ochikubo spoke Japanese with his parents at home until he was around six years old, when he started school, but after that moment he spoke to them almost exclusively in English. His parents tried sending him to an after-school Japanese language program, but he was kicked out for too often cutting class in order to play baseball with his friends. As a result, he spoke Japanese only very poorly and could not read or write it at all.

He attended grammar school and high school in Oakland. Up to the age of seventeen, all of his friends and associates were white. This was not always an easy situation; at times he was excluded from parties and other social activities because of his Japanese face, and he carried these injuries with him for the rest of his life. Ochikubo made his first Japanese American friend when he began attending Oakland Technical High School in his junior year. That friend prevailed upon him to join the Jinshu Kyokai, a social organization for Nisei teens, but he quit the club after just six months when the girls refused to authorize an expenditure of $100 for the boys to travel to Los Angeles to play in a basketball competition.

Ochikubo attended the University of California at Berkeley, graduating in 1931, and then the University of California Dental College from 1934 to 1938. During that time, he met and married a woman from Montana whose mother was white and whose father was Japanese. They had two children together. After graduating from dental school, Ochikubo had some trouble passing the state licensing examination and therefore spent the two years from 1938 to 1940 working with his father in the gardening business. He passed the dental exam in 1940 on his second try, and then accepted a job offer from a relative of his wife's, an Issei dentist who was about to leave the country for Japan and needed someone to replace him. He continued to work as a dentist for almost two years, until the Japanese attack on Pearl Harbor. Even during this time of professional success, he continued to be dogged by painful discrimination, as he had been in childhood: the Hotel Columbia in San Francisco once refused to let him in for a function because of his ancestry, and several clubs to which he had been invited by white doctors refused him admission as well.

Two days after the Japanese attack at Pearl Harbor, Ochikubo walked into an Oakland recruiting station to volunteer for the army. The recruiting officer courteously told him that he was not eligible because he was "an Oriental." Then, in the spring of 1942, Ochikubo and his wife, children, and parents were forced from their Oakland home and into the temporary "assembly center" at the Tanforan racetrack just south of San Francisco pursuant to General DeWitt's mass orders. At summer's end, the entire family was shipped off to a barrack at the Topaz Relocation Center in the Utah desert.

At Topaz, Ochikubo poured his energy into community politics, quickly securing election to the Topaz Community Council, the body of self-governance that the WRA allowed the internees to set up at the camps. The energy that Ochikubo poured into camp politics was not invariably positive, at least in the eyes of the camp's WRA administrators. In the opinion of Topaz's project director, Charles Ernst, Ochikubo's frequent brushes with discrimination earlier in his life were "sores" that "festered" behind the barbed wire at Topaz, "thrust[ing themselves] into much of [his] actions and thought" while he was in camp. In the spring of 1943, when the government pressed the internees at Topaz to fill out the loyalty questionnaires, Ochikubo initially encouraged people not to comply until officials more clearly explained the meaning of questions 27 and 28 and guaranteed them that their civil rights would be restored. When officials threatened to imprison those who did not fill out the questionnaires, Ochikubo relented. On his own form, he answered "yes" both to the question about loyalty and to the question about military service.

By the fall of 1943, Ochikubo had risen to the chairmanship of the community council at Topaz. It was a tense time to be in a leadership position, with shockwaves from the riot and strikes at the Tule Lake Segregation Center in early November buffeting all of the other Japanese American camps. One item of business for the Topaz Community Council was a request to send Topaz residents to Tule Lake to harvest crops that the striking Tule Lake workers would not touch. After a stormy meeting on the subject, a confidential informant reported to the FBI that Ochikubo had said he would rather "see the potatoes rot" at Tule Lake than that "Topaz residents harvest them." The informant, undoubtedly a political opponent of Ochikubo's in the internee community, told the FBI that the dentist had a "subversive" influence at Topaz, and that he "viewed himself as being a kind of leader in a great cause." The FBI's investigation, however, turned up "no definite subversive activities" on Ochikubo's part, and the FBI closed its file.

The Japanese American Joint Board (JAJB) recommended against leave clearance for George Ochikubo on November 17, 1943, at the moment when the controversy about sending Topaz residents to Tule Lake was it its peak. The WRA, however, reached the opposite conclusion, and granted him leave clearance. Topaz project director Ernst was of the view that "Ochikubo had something definite to offer America . . . that would never come out as long as he was inside a relocation center"; he hoped that the army would eventually accept him as a dentist. Ochikubo shared that hope. Waiting for the reinstatement of the draft, Ochikubo decided not to relocate out of camp; he did not wish to leave his wife alone in a new and unfamiliar place with their two young children and without work if he suddenly had to go off to war.

Ochikubo was therefore still at Topaz in the summer of 1944. That was when he decided to mount a legal challenge to his continued exclusion from the West Coast under the mass exclusion orders that the WDC had kept in place since General DeWitt had issued them in the spring of 1942. He had several reasons for suing: he wanted to be "among [his] friends again" and knew that he could "get along with Caucasians"; he had read articles by "high authorities" who said that the "military necessity [was] practically nil now on the coast"; and he thought that it was time for the mass exclusion to be lifted.

Representing Ochikubo was A. L. Wirin, a well-known Los Angeles civil liberties lawyer who had come to specialize in legal matters affecting Japanese Americans' civil liberties during the war. Wirin found two other Nisei to join Ochikubo as plaintiffs. One, Ruth Shizuko Shiramizu, was the twenty-four-year-old widow of a Japanese American soldier, a member of the famed 442nd Regimental Combat Team who had received a Purple Heart in January of 1944 just before dying of his war injuries.[2] The other, Masaru Baba, was a twenty-six-year-old U.S. Army veteran whose pre–Pearl Harbor military service had not protected him from evacuation and internment, but had qualified him for a very early release from the Rohwer Relocation Center in Arkansas in December of 1942 to take a job at a beverage bottling company in Nevada.[3] Wirin filed suit on behalf of all three in the Superior Court of California for Los Angeles County in mid-July of 1944, seeking an injunction restraining Gen. Charles Bonesteel, WDC commander, from enforcing the mass exclusion orders against them.

George Ochikubo (center) examines legal papers with his attorney, A. L. Wirin (left), and Saburo Kido, national president of the Japanese American Citizens League. (From the Los Angeles Daily News Negatives [Collection 1387], Department of Special Collections, Charles E. Young Research Library, UCLA.)

"Stalling on Bad Faith Procedural Tactics"

When he filed the suit challenging the continued mass exclusion of the three plaintiffs, Wirin could not have known that a month earlier, President Roosevelt had decided to postpone the end of mass exclusion until after the November elections. The lawsuit, however, threw a wrench in the president's plan. Naturally, the administration did not want to risk the embarrassment of a public judicial repudiation of its program, especially before the election. But the problem ran deeper than that. One of the most crucial of the plaintiffs' factual assertions was that the mass exclusion of Japanese Americans from the West Coast was no longer a military necessity. Uncomfortably for the government, this was also the position of the WDC and the War Department; George Marshall, the War Department's chief of staff, had stated this as early as May of 1944, and Major General Bonesteel had reiterated it to Assistant Secretary of War John McCloy in early July. The most pressing problem facing government lawyers was therefore not that a court might actually decide the *Ochikubo* case on its merits before the election; it was that the government might need to answer the plaintiffs' factual assertions in any way before the election. Obviously, the government could not admit the plaintiffs' allegation that mass exclusion was no longer militarily necessary without blowing up the president's strategy of delaying the end of mass exclusion. But the government could not plausibly deny it, either.

This dilemma left the government's lawyers only two options. One was to delay the lawsuit with any procedural trick available; the other was to make the cases moot by just relenting in these three specific cases and readmitting them to the West Coast. Attorney General Francis Biddle's first reaction was to moot the cases.[4] But Herbert Wechsler, his assistant attorney general in charge of the Justice Department's War Division, had the opposite reaction, and because he was the one dictating strategy, his preference for a strategy of delay initially prevailed. Wechsler instructed Edward Ennis, the lawyer who headed the department's Alien Enemy Control Unit, to have the U.S. Attorney in Los Angeles wait until the last possible moment and then remove the case from state to federal court. After the case was in federal court, the U.S. Attorney was to "avoid taking a position on the question of military necessity" by moving to dismiss the lawsuit on several procedural grounds. These grounds included a claim that the suit should be dismissed because the plaintiffs had not exhausted all administrative remedies before suing, in that they had never applied to Major General Bonesteel for individual exemptions from the mass exclusion order, and a claim that the federal district court lacked jurisdiction over the case.[5]

Wechsler's approach triggered an outcry from other Justice Department lawyers. On July 18, 1944, John L. Burling, a young attorney on Edward Ennis's staff in the Alien Enemy Control Unit, bluntly informed Wechsler that he found the delaying approach to be completely "unprincipled" and a disservice to "the eighty thousand people [excluded from the coast] whose rights are infringed" by continued mass exclusion. This was a weighty charge indeed against a man who would go on to become one of the leading American legal figures of the twentieth century, largely on the strength of his insistence that the adjudication of constitutional rights must be a rigorously "principled" exercise.[6]

Burling told Wechsler that he favored mooting the cases because this would "at least suggest to [Japanese American excludees] that the Government has no legal right to [continue mass exclusion] and will hint to them that the Government might give up" if a case were filed that could not be mooted. Whereas mooting the cases would have "some of the social effect of a confession of error" in the continued exclusion of Japanese Americans from the coast—a confession of error that Burling supported—"dilatory tactics" of the sort that Wechsler had ordered would "have none of this social effect." It would "just purely and simply delay the adjudication." Burling argued that the contemplated arguments for dismissal of the lawsuit after removal from state court were weak, even "absurd," and that he was therefore "convinced that we must either moot the case before the time to answer [the complaint's factual allegations], make some answer on the merits, or recognize that we are simply stalling on bad faith procedural tactics."[7]

At the same time as Burling was remonstrating with Wechsler over plans for delay, discussions in the War Department were headed in the opposite direction. Assistant Secretary of War McCloy telephoned WDC commander Bonesteel on July 18 to ask him what he would think "of the suggestion that the Department [of Justice] are now pressing on me—that you make moot all of these three cases by permitting all three of them to come in." "I would say no," Bonesteel responded. "The widow is all right," he said, referring to the plaintiff Shiramizu, and Baba was a "borderline case and could go either way," but Ochikubo, whom McCloy described as "something of an agitator," was simply unacceptable. "If he was ruled on [for readmission to the coast] right now," Bonesteel said, "he wouldn't be allowed in." It would not be possible to make the issue go away by mooting all of the cases, so delay through procedural tactics was the only option.[8]

The War Department's insistence on a strategy of delay infuriated John Burling, and his fury soon infected his boss, Edward Ennis, as well. They threw down the gauntlet at a meeting on August 1, 1944, at the Office of the Assistant Secretary of War, attended by McCloy and his top assistant and by the top policy-making brass of the Justice Department—Solicitor General Charles Fahy, Herbert Wechsler, Ennis, and Burling. Ennis and Burling bluntly summarized the merits and demerits of the three possible responses to what they referred to as "the dentist's case"[9]—mooting it, mounting what they called an "espionage and sabotage defense" to it on the merits, and mounting what they called a "social resistance defense" to it.[10]

Mooting Ochikubo's case, the lawyers said, would have the benefit of avoiding a legal defense of "a legally indefensible governmental action," the continued mass exclusion of Japanese Americans, thereby "avoid[ing] the necessity of adopting a legally indefensible position in court." On the downside, they noted, it would provide only a temporary fix; other Japanese Americans would undoubtedly file their own identical suits in short order if

Ochikubo's were mooted. Furthermore, mooting the case might stir up "editorial clamor" in West Coast newspapers, and it might further depress the spirits of Japanese Americans if they felt that they were "being denied a judicial decision which is generally held forth as so essential a part of our form of government."[11]

Ennis and Burling could not contain their scorn for the second option, the "espionage and sabotage defense." This approach would require government lawyers to prove the proposition that Japanese Americans whom the WRA had already cleared as loyal nonetheless presented such a danger that the military was justified in continuing to exclude them all from the coast. On the plus side, the lawyers noted, such a defense, if believed, would arguably fit within the four corners of Executive Order 9066, the president's February 1942 order that had set the entire Japanese American program in motion. It would also give the litigants their day in court, and might produce an elucidating opinion from the Supreme Court in "an unclear field of constitutional law." "This course would probably be most popular in California," they somewhat sardonically noted.[12]

But the potential downside to this option was disastrous. First, they argued, "[i]t is unlikely that any court could be persuaded" to accept the military's claims about the military situation—especially because no "informed and responsible Government officials, including [War Department chief of staff] General Marshall," actually believed them. Second, the lawyers reported that "trial experience" suggested that military witnesses, in the "contest atmosphere of a trial," would make statements "of the military situation and an estimate of the loyalty of the Japanese Americans which would go beyond and not correctly reflect the military judgment of the Commanding General [of the WDC] and the General Staff [of the War Department]." In other words, in a tense courtroom confrontation, military witnesses would probably bend and exaggerate their testimony. Finally, if military officers testified in court that Japanese Americans continued to pose a risk of sabotage and espionage *even after the* WRA cleared them to leave the camps, this testimony would make it much harder for the WRA to find welcoming communities for them in other parts of the country.[13]

The option that Ennis and Burling preferred was the third one—the "social resistance defense." This defense on the merits would require testimony by military authorities that returning Japanese Americans to the coast "is so contrary to the wishes of the overwhelming majority of the population at this stage of the war with Japan . . . that there is reasonable cause to apprehend social unrest, publicly expressed agitation and opposition, and even violence." This would "be undesirable militarily" to the extent that the violence would interrupted war production or prompt reprisals against American war prisoners in Japanese custody.[14]

The central problem with this approach, the lawyers noted, was that it would "require[ ] the Government to take the position that social resistance is a legal reason for preventing the return of Japanese Americans to California." It would force the government to admit, in other words, "that the course which [the government] is pursuing is contrary to our constitutional traditions." On the other hand, Ennis and Burling argued, "[p]ublic resistance to the return of the Japanese Americans *is in fact the real and only reason they are not now being permitted to return.*" Unlike the mooting and military necessity options before them, the social resistance defense had the virtue of being "the closest possible approximation of the truth."[15]

The truth may have been appealing to Ennis and Burling, but the policymakers above them had other things on their minds. Fahy and Wechsler wanted to make Ochikubo's case go away, clearing it from the president's path to the November elections with minimal embarrassment to the Justice Department. McCloy, for his part, wanted to back up his West Coast commander, who was insisting that Ochikubo should not be permitted to return. The August 1 meeting therefore closed without agreement; the top Justice Department lawyers pressed for mooting the case, while the assistant secretary of war thought an espionage and sabotage defense was the best option.

Two weeks later, the logjam was still in place. McCloy therefore convened another meeting—an all-day affair on a Saturday—in order to break it. This time, Major General Bonesteel came in from the coast to join the discussions. And in no uncertain terms, the WDC commander told McCloy and the Justice Department lawyers that George Ochikubo "appear[ed] to be an individual who possesses the qualities and connections essential to an enemy agent."[16] Bonesteel simply could not see his way clear to allowing Ochikubo into the exclusion zone in order to moot his legal challenge. Some sort of legal defense would therefore be necessary; the question was what that defense would be.

The military officials at the meeting urged the Justice Department lawyers to defend the mass exclusion order, as applied to Ochikubo, on the basis of the supposedly incriminating details in Ochikubo's file, but this posed two problems. First, Solicitor General Fahy made clear both that he did not share Bonesteel's dour assessment of Ochikubo's loyalty and, more importantly, that he did not think a court would be likely to see Ochikubo as disloyal. Second, Justice Department lawyers did some quick legal research during the day and decided that they could not defend the legality of a *mass* exclusion order on the basis of *one individual's* conduct, however nefarious it might be. Again the negotiators were at an impasse.

Late in the day, a lawyer from the Judge Advocate General's office came up with an idea that appealed to both sides: the Justice Department would continue to delay the *Ochikubo* case and avoid responding to it on the merits by filing a motion to dismiss it for lack of jurisdiction. In the meantime, the WDC would secretly set in motion a process to secure an order of *individual* exclusion against Ochikubo. If the motion failed in court, and the Justice Department was left with no choice but to respond on the merits to the allegations in Ochikubo's complaint, the WDC would announce Ochikubo's individual exclusion, something that the lawyers thought they could plausibly, even if not enthusiastically, defend.[17] And Major General Bonesteel would allow the other two plaintiffs, Shiramizu and Baba, to return to the West Coast, thereby mooting their cases.

For a time, things went more or less according to plan. Letters were delivered to Baba and Shiramizu late in August, informing them that they could return to the exclusion zone.[18] The government filed its motion to dismiss Ochikubo's suit on jurisdictional grounds, which the district court set down for a hearing on September 11, 1944. However, at the end of August, A. L. Wirin outsmarted the government lawyers. He filed a motion seeking an immediate preliminary injunction barring Major General Bonesteel from enforcing the mass exclusion order against Ochikubo. It too was calendared for September 11. This tactic changed everything. Whereas the government could litigate its jurisdictional motion without taking any position on the merits of mass exclusion, Assistant Attorney General Herbert Wechsler informed Assistant Secretary of War John McCloy that it would be "exceedingly embarrassing" to resist a preliminary injunction "without indicating the nature of the defense on the merits." The government now had no choice but to respond. The time had therefore come for what John Burling had called the Justice Department's "bad faith procedural tactics"; Wirin had outfoxed the government lawyers, and the WDC now had no choice but to commence individual exclusion proceedings against George Ochikubo, and to do it quickly, before the September 11 hearing in federal district court on Wirin's motion for a preliminary injunction.

The Individual Exclusion of George Ochikubo

On September 6, 1944—just a few days before the scheduled oral argument on Ochikubo's motion for a preliminary injunction—a specially appointed board of officers gathered in Los Angeles to consider "the question whether military necessity require[d] the issuance of an order excluding George Ochikubo from military areas" along the West Coast. Ochikubo appeared and testified at the hearing, represented by A. L. Wirin and Saburo Kido, a prominent Nisei attorney and the national president of the Japanese American Citizens' League. The three military officers hearing the case were Col. John T. Rhett, Col. William F. Lafrenz, and presiding officer Col. Oliver Perry Morton Hazzard of the U.S. Cavalry.

Colonel Hazzard played an influential role in the WDC's individual exclusion program, not just because he chaired Ochikubo's hearing board, but also because he trained all of the WDC's other hearing officers on Japanese social and national customs and their bearing on exclusion from the West Coast. Hazzard was a man with a fabled military career. Born in Indiana in 1876, Hazzard enlisted in the army at the start of the Spanish-American War and was among the men handpicked by Gen. Frederick Funston in 1901 to assist in the capture of Filipino resistance leader Emilio Aguinaldo. Stationed in San Francisco in 1906, Hazzard played a leading role in emergency operations after that city's great earthquake. In April of 1916, as commander of the Tenth Cavalry, Hazzard led a band of twenty Apache Indians on a horseback expedition from El Paso to track down Pancho Villa. He commanded a squadron of the Second Cavalry Regiment at the Marne offensive in the First World War and after the war served on a number of missions in the Far East.[19] In World War II, nearing the age of seventy, Hazzard returned to service with the WDC to share his experience in the Far East with the WDC's individual exclusion program, as both an adjudicator and a staff trainer.

The lessons that Colonel Hazzard taught at these training sessions so unapologetically deployed the eugenics-inflected racial nativism of the day that they defy paraphrasing:

> The Japanese people claim to have a civilization of two or three thousand years back. That civilization is different from what we call civilization among Western people. Some psychologists and students of the human brain say the Japanese are considered a very primitive people so far as racial characteristics are concerned and so far as brain development is concerned. . . .
>
> A famous Scotch surgeon once [told me] that he could tell the year that a Japanese surgeon graduated from a medical school or probably could tell you the school he graduated from by the way he did certain op-

erations. . . . I said, "Why does he differ from a Westerner?" He said, "Because there is a group of brain cells which, when highly developed or among civilized people, they can visualize an incident from a word picture. The Japanese have not yet developed that particular group of brain cells[.] [P]robably a few thousand that would represent a small section of one percent of the people, who by association of several generations with Western people and by being educated in Western universities, have developed their brain cells. The Western man, two years after graduating, reads in the Surgical Journal of the improved way of doing a certain operation. He doesn't have to see someone do it. From the word picture he can see it just as if he had seen the operation itself. The Japanese don't do that.["] . . .

We run up against a lot of things which are difficult to understand in conducting these [Japanese American exclusion] hearings and trying to evaluate their answers. The matter . . . of face-saving—face-saving is just the result of a training that they have had since childhood—a very primitive training which is more or less mechanical and which does not develop individuality because with the exception of these two or three thousand Japanese leaders you will find very little individuality among the Japanese people.

Although "legally some of these people are American citizens," Colonel Hazzard explained to his trainees, "they belong to an alien race, an enemy alien race." He stressed that this fact alone was not a sufficient basis for exclusion, but "as long as you are working on these Boards with the military situation that you have been given[, . . .] you must enter into that hearing with a certain amount of suspicion because of . . . the personal characteristics you know about them," characteristics that "thousands of students have discovered from associations with these Japanese people over a long period of time." "Therefore," Hazzard instructed his loyalty-screeners-in-training, "do not evaluate their practices and denials as you would that of a Western man."[20]

These were the words and views of the officer who interrogated George Ochikubo about his loyalty in September of 1944. Not surprisingly, the interrogation resembled a cultural and political reeducation session as much as it did a hearing. Interspersed with questions in which Hazzard sought clarification about Ochikubo's life and family were questions of this sort:

Have you followed pretty closely, in relation to your parents, the Japanese custom of paying special attention to their influence, of accepting their viewpoint about various things to an extent probably greater than American children do as a rule? . . .

. . . As the penetration of the Japanese Army into China proceeded, did you have any particular feeling in the matter at all as a descendant of the Japanese people? . . .

. . . In the event of any of these American boys [in college or dental school] making derogatory remarks about the Japanese race or nation or that sort of thing, was your inclination to defend the Japanese people? . . .

. . . Do you know if you were ever looked upon by the [Topaz] Relocation Center authorities as an aggressive leader, more or less objecting to the policies of the camp at different times? Did you feel any resentment as to your being in this camp that would lead you to be non-cooperative with the authorities? . . .

. . . In your opinion now do you think that military necessity is what governed the action of the Commanding General, Western Defense Command [in ordering evacuation and internment]? . . .

. . . Do you consider that all Japanese who might follow the precedent established in your case could be trusted as to their loyalty as an entire class to be accorded the same privilege? Do you believe every other individual could be trusted to the same extent that you would trust yourself here? . . .

Assume that you were the Commanding General of the Western Defense Command here and had the responsibility of 135 million people more or less on your shoulders for the protection of this coast line, in your opinion, assuming you were in such a position, do you believe that you would be justified in permitting the wholesale return of all Nisei Japanese back to this zone, considering that you would have a belief that there still was some danger [to the coast]?[21]

Colonel Hazzard also grilled Ochikubo about his displeasure with the loyalty questionnaire of early 1943, his conduct as a member of the Topaz Community Council, his alleged comment about "letting the potatoes rot" at Tule Lake, his relationships with certain family members and acquaintances, and a comment that an informant had said Ochikubo made at a dental school alumnae function in 1937 or 1938 to the effect that Ochikubo had an uncle who was an admiral in the Japanese navy and who one day would "come over and blast hell out of San Francisco bridges." The dentist denied or rebutted all of Colonel Hazzard's suggestions of disloyalty, but especially this last

OCHIKUBO, George Akira   CONFIDENTIAL
Central Utah Relocation Project,
Delta, Utah

A federal investigative report dated 8 May 1942
states that Subject, a dentist in Oakland, is
reported (Rating "B") to be resentful of American
discrimination against Japanese and to have once
struck an unknown white man because he made derogato
remarks about the Japanese. Another confidential in
formant stated (Rating "B") that Subject had justifi
the Japanese invasion of China. Subject boasts of
some ability in jiujitsu. He is also reported
(Rating "C") to be very critical of the American
government for the Japanese evacuation.
A federal investigative report dated 10 May 1943

OCHIKUBO, George Akira   CONTINUED

states that Subject, a Nisei, stated that he felt a
great wrong had been done to the Japanese-Americans
by the U. S. Government, and prepared a memorandum
of fine points, stating what rights he thought the
Government should restore to them, in a speech made
at a meeting held at the Relocation Center. An
informant stated that Subject was considered a leade
in the opposition against registration, but later
publicly reversed his position and personally led
his Block to register when scheduled. He stated
that he had offered his services to the U. S. Army,
but that his services were not accepted.
A federal investigative report dated 8 May 1942
states that Grace OCHIKUBO, Subject's wife, stated

OCHIKUBO, George Akira   CONTINUED

in an interview with a confidential informant that
Subject was approached "to do some work". Subject's
wife gave the impression that the "work" referred to
espionage activities. Subject is held in ill repute
because of his gambling.

Oct. 27, 1943   jh

A confidential compilation of military intelligence data on George Ochikubo that was used to support his individual exclusion from the West Coast. (National Archives [College Park, Maryland], Record Group 60, File 146-42-107, series 1. Courtesy of the National Archives.)

one. Ochikubo explained that he had no uncle in the Japanese navy, recalled no such alumnae dinner, was not yet a dental school alumnus in 1937 or 1938, and never made such a statement even in jest.

Shortly after the hearing concluded, the Board of Officers voted to recommend Ochikubo's individual exclusion from the West Coast. "From all evidence presented to it," Hazzard's board explained in their findings, Ochikubo was "a man of very keen intelligence, with outstanding characteristics of dominant leadership." The board found that the dentist's "expressed opinions and policies for a time did delay the submission of questionnaires and offers to volunteer for military service, and did also obstruct the employment of excludees in his Center in harvesting crops in the Tule Lake project." Ochikubo had been "indoctrinated by his parents and others with a belief in Buddhistic creeds based primarily on loyalty to the Japanese Emperor and his divinity, and in other Japanese traditions, culture and ethics, to such an extent as to create a doubt as to his complete renouncement of obligation to the Japanese Government." The board found "an accumulation of bitterness" in Ochikubo that "resulted in his obstructive activities as a member of the [Topaz] Community Council," as well as "a lack of dependability under emergency situations" and other "potentialities which . . . render his presence in the Pacific Coastal Zone of the United States a decided menace to military security."[22]

In light of the views of the hearing board's presiding officer, this was hardly a surprising outcome. Colonel Hazzard was primed to see George Ochikubo as a member of an enemy alien race, a race that was primitive and biologically inferior, and whose members (save a handful) were more or less identical to one another. That is what he saw.

A bit more surprising, however, was the board's reasoning. Just a day before the hearing, Major General Bonesteel approved a revised "Statement of Policy re Evaluation of Exclusion Cases." This was the policy statement that required "material evidence" that an excluded person was dangerous to national security and confined the categories of potential excludees to "individuals who [had] assumed leadership" of "pro-Japanese societies" and religious groups with "highly nationalistic" teachings, people who had engaged in Japanese cultural and financial activities "to a marked degree," and people who "ha[d] opposed the war effort or urged others to oppose the war effort" in ways other than by "object[ing] to the removal of the Japanese from the West Coast."[23] Nowhere in their findings did Colonel Hazzard and his fellow hearing officers cite any of the provisions of the September 8 policy statement. They mentioned Ochikubo's "outstanding characteristics of dominant leadership" but did not identify him as leading any particular "pro-Japanese society." They suggested that Ochikubo had hindered the administration of the loyalty questionnaires, military recruitment, and the smooth operation of the internee employment system but omitted to mention that Ochikubo's reason for speaking up on these issues was the permitted one: "objection to the removal of the Japanese from the West Coast." In short, the hearing board barely even tried to conform its analysis of the evidence in Ochikubo's case to the WDC's supposedly controlling policy standards.

But this did not appear to trouble Major General Bonesteel. On September 21, 1944, he approved the hearing board's recommendation that George Ochikubo be excluded from the West Coast.[24] The WDC commander had said as far back as mid-August—long before any investigation or hearing—that Ochikubo appeared to "possess[ ] the qualities and connections essential to an enemy agent"; Colonel Hazzard's inquiry merely ratified this foregone conclusion. The point of Ochikubo's hearing had not been to undertake an impartial and even-handed investigation of the dentist's loyalty; it was to prop up a decision that had already been made, and to replace the mass exclusion order with an order of individual exclusion that would be easier to defend in court.

The Trial of *Ochikubo v. Bonesteel*

On October 2, 1944, federal district judge Pierson M. Hall denied Ochikubo's motion for a preliminary injunction barring Major General Bonesteel from enforcing his order of individual exclusion. In order to qualify for a preliminary injunction, the law requires that a plaintiff show, among other things, that he will suffer an "irreparable injury" if the court does not enjoin the defendant from acting. This meant that Ochikubo had to prove to Judge Hall's satisfaction that Major General Bonesteel would use military force to arrest Ochikubo and eject him from the exclusion zone if he were to return. Judge Hall did not believe that military force was sufficiently likely; he noted that a criminal statute was on the books making it a federal crime to defy the WDC commander's military orders. (This was the statute under which the better-known litigant Fred Korematsu had been criminally prosecuted when he tried to evade evacuation and exclusion back in the spring of 1942.) Thus, Judge Hall reasoned, if Ochikubo violated Major General Bonesteel's order and returned to the West Coast, it was possible—indeed, arguably *mandatory* —that the dentist would be subject to civilian arrest and indictment rather than forcible military ejection.[25]

Judge Hall was careful to note in his opinion that he was deciding only the preliminary matter of Ochikubo's entitlement to an injunction and not passing judgment on the merits of Ochikubo's legal challenge to his individual exclusion. "Particularly," he wrote, "I do not wish to be understood as deciding that I do or do not, as a Court, have the power to review the decisions of the military with relation to their conclusions in this case."[26]

This question—whether or not a federal district judge had the power to review the merits of a military commander's exclusion of an American citizen from a region of the country—became a major point of contention among government lawyers as they prepared for trial of the *Ochikubo* case. Military lawyers in the WDC wanted to use the *Ochikubo* litigation to establish the legal principle that a military commander's exclusion orders were categorically unreviewable in civilian courts. Maj. Gen. Henry Pratt pressed this position in a memorandum to the U.S. Army's chief of staff on January 8, 1945. "I believe that a policy should be adopted to the effect that the defense to the suits seeking to restrain enforcement of military orders should be limited to establishing the basic constitutional authority to exclude potentially dangerous persons, and to showing that the exclusion procedure comports with administrative due process," Pratt maintained. What Pratt envisioned was a brief trial at which the U.S. Attorney would prove two things: first, the legal proposition that the war power includes the abstract power of a military official to exclude people from certain territory, and second, the factual proposition that Ochikubo had been given a hearing. That would be all. The merits of the exclusion order would be entirely off-limits, as would all information on which the WDC relied in deciding on Ochikubo's exclusion.[27]

Not only was this a breathtakingly broad assertion of military power, it was also out of step with the approach that other courts had already taken during the war. In cases in Boston and Philadelphia contesting the individual exclusion of naturalized American citizens of German ancestry from the Eastern Defense Command, two federal district judges had decided in 1943 that courts *could* review the merits of a military commander's exclusion orders.[28] Indeed, in the Boston case, a federal district judge had not just reviewed but *overruled* the military's exclusion order, finding that "in light of the conditions prevailing in the Eastern Military Area in April of [1943]," the Eastern Defense Command lacked "a reasonable and substantial basis for [its] judgment" excluding a naturalized American citizen of German ancestry from the East Coast.[29] The government had not appealed that decision. Yet now the WDC was pressing to establish a principle of unreviewable military discretion.

This was more than the War Department itself could bring itself to authorize. On February 14, 1945, Maj. Gen. Myron Cramer, the army's Judge Advocate General, replied to Major General Pratt's proposal. While Cramer agreed with the general proposition that a military commander's orders ought to be final, he noted that the law recognized one "qualification" to this general rule: "If . . . the excluded person alleges that his exclusion was arbitrary or capricious, or without any factual basis whatever, it will be necessary for the Government to present some evidence to the contrary, which may include such parts of the record of hearing as may safely be disclosed." In other words, lawyers in the Ochikubo litigation would have to be prepared to establish that Major General Bonesteel's order of individual exclusion had a basis in fact, and they would need to open the military's intelligence files to that extent. But the Judge Advocate General suggested none too subtly that government lawyers should be crafty in deciding which parts of the file to present. "[T]he government should [not] refrain from putting in evidence those parts of the record of hearing which do not need to be kept secret," he advised, "*if they will help win the case.*" Apparently there was no obligation to share parts of the record that would *not* help win it. Furthermore, the Judge Advocate General stressed that the lawyers trying the Ochikubo case should remind the judge that "the Commanding General had before him other evidence which cannot be disclosed."[30]

Trial of the Ochikubo case began in Judge Hall's Los Angeles courtroom on February 27, 1945.[31] The main issues to be litigated were whether the military situation along the West Coast continued to justify the exclusion of some Nisei, whether the WDC had a procedurally adequate system in place for deciding who was unsafe to readmit to the coast, and whether Major General Bonesteel's order excluding Ochikubo and General Pratt's order reaffirming it were arbitrary. It is noteworthy that on all three of these scores, especially the first two, the records of the WDC and War Department were quite clear. Back on August 8, 1944, Major General Bonesteel had written unequivocally to army chief of staff George Marshall that "many of the conditions which [had] motivated the decisions of two years ago [on evacuation and exclusion] no longer exist." Neither "a major attack" nor "an attack on a relatively large scale upon the Pacific Coast" was possible. The most that might be contemplated was the "shelling of shore installations from submarines," "minor-scale bombing of vital installations and war plants," and "minor-scale" action by saboteurs landed by submarine. As for the capabilities of "Japanese now in the United States," Bonesteel had noted the possibilities of "the lighting of forest fires," "sabotage against vital installations," and "dispatch of information to waiting submarines as to the departure of troop ships, etc." The "sum total" of all of these risks, however, could not be "considered as greater than action of a secondary nature." None of it, he had stated, could "seriously change the final outcome of the war."[32] Certainly, between August of 1944, when Major General Bonesteel had offered his assessment to Marshall, and the end of February of 1945, when military witnesses testified at the *Ochikubo* trial, the military situation along the coast had improved, not worsened.

As for whether the WDC had a system in place for adjudicating who could return to the coast and who could not, the record was even clearer. In August and September of 1944, the WDC had issued policy statements setting standards for individual exclusion cases and identifying exactly which aspects of a Nisei's record would qualify him or her for exclusion. In December of 1944, the WDC had been forced to narrow those standards dramatically in order to reach the negotiated limit of 10,000 excludees. Women could not be excluded at all; men could not be excluded unless they had answered "no" to the loyalty question in 1943, renounced their citizenship, demanded expatriation to Japan, or served as a prewar leader of a nationalistic Japanese group.

At trial, the military witnesses testified as if they were speaking of an entirely different military situation—one of mounting rather than subsiding peril—and an entirely different adjudication system—one of subjective and largely standardless military discretion. The government's military expert at the *Ochikubo* trial was Brig. Gen. William H. Wilbur, chief of staff of the WDC.[33] Wilbur admitted that American military efforts against Japan had been "uniformly successful" for a long time, that the WDC had ceased being a theater of operations well over a year earlier, that the dangers of espionage and sabotage along the West Coast were lesser than they had been in the spring of 1942 when General DeWitt had ordered the mass exclusion of Japanese Americans, and that the overall improvement of the military outlook had been one of the factors that led the WDC commander to rescind the mass exclusion of Japanese Americans in 1944.

Yet General Wilbur testified that in his opinion, the danger of sabotage and espionage by Japanese Americans in the WDC was *increasing* rather than decreasing, as was the peril that such sabotage and espionage would create. He testified about the "capabilities" of the Japanese military along the West Coast, and his testimony ranged far beyond what Major General Bonesteel had described nearly seven months earlier. He spoke at length about the risks that enemy submarines allegedly continued to pose at that point in the war: that they would shell coastal installations, station themselves in shipping lanes to destroy crucial convoys, release mines near major U.S. ports, and even land "small forces of a commando type on our shores." He spoke of a risk—entirely unmentioned in any contemporaneous security assessment—that Japan would "send a carrier to some point 800 or 1000 miles away from our coast and launch planes which will come to this area" on missions from which they would not return. Wilbur also testified about a risk—again, utterly absent from the WDC's own internal assessments—that Japan would "launch small planes from submarines" to drop incendiary bombs and set massive forest fires that would in turn ignite oil refineries and adjacent towns. Most ominously of all, Wilbur testified that "[t]here [were] other military capabilities" that he could not mention because "members of the Press [were] present"—although he did hint that there was an unnamed "type of [enemy] action which ha[d] been inaugurated during the last four months which [was] a very serious consideration."[34]

He also testified about the sorts of sabotage and espionage that Japanese Americans in the WDC could commit, and once again his testimony pressed far beyond anything that had actually been contemplated in internal WDC discussions. Japanese Americans, he said, "could supply valuable information" on troop movements, war plans, and preparations, possibly enabling enemy submarines to attack departing troop convoys at a cost of "many thousands of lives of soldiers." They could collaborate with paratroopers and commandos by supplying and guiding them. They could "cut communication wires," "blow bridges," "set fires," and "otherwise create confusion."

And even though Wilbur admitted that the Japanese military situation was continuing to collapse and the Allies' position to strengthen, he argued that the likelihood of sabotage and espionage was increasing rather than decreasing. "The Japanese are well known to be a nation of face-saving people," he asserted, as if quoting directly from one of Colonel Hazzard's training lectures on the monolithic racial characteristics of the Japanese. "As we bring the campaign home to the Japanese, to the main Japanese islands, it is practically certain that the Japanese people will raise a cry for some action against the United States." The military, he said, had to consider "the definite psychology among the Japanese," a "banzai," "face-saving attitude." That attitude meant that "Japanese leaders w[ould] attempt to send something, to make some effort against the United States." The military, he maintained, therefore needed to be even "more watchful" than ever for sabotage and espionage.

In August of 1944, Justice Department lawyers John Burling and Edward Ennis had warned that in the "contest atmosphere" of a trial, military witnesses tended to make statements "of the military situation . . . which would go beyond and not correctly reflect the military judgment of the Commanding General [of the WDC] and the General Staff [of the War Department]." General Wilbur's outlandish trial testimony about the increasing risks of Japanese American treachery on the West Coast and the broad array of Japanese military capabilities just a few months before the war's end shows that Burling and Ennis were right. Or perhaps their prediction was not quite dour enough; their reference to the "contest atmosphere" of a trial implied that military witnesses tended to exaggerate and lie when "contested"—that is, on cross-examination. General Wilbur volunteered many of his most outrageous exaggerations on *direct* examination by the government's own lawyer.

But this was not the worst of it. Col. Harold W. Schweitzer, the executive officer of the WDC's Civil Affairs Division, testified at the *Ochikubo* trial about the WDC's loyalty adjudication system.[35] Only Schweitzer's own sworn words from the witness stand can convey how far his account deviated from reality:

> Q. Is there any rule or regulation which sets up the standard used by the Civil Affairs Division, of which you are Executive Officer, as to what constitutes a potential security risk?
>
> A. No, sir. . . . We attempt to ascertain whether the presence of an individual in the sensitive zones or exclusion zones of the West Coast might be a source of potential danger to the security thereof.
>
> Q. Now, in attempting to ascertain that, is there some definition or standard or criterion as to what is a potential danger which either the Commanding General or any other officer within the Western Defense Command has outlined, or do you just use your own judgment?
>
> A. Each case is decided on an individual basis, and . . . the Commanding General, of the information of the officer in charge of the Civil Affairs Division, has given to the officer in charge certain examples of types of persons who might be considered potentially dangerous. It is not [conclusive].[36]
>
> Q. In other words, the Civil Affairs Division, in making a recommendation in an individual case to the Commanding General, exercises its best judgment in the individual case?
>
> A. That is right.

Attorney Wirin tried to pin Schweitzer down on whether the WDC had fixed standards of any kind for adjudicating the loyalty of Japanese Americans:

Q. Is there a way that you, as Executive Officer of the Civil Affairs Division, can find the standard which the Commanding General uses as to what constitutes a potential security risk? Is there any memorandum or document which defines or prescribes a standard?

A. From time to time, we are given certain examples of the types of individuals who might be considered potentially dangerous. I might say that the standard, if there is such a standard, would be changed from day to day. The whole thing is relevant. It depends on the military situation at the present time. A lot depends on enemy activity or anything else that happens.

Perhaps finding Schweitzer's testimony difficult to believe, Wirin pressed him again on whether the WDC had any sort of standards for its adjudications:

Q. Is there a general standard applicable to all cases, or is there a standard used in each individual case for each individual?

A. The standard is not applicable to all cases. . . . Each case is decided on its own individual basis.

At this point, Judge Hall himself cut in:

THE COURT: Mr. Witness, isn't there some standard which is common to all of them? I don't mean a multiple standard, but isn't there some standard which is taken by the Commanding General as to whether or not it is safe for the country, or there will be espionage or sabotage or something?

THE WITNESS: The general standard is whether the man's presence in the exclusion areas would be a source of potential danger to the security thereof.

THE COURT: That is the general standard?

THE WITNESS: Yes. Then, keeping that in mind, each case is decided upon its own basis. Individual determination is made in each case.

THE COURT: The variant then comes with relation to the particular individual. Is that it?

THE WITNESS: That is right.

THE COURT: Or does the variant come with the standard?

THE WITNESS: The variant comes with consideration with respect to the particular individual, based upon the facts that are presented that pertain to that individual.

THE COURT: Applied to what is or is not safe?

THE WITNESS: Yes, that is right.

In case there was any doubt that the adjudication system Schweitzer was describing came from the pages of Kafka, Wirin clarified the matter with his last question on the subject:

Q. Let me ask you this. How is a subject before the Hearing Board to know the standard which the agencies of the Western Defense Command use in determining what, and I quote from [a WDC memorandum], "constitutes a potential security risk?"

A. I know of no way for him to know.

Barely a word of Colonel Schweitzer's testimony was true. He was asked if the Civil Affairs Division of the WDC had "any rule or regulation" that set up a "standard" for judging who constituted a security risk. He said "no." This was false. By the time of the *Ochikubo* trial in late February, the WDC had been using the specific screening criteria that had been tailored to produce a maximum of 10,000 excludees for at least two months. General Wilbur, for his part, had briefly alluded to these screening criteria in his testimony, although he had declined to elaborate on them or even list them all because it was not "in the public interest that they should be discussed." Colonel Schweitzer did not even see fit to mention them.

Schweitzer was asked whether the WDC commander had issued any sort of "definition or standard or criterion as to what is a potential danger," and he replied that each case was decided on an individual basis, with the assistance of certain "examples" of types of dangerous people that were not conclusive. This was deeply misleading. Most cases of individual exclusion were *not* decided on an individual basis; most were decided on the basis of rigid criteria that removed from consideration huge categories of Nisei—for example, women and people whose questionable conduct occurred before the Pearl Harbor attack. And these criteria *were* conclusive.

Pressed by the judge himself on whether there was not *some* general standard for determining dangerousness, Schweitzer said that the general standard was "whether the man's presence in the exclusion areas would be a source of potential danger to the security thereof." This was incomplete; the WDC's policy statement of September 1944 insisted on "*material evidence* which indicates that the individual being considered is dangerous to military security*." The judge wanted to know whether there were adjudication criteria at a level beneath that general standard, or whether instead the decision was a discretionary one that turned entirely on the details of each case; Schweitzer said it was the latter. This was false. In order to bring the number of supposedly dangerous people down to 10,000, the WDC had been compelled to adopt a handful of concrete criteria centered on very specific types of post–Pearl Harbor conduct and statements, and it was these criteria that mechanically identified virtually all of the individual excludees.

Attorney Wirin asked Schweitzer how a potential excludee could even know the standards by which he would be judged, and Schweitzer replied that he knew of no way. This was, at best, misleading; one obvious way for a potential excludee to learn the WDC's standards was for the WDC to tell him. The WDC might not have wanted to do that—General Wilbur's refusal to elaborate on them would tend to suggest that it did not—but Schweitzer was nonetheless less than truthful when he claimed to know of no way for a potential excludee to learn of the WDC's standards.

This final claim—that an excludee could not know the criteria of judgment—was perhaps the most importantly deceitful representation that Colonel Schweitzer made at the Ochikubo trial. Schweitzer was suggesting that the WDC's exclusion standards were essentially unknowable. They were just too ephemeral to be communicated, too discretionary and subjective and dependent on context. They "changed from day to day," fluctuating as a function of "the military situation at the present time" and "enemy activity or anything else that happens." While much of Schweitzer's testimony was false, these words were unconscionable. Whatever else might be said of the WDC's screening program, it did not change from day to day, and it was not a function of a shifting military situation—much less of "enemy activity" along the coast, of which there was, at this point in the war, none.

Colonel Schweitzer's misrepresentations played an important role at the Ochikubo trial. Not only did they conceal the true nature of the WDC's screening system from Judge Hall, but they also turned the judge's attention away from a crucial fact: even if all of the WDC's insinuations about George Ochikubo were true, the WDC's regulations would not have placed him among the 10,000 individuals meriting exclusion. On February 9, 1945, in anticipation of trial, WDC commander Henry Pratt signed an order reaffirming Ochikubo's individual exclusion and endorsing the findings of Colonel Hazzard's hearing board. By that time, the standards governing individual exclusion were the stripped-down, bare-bones standards that the WDC had been forced to adopt in order to limit the number of excludees. Those standards allowed the exclusion of male Nisei who had renounced their citizenship, applied for expatriation, answered "no" to the loyalty question on the 1943 questionnaire, or, in the years before Pearl Harbor, led certain Japanese nationalist groups. None of these applied to George Ochikubo. He had answered "yes" to the loyalty question, had never renounced his citizenship or sought expatriation, and had never led any sort of Japanese group before Pearl Harbor. The government's courtroom defense of George Ochikubo's individual exclusion was therefore fraudulent.[37]

It also turned out to be irrelevant to the outcome of the case as Judge Hall saw it. On June 1, 1945, Judge Hall issued his decision in *Ochikubo v. Bonesteel*. It was a decidedly odd opinion that reached conclusions that neither party had pressed on him. Judge Hall concluded that Executive Order 9066, President Roosevelt's original order authorizing the military to remove people from the West Coast, created a form of martial law. That martial law, however, was not limitless; Congress had limited it by passing a statute authorizing the Justice Department to bring criminal prosecutions in civilian courts against people who resisted military orders. Therefore, Judge Hall reasoned, the commanding officer of the WDC lacked the power to enforce an exclusion order by arresting the excludee and evicting him from the exclusion zone. The only lawful way for him to proceed was to arrest the excludee and turn him over to the U.S. Attorney for criminal prosecution. And it was in *that* setting—rather than a suit for an injunction of the kind that Ochikubo had brought—that an excludee could challenge the lawfulness of his exclusion order. Ochikubo was seeking an order from Judge Hall enjoining General Pratt from enforcing what Ochikubo maintained was an illegal exclusion order, but General Pratt had no authority to enforce *any* exclusion order, legal or illegal. By seeking a ruling that his individual exclusion order was illegal, Ochikubo was, in effect, jumping the gun. There would be time enough for a court to assess the legality of the exclusion order if Ochikubo violated it and were prosecuted for doing so.[38]

The military's misleading defense of Ochikubo's exclusion order did not matter to the case's outcome, but that does not mean that it was inconsequential. It was a stunning courtroom bluff, more brazen and extensive than the now-notorious concealment that marred and eventually undid the convictions of Fred Korematsu, Gordon Hirabayashi, and Minoru Yasui for violating curfew and evacuation orders.[39] What could have led military officials to misrepresent the military risks facing the West Coast and the truth about their screening system, and to defend an order of exclusion that was groundless?

It is impossible to know for sure, but General Pratt's memorandum of January 8, 1945, to War Department chief of staff George Marshall provides a hint. That was the document in which Pratt insisted that the government should try to use the *Ochikubo* case to establish the legal proposition that a military commander's exclusion order is unreviewable on its merits in a civilian court. Pratt made clear in that memorandum that his concern was not really George Ochikubo; his concern was protecting the power of military commanders. The WDC's chief of staff, Brigadier General Wilbur, expanded on Pratt's memorandum a few days later, explaining that it was "important, not only in the present situation but particularly in the event of another war, that the right of the military to discharge its emergency powers and responsibilities in wartime, without undue interference by the courts, be fully established and emphasized."[40] Pratt wanted his lawyers to argue that a civilian court could do nothing more than ascertain that a military commander was empowered to exclude civilians and that he gave them a hearing.

The War Department turned Pratt down, at least in part; the Judge Advocate General determined that the WDC would have to prove that its exclusion of George Ochikubo had a foundation in fact and was not arbitrary. Perhaps, then, the WDC's courtroom deceptions were a way of reclaiming a bit of what the Judge Advocate General had taken away. If the WDC could persuade a court that its individual exclusion system was a subjective and discretionary process, constantly recalibrated to fluctuating, secret nuances of military intelligence, the WDC would accomplish much of what it wanted. It would place an insurmountable wall around the discretion of a military commander to exclude whichever civilians he pleased, without having to open his process to the eyes of a civilian judge. That would be an attractive ruling to General Pratt, of course, but with the war nearly over, it would be more than that: it would be a very useful precedent for future commanders in future conflicts.

There is one additional piece of evidence that supports this supposition about what might have motivated WDC officials to defend a very different exclusion procedure in court from the one they actually used. After Judge Hall issued his *Ochikubo* ruling, General Pratt insisted that the Justice Department take an appeal to the Court of Appeals for the Ninth Circuit. Pratt objected to Judge Hall's conclusion that the military lacked power to enforce its own civilian exclusion orders, and wanted that ruling overturned.[41]

In August, while the appeal was pending, Japan surrendered. All outstanding orders of exclusion from the West Coast—including George Ochikubo's—were rescinded. In the views of both the Justice Department and the Judge Advocate General's office, the government's appeal of Judge Hall's decision was now moot.[42] But General Pratt did not agree; he wanted government lawyers to grind on with the appeal of Judge Hall's decision even though there was no exclusion order left to defend. "It was the policy of my predecessors in command and it is my policy," he explained in a memorandum to the Judge Advocate General, "to endeavor in every proper way to establish and preserve legal precedents favorable to the employment of such emergency powers by a military commander as the dictates of military necessity may at any time require."[43]

For the WDC, it seems, the *Ochikubo* case was not really about George Ochikubo, or his loyalty to the United States, or the danger that he—or, for that matter, Japan—actually posed to the West Coast. The *Ochikubo* case was instead mostly about making law. It was about creating legal precedent favorable to the unfettered deployment of military power against American civilians on American territory, at a moment that the military deemed an emergency. Misrepresenting the nature of its individual exclusion program to a federal court might have been one way to do that.

George Ochikubo returned to the West Coast after the war was over and reopened his dental practice. In later years, he would sometimes tell his children how much he resented his government's having taken away his name and replaced it with a number at the gates of the Topaz Relocation Center. Other than that, he would say very little about his wartime experiences, and nothing at all about his failed effort to establish his loyalty to the United States in a federal courtroom in Los Angeles.

He would, however, often boast that he served his country with honor in the Korean War just a few years later, doing triage on his wounded fellow Americans after his unit's medical officer was killed.[44]

CONCLUSION

WHAT CAN WE learn from the federal government's war-time misadventures in assessing the loyalty and disloyalty of Japanese Americans? One thing that we do *not* learn from this episode is that times of crisis and war tend to trigger a panic about the loyalty of American citizens that subsides in quieter moments. To be sure, the Japanese American experience in World War II does corroborate this thesis. But the thesis itself is something that we already knew. From the nation's very beginnings, wars and crises, both domestic and international, have unleashed anxieties about the loyalties of American citizens.

The country was but six months old when it saw its first military screening of the loyalty of civilians. In January of 1777, Gen. George Washington issued a proclamation giving all New Jersey residents who had expressed Tory sympathies thirty days to appear before a military official and swear their loyalty to the United States; those who refused would be treated as enemies. With explicit congressional approval, Washington also demanded loyalty oaths from every soldier in the armed forces. By 1778, each of the thirteen former colonies had a loyalty oath for its residents to swear, and the young states also invoked the law of treason and other criminal measures against those deemed disloyal. And just a decade later, Federalist concerns about disloyalty and the influence of revolutionary ideas from blood-soaked France led to the disastrous and short-lived Sedition Act, which came closer to equating simple political dissent with disloyalty than any legal provision in the nation's entire history.[1]

The Civil War was, at a basic level, a battle over loyalty, and the war's aftermath included a sizable federal review of the loyalty or disloyalty of many residents of the formerly seceded southern states. Both Union army orders and congressional legislation during the war provided that southerners who remained loyal to the Union during the period of secession and who furnished supplies to the advancing Union army would be entitled to compensation after the war for the value of what they had furnished. The trick after the war was to determine which southern claimants had actually remained loyal and which had not. In 1871, Congress created the Southern Claims Commission and empowered it to make loyalty findings in cases brought by southern claimants for compensation. Its standards were rigorous: as Frank W. Klingberg explains in his valuable volume *The Southern Claims Commission*, the agency found disloyalty in such simple actions as "[v]oting for secession candidates, furnishing a horse for a Confederate soldier, and even paying Confederate taxes or selling goods to the Richmond government."[2] Of the almost 17,000 southerners who pursued their claims to conclusion, nearly 60 percent failed the commission's loyalty test.

World War I and the Russian revolution of 1917 triggered new anxieties about the loyalties of Americans. First pro-German pacifists came under suspicion, and then pro-Bolshevik political radicals. The federal government itself carried out only the smaller part of the program of loyalty inquisition, bringing prosecutions under the Espionage Act of 1917 and the Sedition Act of 1918.[3] The larger share of loyalty investigation during this turbulent time was the business of a huge network of private undercover investigators known as the American Protective League, which worked in close cooperation with, but formally independent of, the Justice Department and the Bureau of Investigation. To these amateur investigators the government left much of the business of hunting for German spies and subversives and doing background loyalty investigations for security clearances and civil service jobs. As might have been expected, this untrained network of amateur agents was "too credulous in accepting unsupported allegations of disloyalty," often "equat[ing] labor-union connections, minority ethnic descent, or racial factors with lack of allegiance" to the United States.[4]

And as noted at this book's beginning, the country weathered a loyalty crisis of great magnitude in the wake of World War II, as our relations with our erstwhile ally the Soviet Union froze into cold war and Communist forces took control of China. This crisis was the loyalty scare of the Truman and Eisenhower years, which some call, a bit misleadingly, the "McCarthy era."[5] What most people best remember of this era is its theatrical public inquiries—the investigation by the House Committee on Un-American Activities into communist infiltration of Hollywood, and the numerous hearings and investigations of the Senate Permanent Subcommittee on Investigations under the attention-grabbing leadership of Senator Joseph McCarthy and his aide Roy Cohn. Far more pervasive and systematic, however, were the largely unseen loyalty investigations of federal employees and job applicants undertaken across the federal bureaucracy by command of President

Truman's Executive Order 9385 of March 1947, "prescribing procedures for the administration of an employees loyalty program in the Executive Branch of government."[6] The scope of the loyalty-security program was simply enormous; it covered every federal job in the country. In its first six years of operation, some four million people were screened by various federal loyalty boards. And while only 519 people suffered findings of disloyalty, the most careful student of the boards and their work has concluded both that "[t]rivial allegations, rumor, and gossip" led to many accusations of disloyalty and that many innocent people were scrutinized and threatened with dismissal or other punitive measures for mere affiliation with organizations that the attorney general designated as subversive by fiat.[7]

This very brief synopsis of the high points—or perhaps they are the low points—of the American experience with loyalty inquests during times of crisis shows that in one basic sense, the loyalty screenings of Japanese Americans in World War II were nothing new. For well over 200 years, Americans have reacted to war and crisis by doubting the loyalty of other Americans.

Yet in some important ways, the loyalty bureaucracy for Japanese Americans in World War II was new. Many of the earlier episodes began and ended with the simple administration of a loyalty oath and involved no system of investigation and adjudication; for Japanese Americans, the government was not content with avowals of loyalty, and it set up multiple, sometimes overlapping systems of bureaucratic investigation to probe behind them. Some of the earlier investigative loyalty bureaucracies—particularly the Southern Claims Commission after the Civil War—focused on whether the subjects of their investigation had been disloyal in the past; the Japanese American bureaucracy tried to discern what its subjects' *current* allegiances were, and from those to predict whether its subjects were likely to act subversively *in the future.* Many of the other systems primarily examined their subjects' *conduct;* the Japanese American inquests focused, to varying extents in different agencies, on their subjects' *cultural and religious identity.* And, of course, the impact of the Japanese American loyalty adjudications on their subjects was unique in American history. At other times and in other crises, a finding of disloyalty could cost a citizen his job, or a claim to compensation. In World War II, a finding of disloyalty could cost a Japanese American his freedom of movement or his right to enter an enormous swath of American territory.

The loyalty bureaucracy of World War II was therefore not just a repetition of typical wartime jitters but in many respects unique. We can draw a number of lessons from it. Chief among them is the basic observation that civilian and military agencies took strikingly different views of the capacity of the Nisei to be loyal to the United States.[8] The Provost Marshal General's Office took the presumption of Nisei disloyalty that the Western Defense Command had created in the late winter and spring of 1942 and carried it forward throughout its work. Then, as mass exclusion ended and individual exclusion began, the PMGO passed the baton of racially presumed disloyalty back to the WDC, which ran with it until war's end. To be sure, the military was not a monolith on this issue; often the War Department's civilian leadership proved itself able to see that Nisei loyalty could be a product of something other than race and family. The military's main Japanese American security branches, however, never really progressed far beyond General DeWitt's early assessment that there was "no such thing" as a loyal Japanese American.

By contrast, the War Relocation Authority, staffed as it was by civilian bureaucrats, many of whom had backgrounds in the Department of Agriculture, the Department of the Interior, and the Office of Indian Affairs, tended to see the Nisei as a group of mostly loyal Americans more sinned against than sinning. It is, of course, impossible to say with absolute confidence that the civilian agency's sight was clearer than the military agencies'. Perhaps segregation, exclusion, and war plant disqualification as directed by the PMGO and the WDC really were the only things that stood between some Nisei and treason. But this is quite doubtful. The sterling record of the Nisei who were in fact released from camp and who did work in war plants tends to suggest that between the WRA on the one hand and the PMGO and WDC on the other, the civilian agency more nearly captured the truth about Nisei loyalty than the military agencies.

These agencies were aware—sometimes painfully aware—of their vastly different outlooks. Each tended to ascribe the other's viewpoint to something in that agency's basic nature. To the WRA, the PMGO and WDC were too military in their approach; to the military agencies, the staff of the WRA were bleeding-heart bureaucrats and social workers who never managed to become sufficiently "war-minded" for the task at hand. Undoubtedly these caricatures were grounded in something quite real about the essential differences in the agencies' backgrounds and missions. Yet another important difference suggests itself: the nature and the amount of interaction that each agency had with the American citizens whose loyalty they were judging. The staff of the PMGO and the WDC had precious little direct and personal experience with American citizens of Japanese ancestry. The PMGO and the WDC knew the Nisei mostly through paper and files—the answers to questions on the registration questionnaire, the paper reports of intelligence agencies, and the listings of bank deposits and club memberships compiled by the WDC's Civil Affairs Division. Some PMGO and WDC staff members were on the teams that administered the registration questionnaires at the camps, but those experiences were brief, tense, and often at least mutedly adversarial.

The WRA, by contrast, came to know the Nisei rather well. WRA staff members lived and worked alongside the internees in the camps; headquarters staff members in Washington made frequent trips to the camps and were in daily contact with their colleagues in the field. To be sure, the attitudes of WRA staff toward the Nisei were often paternalistic and sometimes suspicious. But as an agency, the WRA came to know the Nisei as human beings and as a human community, and understood the pressures on that community from personal experience. The comparatively greater trust that the WRA was willing to extend to the Nisei may derive from the simple fact of greater personal exposure, and if it does, this would suggest the danger of a policy that places the responsibility for judging the loyalty of citizens in the hands of an agency that does not know them, or encounters them only adversarially.[9]

Another lesson from the wartime adjudications of Japanese Americans' loyalty is the importance of identifying their precise purpose. The Japanese American Joint Board was charged with two responsibilities that were arguably quite different: making recommendations about who was loyal enough to leave a relocation center, and determining who was loyal enough to work in a plant or industry doing sensitive war work. It would not be unreasonable for the government to handle these two judgments quite differently: surely it is sensible to apply more rigorous security standards to those who wish to build bombs than to those who wish simply to enjoy freedom of movement in places of no special military significance. Yet the JAJB tried to handle both of these tasks simultaneously and, more importantly, tried to do so with information gathered and collated by a military office whose core mission was industrial security. To make matters worse, much of that military office's information came from the files of the WDC, whose utter disbelief in the very idea of Nisei loyalty had launched the entire program of mass exclusion and detention in the first place. It was perhaps not surprising that the military's deeply suspicious standards came to dominate the Joint Board's review of both war plant and indefinite leave cases. But it was also wrong—and damaging to the lives of many American citizens.

Yet another lesson from the experience of the JAJB, the PMGO, the WRA, and the WDC in adjudicating Nisei loyalty was the subtle yet pervasive influence of the agencies' own biases, needs, and goals on the matter they were studying. The JAJB may have been envisioned as a laboratory where loyalty could be distilled and tested, but in reality it was not an antiseptic setting. Board members carried the spores of prejudice, fear, opportunism, and politics into that laboratory from their home agencies, and those spores invisibly but thoroughly contaminated the JAJB's loyalty testing process. The WRA strove for a more contextualized and compassionate system of adjudication, but it never managed to wring from that system its own needs to manage its captive population, bolster its struggling relocation program, and defend itself in court. And the PMGO and WDC ultimately abandoned the notion of evenhanded inquiry entirely, with the chief of the PMGO's Japanese-American Branch insisting that the Nisei were not "morally entitled" to the protections of the U.S. Constitution and the WDC presenting a deeply misleading account of its adjudication methods to a federal court. The experiences of these agencies suggest that it will always be surpassingly difficult for government to wring bias, fear, and politics from the business of gauging loyalty during times of crisis.

In the sorry story of the *Ochikubo* trial, there is at least the hint of an additional lesson: some military security officials will be tempted to distort and dissemble—even under oath—when questioned about security matters in court. On every key point—the nature of the military threat to the West Coast, the degree of security risk that Japanese Americans posed, and the methods the WDC used to sift the loyal from the disloyal—military witnesses testified to things that were not true, or stretched the truth beyond recognition. It is, of course, potentially unfair to generalize the behavior of military witnesses at the *Ochikubo* trial to all military witnesses providing evidence about security matters during times of war. *Ochikubo* supplies just one data point on this question. But it is crucial to remember that before *Ochikubo*, top Justice Department lawyers predicted that military officials would behave on the witness stand precisely as they ended up doing. This was one of the main reasons that Justice Department lawyers were so insistent that the government should not defend the *Ochikubo* litigation on the grounds of a military necessity to combat espionage and sabotage. By the spring of 1945, they had tried quite a few cases concerning curfew and exclusion orders directed at U.S. citizens. They knew from personal experience what their military witnesses tended to do when wartime security measures came under critical scrutiny in a courtroom. The lessons of experience that these Justice Department lawyers learned are probably lessons to keep in mind in every situation where litigants challenge military security measures during times of war.

Yet it may be wrong to blame all of these problems and difficulties wholly on the government agencies that sought to sift the loyal from the disloyal. Perhaps many of the difficulties they encountered had at least as much to do with the slipperiness of the criterion that the agencies were judging. Perhaps the problem lay most of all in the effort to hinge a wartime security program on the ephemeral and ambiguous concept of "loyalty" rather than on dangerousness.

This idea is suggested in a vignette from the Poston Relocation Center in March of 1944. Edward Spicer, an anthropologist on the staff of the WRA's Community Analysis Section, dropped in one evening for an unannounced visit to the barrack of Richard Nishimoto, an influential Issei internee at the Poston Relocation Center in Arizona.[10] Nishimoto was, among other things, a field researcher for the Japanese Evacuation and Resettlement Study (JERS), a major social science study of the internment that was being run by Berkeley professor Dorothy Swaine Thomas.[11] More than many internees, Nishimoto had his eyes and ears trained on the internee community at Poston, and Spicer wanted to talk with him about the currents of cooperation and dissent that were swirling at the camp. As they talked, a storm blew in and knocked out all the lights. The two men talked late into the night in darkness. Their subject was loyalty.

"Spicer thought loyalty was hard to define," Nishimoto wrote in his diary late that night. It was something one found only among "the fanatical people" and the "simpler people," something more extreme than the eagerness of "naturalized citizens . . . to bend their backs to wave the flag." It was easier, these two close observers of the Japanese American wartime experience agreed, "to describe pride in [one's] own race." "Those Japanese here [at Poston] who wished for [a] Japanese victory," Nishimoto pointed out, "were not necessarily loyal to Japan and disloyal to the United States." He and Spicer agreed that most who supported Japan did so "because they would gain personal advantages out of it" and because of their "racial pride," not because of a feeling of loyalty to the emperor. Yet, unfortunately, the men observed, "many people were mistaking or intermingling . . . loyalty and . . . [racial] pride."[12]

The two men's observations about racial identity and loyalty retain their bite more than sixty years later. None of the agencies adjudicating Japanese American loyalty in World War II ever managed to break these two things apart. The WRA tried to separate them in many cases but often fell short. The JAJB, PMGO, and WDC never even really tried. All of the agencies were content to use their imaginings about loyalty as a proxy for danger to national security, and this was their central mistake.

The risk that American citizens of Japanese ancestry posed to the United States—if they posed a risk at all—was a risk that they would *do something* against the United States, not that they would *feel or think something* about the United States. This was what Scott Rowley, the project attorney at the Poston Relocation Center, may have been trying to bring to the attention of his Washington, D.C., superiors when he complained in 1943 that he did not understand why he and his fellow camp administrators were being asked to divine the loyalty of internees rather than the risk they posed to national security. Rowley here glimpsed the crucial flaw in the loyalty screening program, something that his boss in Washington entirely missed when he replied that disloyalty and danger amounted to the same thing.

This confusion between feelings of disaffection or disaffiliation and acts of betrayal continues to mark even some of the best thinking about national loyalty. In *Loyalty: An Essay on the Morality of Relationships*, the leading recent work on loyalty and the law, legal philosopher George P. Fletcher conceives of loyalty as a spectrum stretching between (and including) two poles. At one end is what Fletcher calls "minimal loyalty," which is a refusal to betray the object of one's loyalty. At the other end is what he calls "maximum loyalty," which is "devotion, an affirmative feeling toward the object of loyalty[,] . . . affection." And in between these two poles are "degrees of loyalty," conditions that "oscillate[ ] between a passive minimum and a fervent maximum."[13]

Fletcher is surely right to note the important difference between non-betrayal and devotion. But by placing them on a continuum, he invites the same confusion that marred the government's wartime adjudications of Japanese American loyalty. For Fletcher, non-betrayal and devotion are both breeds of loyalty: they are fundamentally the same thing appearing in alternate states. Just as a single molecule of water can take the form of steam, water, or ice, the single attribute of loyalty can take the form of non-betrayal or devotion. But this is true only in the loosest of ways. To be sure, non-betrayal and devotion both relate in some way to the connection between citizen and country. But the two are crucially different. Minimum loyalty entails a certain kind of *action*, namely, a forbearance of betrayal of one's country. Maximum loyalty entails certain kinds of *feelings*, namely, devotion to, identification with, and affection for one's country. Just as love and murder are not polar manifestations of the same underlying attribute, nei-ther are patriotic devotion and non-betrayal. One is a feeling, the other, an action.

It is a dangerous mistake to depict loyalty as ramping down by degrees from a maximum state of fervent devotion to a minimum state of non-betrayal. For some people, feelings of deep disaffection for and alienation from their country may contribute to a willingness to undertake dangerous acts of betrayal. But there are many other possibilities. People can be utterly disgusted with their nation and yet have not the faintest inclination to betray it. People can be entirely disenchanted with their nation yet in no way at-tracted to its enemy. People can feel strong affection for another nation and its culture—think, for example, of an American Anglophile—without risking subversive conduct. And people can be quite attached to their own country and nonetheless betray it for other reasons, such as love or money. The two attributes—feeling and action—simply do not belong on a single continuum.

It was the central error of the various Japanese American loyalty programs of World War II that they calculated the risk of subversive and criminal acts largely as a function of a Japanese American's cultural assimilation and racial or ethnic identity. All of the agencies adjudicating the loyalty of cit-izens in World War II—the WRA, the JAJB, the PMGO, and the WDC—were in the business of making predictions about how people would *behave*: how likely and how willing they would be to commit crimes of espionage, sabo-tage, or violence to support the Axis powers and injure the United States and its allies. Over recent decades, with the rise of preventive detention and the growth of civil commitment, the fields of criminology and psychiatry have seen vigorous debate over whether it is possible to predict that a person will commit dangerous or violent acts in the future.[14] There is, naturally, dis-agreement: some maintain that scientific efforts at assessment and predic-tion cannot beat a coin toss; others insist that at least moderately accurate prediction of certain kinds of behaviors by certain types of individuals is possible. But one thing is beyond doubt: any prediction method with even a remote chance at accuracy must take into account a welter of information about an individual's past conduct, environment, and psychology. Hinging a prediction of a person's future risk of dangerous or illegal behavior on one or two rudimentary facts about him is unthinkable.

And when those facts are a person's ancestry and cultural practices and ties, the prediction is uniquely dangerous. Of all of the attributes that mark a person's identity—gender, physical appearance, personality, intellect, man-ners of speech, educational pedigree, job, and on and on—few are more pernicious predictors than ancestry and cultural practices. They are the basis of some of our society's crudest caricatures and most powerful stereotypes, not to mention our most intense fears and most destructive antagonisms. Focus on a person's ancestry and cultural practices is far likelier to corrupt an inquiry into his loyalty and dangerousness than to enhance it, precisely by misleading the investigator into assuming that feeling and conduct correlate more closely than they really do.

A subtler depiction of loyalty and disloyalty than Fletcher's appears in the late University of Chicago sociologist Morton Grodzins' half-century-old work *The Loyal and the Disloyal: Social Boundaries of Patriotism and Treason*.[15] For Grodzins, loyalty and disloyalty were not polar points on a single continuum but points of intersection among swirling circles of timing, personality, chance, and a person's life circumstances. "Modern man has a variety of groups, causes, and leaders to choose from," Grodzins maintained; "[h]is loyalties are as fluid as his career and as numerous as the segments of his life."[16] In a democracy, national loyalty arises for the most part indirectly, as a function of the support that the nation devotes to the more direct and primary loyalties to family, friends, career, faith, and social and recreational organizations that people experience in their daily lives. It is only "when state policies conflict with the welfare of [these] primary groups[,] and choices have to be made[,] that the stage is set for crisis, and national disloyalty is more likely to result."[17]

But even in this unusual scenario, the stage is merely set; the precise lines of disloyalty remain unscripted. "When sorrows overbalance joys, when the cause of sorrow can be traced to an existing allegiance, and when an alternative is available, the stage is set for a shift in loyalty,"[18] Grodzins argued, but still disloyal action defies prediction. "Future advances in scientific analysis may satisfactorily explain political accidents, individual differences in personality, and the varying extent to which ideas and ideals influence action," Grodzins noted. But he was doubtful; he saw just too many other options for the alienated person: "He may become indifferent or withdrawn[,] . . . alter his expectations for life[,] . . . become sick or turn to hoboism[,] . . . conform completely because he has no other alternative[,] . . . [or] follow other courses of deviance."[19] Ultimately, Grodzins concluded, "individuals . . . exercise freedom,"[20] a freedom that would confound simplistic efforts at predicting who would act to betray his nation.

Morton Grodzins knew whereof he spoke. As a graduate student employee of the Berkeley JERS project, Grodzins spent the years 1942 to 1945 closely observing the exclusion, detention, relocation, and segregation of the West Coast's Japanese Americans.[21] From that experience, Grodzins came to understand that "[t]he Japanese American case illuminate[d] the wide range of ambiguities contained in the concept of national loyalty."[22] At the pivotal moment in early 1943 when the government circulated the loyalty questionnaires, "some evacuees regarded the fact of evacuation itself as the crucial point of judgment: the [evacuation] program and nation were equated," and "[t]he United States was rejected in favor of family solidarity, security, or an uncertain future in Japan."[23] Other internees "regarded evacuation as an aberration of the democratic norm and preserved faith in a later return to it"; these people, according to Grodzins, "answered 'Yes'" to Question 28.[24] Still others agreed that the government's program was an aberration, a "distortion of democratic principles," but "declared their disloyalty to America as an expression of their commitment to those principles or as a protest against the discrepancy between program and principles."[25] The range of responses to the questionnaire was, in other words, as rich and diverse as the population it surveyed. The simple dyad of "loyal/disloyal" that the government foisted on the Japanese American community did not come close to capturing its human diversity and complexity.

The government's various loyalty screening programs in World War II bequeathed us many lessons. Their most important lesson, however, is also their most basic: Loyalty is too ephemeral and ambiguous a criterion to support a national security program, especially in a racially or ethnically charged setting. When government officials on a loyalty inquest screen citizens for hidden biases and motivations, they are likeliest to find their own.

JUST A FEW YEARS after this sorry chapter in the history of the government's treatment of its citizens closed, a new one opened. By March of 1947, the threat of a new national enemy—Communism—led President Truman to prescribe a loyalty investigation for every federal employee and every applicant for a federal job.[26] The mistakes and excesses of that period have been quite fully documented, and they share certain features with the Japanese American episode, guilt by association chief among them. At one very telling moment, however, the later episode was chillingly foreshadowed in the former. In mid-1943, while the WRA's plans for segregating "the disloyal" were taking shape, Dillon Myer decided that it would benefit the WRA's segregation and leave clearance program to set up a quasi-independent review board to hear appeals from segregees at Tule Lake whose applications for indefinite leave had been denied.[27] The idea was to bring in well-respected judges and lawyers from outside the WRA to hear appeals, in order to bolster public confidence that only the truly and certifiably loyal were being released from camp.

WRA lawyers generated a list of possible candidates for the board. Near the top of their list was James H. Wolfe, chief Justice of the Utah Supreme Court.[28] Before inviting him, however, Dillon Myer thought it wise to send his name to the Justice Department for a background check.[29] On October 26, 1943, FBI director J. Edgar Hoover replied. Chief Justice Wolfe, Hoover reported, was suspected of being a Communist: "It has been reported that he is a member of the Board of Directors of the League for Industrial Democracy. It has also been alleged that Chief Justice Wolfe has been sympathetic with and possibly one of the leaders behind the local Communist party. . . . Mrs. Wolfe, wife of the Chief Justice, is a local officer of the Russian War Relief Incorporated in Salt Lake City, Utah."[30] The ironies here are rich. The WRA, looking for a well-regarded white man from outside its own ranks to adjudicate the loyalty of the Nisei, turned to the FBI. The FBI, using the very tactics of guilt by membership, guilt by association, and guilt by family ties that marked the Nisei investigations, labeled the chief justice a suspected Communist.

The WRA tapped the chief justice for service on the appellate panel anyway, and he served on that body, but the suspicion of communism was not behind him. On August 31, 1947, the House Un-American Activities Committee publicly accused Chief Justice Wolfe of being a member of a communist front organization.[31] He lived under this shadow of suspicion for six years, until he was finally cleared by a special investigative committee of the Utah House of Representatives.[32]

Nisei subversives, communist subversives: the face of the "disloyal" American changed, but the method of identifying him stayed the same. And now we again find ourselves facing a foreign enemy who is thought to have domestic support among American citizens. While the Arab Muslims who attacked the United States on September 11, 2001, were all aliens, in the years since then American citizens of Arab ancestry and Muslim faith have been implicated in supporting al-Qaeda in the United States. As well, four British Muslim citizens of Arab ancestry blew themselves up on London buses and subways in July 2005, and a number of Canadian citizens of Arab ancestry were arrested in June of 2006 and charged with planning terror attacks in Toronto. Threats to national security since September 11 have crossed the line between aliens and citizens.

In this environment of fear, familiar old suspicions are growing. In a disheartening Gallup poll of over one thousand Americans in August of

2006, four in ten admitted to feeling at least some prejudice against Muslims. Forty percent also supported the idea of requiring all Muslims—U.S. citizens and aliens alike—to carry a special identification card "as a means of preventing terrorist attacks in the United States." One in three of the respondents reported believing that Muslims in the United States are sympathetic to al-Qaeda.[33] And at criminal trials of Muslims in the United States, prosecutors have pointed to wallet cards printed with Islamic prayers as evidence of their owners' "jihadist intent."[34]

Sadly, conditions appear to be ripening for new presumptions of disloyalty. There is no telling what the future holds—whether another domestic terror attack will occur, or whether the government might again feel the need to assemble a program to judge the loyalties of masses of American citizens. Should such a moment arrive, the sorry experiences of the Japanese American Joint Board, the Provost Marshal General's Office, the Western Defense Command, and the War Relocation Authority leave little reason to hope for much more than prejudice, misjudgment, and mistake.

NOTES

CHAPTER ONE

1 Executive Order No. 9835, p. 1935. Information about the scope of the loyalty-security program comes from Parrish, "Lawyer in Crisis Times," pp. 1809–11.

2 Terminology for the government's actions against Japanese Americans in World War II is a sensitive topic. Certain historically authentic terms, such as "concentration camp," can cause confusion and misunderstanding for modern readers; other historically authentic terms, such as "evacuation" and "relocation," were euphemisms whose continued use can mislead modern readers about the real nature of what the government did. Any reader seeking clarity on these important questions of terminology should consult Daniels, "Words Do Matter," pp. 190–214. In my writing, I find it effective to avoid euphemistic terminology when possible while at the same time continuing to use certain words such as "internment" that, although inaccurate, have achieved overwhelming popular currency and recognition.

3 Among the best works on the Japanese American community's reaction to the 1943 loyalty questionnaires are Weglyn, *Years of Infamy*, pp. 134–55; Thomas and Nishimoto, *Spoilage*, pp. 53–83; and Spicer et al., *Impounded People*, pp. 142–78. Works that at least briefly describe the government's loyalty adjudication process include Ten Broek, Barnhart, and Matson, *Prejudice, War and the Constitu-*

tion, pp. 153–57; and Commission on Wartime Relocation and Internment of Civilians, *Personal Justice Denied*, pp. 201–4.

4 The debate in the Holocaust literature is often termed a debate between "intentionalists" (who believe that Hitler's will chiefly explains the Nazi genocide) and "functionalists" (who locate the genocidal plan chiefly in the Nazi bureaucracy). A leading intentionalist work is Bracher, *German Dictatorship*; a principal structuralist work is Broszat, *Hitler State*.

5 There is, for example, but one book-length study of the War Relocation Authority, Richard Drinnon's *Keeper of Concentration Camps*, but it principally examines (and demonizes) Dillon S. Myer, the man at the top of the agency, rather than devoting serious attention to the midlevel officials within the WRA who were responsible not just for the day-to-day operation of the agency and its camps but also for major policy choices.

6 "Concentration camps" was the term that the state officials used. For more on the demands of the Western governors and attorneys general for harsh conditions of confinement for Japanese Americans, see Muller, *Free to Die for Their Country*, pp. 32–33.

7 A recent and valuable book that shares this study's concern for the inner workings of the internment episode is Austin's *From Concentration Camp to Campus*. While Austin's concern is the National Japanese American Student Relocation Council, a private organization that helped young Japanese Americans leave the camps for college, his study ably documents that organization's complex and often frustrating interactions with a variety of government agencies.

8 On these mechanisms in the Truman and Eisenhower years, see Commager, *Freedom, Loyalty, Dissent*; Abbott, "Federal Loyalty Program"; and Bernstein, "Loyalty of Federal Employees."

9 "Final 'Buffalo Six' Member Pleads Guilty"; "'I Plead Guilty'"; "Two Plead Guilty in Oregon Terror Case."

10 The only wartime conviction of any Japanese American for anything even remotely like sabotage in the United States was the conviction of three Japanese American sisters in 1944 for conspiracy to commit treason. See Muller, "Betrayal on Trial." The sisters developed romantic relationships with German war prisoners who were working on the same Colorado onion farm and helped the men escape from their prisoner-of-war camp. Their conviction for conspiracy to commit treason is, however, highly suspect because the government presented no evidence at all of the sisters' intent to betray the United States. Ibid., pp. 1776–86, 1797–98.

11 Any list of the most influential titles on the overarching story of the eviction and incarceration of Japanese Americans in World War II would have to include Weglyn, *Years of Infamy*; Commission on Wartime Relocation and Internment of Civilians, *Personal Justice Denied*; Daniels, *Concentration Camps USA*; and Ten Broek, Barnhart, and Matson, *Prejudice, War, and the Constitution*.

12 Readers interested in the complex transnational lives and identities of the immigrant generation should consult Eiichiro Azuma's important book *Between Two Empires*.

13 Among these are Irons, *Justice at War*; Commission on Wartime Relocation and Internment of Civilians, *Personal Justice Denied*; Robinson, *By Order of the President*; Kashima, *Judgment Without Trial*.

CHAPTER TWO

1 "Nikkei" is a generic term for people of Japanese ancestry. It does not distinguish between aliens and U.S. citizens.

2 Daniels, *Asian America*, p. 115.

3 Japanese Americans use Japanese terms to number their generations; "Issei" means "first-generation."

4 The generational makeup of the prewar Japanese American community is summarized in Daniels, *Prisoners Without Trial*, p. 16. For a provocative article exploring questions related to the citizenship of Asian Americans, see Volpp, "Obnoxious to Their Very Nature."

5 On the loyalties and assimilation of the Issei, see Ichioka, *The Issei*, pp. 176–96, and Azuma, *Between Two Empires*. There were certainly cases in which the presumption of primarily Japanese, rather than primarily American, identity was false. For a moving account of one such case, see Fiset, *Imprisoned Apart*.

6 Recent work on the prewar lives of the Nisei is rich and considerably complicates the rather simple story of all-out Americanism that dominated the postwar telling of the Nisei story. The conventional narrative is most succinctly stated in Hosokawa, *Nisei*. The recent work includes Yoo, *Growing Up Nisei*, and Azuma, *Between Two Empires*, pp. 111–34. Prewar Nisei life also features prominently in many of the oral histories in Tateishi, *And Justice for All*. Issei attire is described in Ichioka, *The Issei*, p. 185. Information about Nisei school performance and truancy rates can be found in Daniels, *Asian America*, pp. 173–74.

7 Miyamoto, *Social Solidarity Among the Japanese in Seattle*. Useful material on the prewar Japanese Associations is in Ichioka, *The Issei*, pp. 156–64; Daniels, *Asian America*, p. 165; and Hayashi, *Democratizing the Enemy*, pp. 41–53.

8 The leading, albeit not entirely dispassionate, history of the JACL is Hosokawa, *JACL*. Two recent documentaries depict the wartime JACL in a rather more negative light: Omori, *Rabbit in the Moon*, and Abe, *Conscience and the Constitution*.

9 Daniels, *Asian America*, p. 169.

10 On religion in prewar Japanese America, see ibid., pp. 169–71; Yoo, *Growing Up Nisei*, pp. 44–45; and Hayashi, *Democratizing the Enemy*, p. 67. A roughly contemporaneous source is Kenneth D. Ringle, "The Japanese Question in the United States," June 15, 1942, NARA Washington, RG 210, Entry 116, Box 511, p. 18.

11 Under the 1916 amendment to Japanese citizenship law, Nisei older than sixteen could retroactively renounce their Japanese citizenship only if they had

completed Japanese military service. See Ichioka, *The Issei*, p. 204. A common reason that Issei parents had for registering the birth of a child was a desire to make it possible for that child to receive an inheritance from Japan. See Ringle, "Japanese Question in the United States," p. 9.

12 It is difficult to assess the actual number of dual American/Japanese citizens at the time World War II began because we do not have records of how many Nisei (or their parents) retroactively renounced citizenship between 1916 and 1924 under the 1916 amendments, or of how many newborn Nisei after 1924 were registered as Japanese citizens by their parents. We do know that of the 71,531 Nisei in the WRA relocation centers on January 1, 1943, 11,919 (or 16.6 percent) were born before 1917. See War Relocation Authority, *Evacuated People*, p. 96. These Nisei, as a technical matter, would have held Japanese citizenship unless they renounced it. At the other end of the Nisei age spectrum, 40,008 people in the camps—56 percent of the total number of Nisei—were born after 1924, and would have been Japanese citizens only if their parents went to the effort of registering them as citizens within two weeks of their birth.

13 For more on the Japanese language schools, see Asato, *Teaching Mikadoism*; Daniels, *Asian America*, p. 175; Ichioka, *The Issei*, p. 203; Azuma, *Between Two Empires*, pp. 126–29; and Yoo, *Growing Up Nisei*, p. 28.

14 Ichioka, *The Issei*, pp. 200–202; Azuma, *Between Two Empires*, pp. 122–34. Azuma's subtle analysis teases out the important distinction in the minds of the Issei between the racial identity and the citizenship of their children. The Issei saw their children as members of the Japanese race—a view that was strongly, even if oppressively, reinforced by the white American culture in which they lived. They thought a Japanese moral and spiritual education was crucial to sustaining the Japanese racial qualities that were their birthright. Yet they also understood that the Nisei's citizenship was American, and that the Nisei's future was as racially Japanese people in America. For this reason, the Issei designed a Japanese education for their children that they hoped would serve rather than conflict with American citizenship.

15 Daniels, *Asian America*, pp. 175–76; Yoo, *Growing Up Nisei*, p. 33.

16 Kendo America, "About Kendo"; "What Is Kodokan Judo?"; "FBI Reports on Kendo"; Svinth, *Getting a Grip*.

17 Azuma, *Between Two Empires*, pp. 163–65; Hayashi, *Democratizing the Enemy*, pp. 58–60.

18 By the end of the 1930s, as conflict between Japan and the United States began to grow, the Issei largely terminated their support for the Japanese military in an effort to bolster their unstable position in America. See Azuma, *Between Two Empires*, pp. 166–69, 183–86.

19 Memorandum, Frank Sweetser to Robert Frase, August 24, 1943, JERS, reel 22, frame 211.

20 Azuma, *Between Two Empires*, p. 170.

21 This practice is described in *In re Yokohama Specie Bank, Ltd.*

22 See several Nisei's recollections of cultural clash and discomfort upon visiting Japan in Muller, *Free to Die for Their Country*, pp. 11–12.

23 Leighton, *Governing of Men*, pp. 79–80.

24 This is the estimate in Daniels, *Asian America*, p. 176. In 1942, a survey was performed on a sample of around 22,500 internees—about a quarter of the residents of eight of its wartime relocation centers—to determine the extent of schooling in Japan among the Nisei. See "Residence in Japan and Schooling in Japan for 22,500 Residents of Eight Relocation Centers (Approximately 25% Sample) by Age and Nativity 1942," JERS, reel 22, frame 98. Of the people in the sample, 14,939 were American-born. Of those, 12,945, or 87 percent, had had no schooling in Japan at all. One hundred twenty, or less than 1 percent of the Nisei in the sample, had had between one and three years of schooling in Japan. Thirteen percent of the Nisei (1,874 individuals) had had three or more years of education in Japan. Around half of that group, or around 6 percent of the total number of Nisei surveyed, had received their three or more years of Japanese education entirely in elementary school. If these WRA numbers can safely be extrapolated to the entire Nikkei population of the West Coast, then the numbers of Kibei among the Nisei are actually smaller than has traditionally been supposed.

25 Daniels, *Asian America*, p. 177; Thomas, "Some Social Aspects of Japanese-American Demography," pp. 466–67; Diary of Richard S. Nishimoto, March 13, 1944, JERS, reel 236, frame 280; Azuma, *Between Two Empires*, p. 137.

26 Eiichiro Azuma has recently written of the considerable efforts mounted by some Issei in the United States to persuade the Kibei in Japan to return to the United States to continue the Issei's achievements in farming and to take Nisei brides. See Azuma, *Between Two Empires*, pp. 118–22.

27 The most notorious of these was Tom Kawakita, who taunted and abused American war prisoners in Japan during the war. Upon his return to the United States after the war, he was convicted of treason. See *Kawakita v. United States*.

28 Kiyota, *Beyond Loyalty*; Daniels, *Asian America*, p. 177.

29 Dillon S. Myer to John J. McCloy, June 8, 1943, JERS, reel 22, frames 206–8.

30 Daniels, *Asian America*, pp. 100–154.

31 Mike Masaoka, "JACL Creed," quoted in Daniels, *Asian America*, p. 181.

CHAPTER THREE

1 The Munson and Carter memoranda are quoted in Robinson, *By Order of the President*, pp. 65–68, and in Daniels, *Concentration Camps USA*, p. 28.

2 Commission on Wartime Relocation and Internment of Civilians, *Personal Justice Denied*, p. 54; Robinson, *By Order of the President*, p. 79.

3 Robinson, *By Order of the President*, p. 62 (quoting FBI Memorandum, Nov. 15, 1940, FBI Records 65-286-61, rpt. in CWRIC Records, reel 3, pp. 3602–3).

4   Robinson, *By Order of the President*, p. 62.

5   Ibid., pp. 78–81, 100; Commission on Wartime Relocation and Internment of Civilians, *Personal Justice Denied*, p. 55.

6   This is not to absolve President Roosevelt of responsibility for the wartime exclusion and detention of American citizens of Japanese ancestry. As Greg Robinson persuasively argues in *By Order of the President*, Roosevelt had decidedly negative views of Japanese Americans, and these views both "contributed to his failure to intervene to protect their liberty and property rights in the face of public hysteria" after Pearl Harbor (ibid., p. 243), and helped explain his "remarkable lack of interest in the consequences of his policies" (ibid., p. 245). Ultimate responsibility for the episode unquestionably lies with him. However, the impetus for the program came from the military, as did much of the planning and execution.

7   Executive Order 9066. The story of how President Roosevelt came to sign Executive Order 9066 is well told in Irons, *Justice at War*, pp. 25–64, and Robinson, *By Order of the President*, pp. 73–124.

8   DeWitt simultaneously ordered the exclusion of all Japanese aliens from those zones.

9   Memorandum, DeWitt to the Secretary of War, February 13, 1942, rpt. at <http://www.unc.edu/~emuller/isthatlegal/DeWitt1.jpg> (accessed August 5, 2006) and <http://www.unc.edu/~emuller/isthatlegal/DeWitt2.jpg> (accessed August 5, 2006).

10 John L. DeWitt, Letter of Transmittal to Chief of Staff, U.S. Army, June 5, 1943, for *Final Report: Japanese Evacuation from the West Coast, 1942*, rpt. at <http://www.sfmuseum.org/war/dewitto.html> (accessed August 8, 2006).

11 DeWitt, *Final Report*.

12 DeWitt was not alone in these views among the military's leadership. In his diary, Secretary of War Henry Stimson asserted as a "fact" that the "racial characteristics" of the "second generation of Japanese" were "such that we cannot understand or trust [them]" (Henry Stimson, Diary Entry of February 10, 1942, quoted in Irons, *Justice at War*, p. 55). Similarly, Maj. Karl Bendetsen, a top legal assistant to the provost marshal general and a chief architect of the exclusion and incarceration of Japanese Americans, argued in a February 3, 1942, memorandum that "by far the vast majority of those who have studied the Oriental assert that a substantial majority of Nisei bear allegiance to Japan, are well controlled and disciplined by the enemy, and at the proper time will engage in organized sabotage, particularly, should a raid along the Pacific Coast be attempted by the Japanese" (Karl Bendetsen to Provost Marshal General Allen Gullion, February 3, 1942, quoted in Irons, *Justice at War*, p. 49).

13 The report is quoted in Robinson, *By Order of the President*, p. 55.

14 Provost Marshal General's Office, "Investigative Procedure: Eighth Hour," n.d., p. 7, NARA College Park, RG 389, Entry 480, Box 1725.

15 Japanese-American Branch, Office of the Provost Marshal General, "History of the Japanese Program," 1945, pp. 10, 72, NARA College Park, RG 389, Entry 480, Box 1756.

16 On the eugenics movement, see Axel, *The Unfit*. On American nativism, see Higham, *Strangers in the Land*.

CHAPTER FOUR

1 The numbers are derived from the chart "Single Years of Age by Sex, Nativity and Marital Status: All WRA Centers, January 1, 1943," in War Relocation Authority, *Evacuated People*, p. 96. All of the nearly 40,000 Issei along the West Coast were also forced from their homes. I do not mention the Issei in the text only because the focus of this study is the government's perceptions of the loyalty of the Nisei.

2 For more on the circumstances of the eviction of the West Coast Nikkei and their incarceration in the assembly centers, see Commission on Wartime Relocation and Internment of Civilians, *Personal Justice Denied*, pp. 104–48.

3 For a comprehensive, if rather self-serving, history of the WRA, see War Relocation Authority, *WRA: A Story of Human Conservation*.

4 For more on the Salt Lake City conference and the WRA's decision to build detention camps rather than CCC-style camps, see Muller, *Free to Die for Their Country*, pp. 31–33, and Irons, *Justice at War*, pp. 71–72.

5 For more on the relocation centers, see Commission on Wartime Relocation and Internment of Civilians, *Personal Justice Denied*, pp. 149–84.

6 War Relocation Authority, *WRA: A Story of Human Conservation*, pp. 31–32; Dillon Myer to Clarence Cannon, Chairman, House Appropriations Committee, June 15, 1943, NARA College Park, RG 107, Entry 183, Box 33. Western farmers were not the only powerful interests to benefit from internee labor. Interior Secretary Harold Ickes caused something of a stir when he hired seven internees from the Poston Relocation Center in Arizona to work on his Olney, Maryland, farm in the early spring of 1943. See "Internees Hired by Ickes for Farm."

7 So intense was the economic pressure for Japanese American farm labor that early in 1943, the Western Defense Command was forced to accede to a westward shift of the line of total Japanese American exclusion in Arizona so that Nikkei laborers could harvest the cotton crop without entering the forbidden exclusion zone. See Chief of Staff George Marshall, Outgoing Message, February 27, 1943, NARA College Park, RG 107, Entry 183, Box 33.

8 Muller, *Free to Die for Their Country*, p. 41; War Relocation Authority, *WRA: A Story of Human Conservation*, pp. 109–10; National Japanese American Historical Society, "The Military Intelligence Service."

9 On the efforts of the JACL and the assistant secretary of war to restore Nisei military service, see Muller, *Free to Die for Their Country*, pp. 41–45, and War Relocation Authority, *WRA: A Story of Human Conservation*, pp. 109–10. General

DeWitt's angry memorandum to the army's chief of staff critiquing these efforts can be found at NARA College Park, RG 107, Entry 180, Box 22.

10 The writ of habeas corpus, "[a]t its historical core, . . . has served as a means of reviewing the legality of Executive detention" (I.N.S. v. St. Cyr).

11 Ex parte Ventura; Ex parte Endo; In re Ernest Wakayama; In re Toki Wakayama. The Wakayamas ultimately abandoned their litigation in favor of a request for expatriation to Japan in 1943. See Irons, Justice at War, p. 115.

12 Memorandum, Edwin E. Ferguson to Edwin Bates, April 22, 1942, NARA Washington, RG 210, Entry 16, Box 237.

13 Maurice Walk to Philip M. Glick, July 24, 1942, NARA Washington, RG 210, Entry 16, Box 230.

14 JAJB Minutes, March 2, 1944, p. 3, NARA College Park, RG 389, Entry 480, Box 1725.

15 "Resolution of Policy towards the Japanese," p. 5.

16 Daniels, "Western Reaction to the Relocated Japanese Americans," p. 115.

17 WRA director Dillon Myer noted the irony in local community support for internee labor furloughs in a 1943 interview with sociologist Morton Grodzins. See Morton Grodzins, Notes of Interview with Dillon Myer, September 29, 1943, JERS, reel 22, frame 399: ("Our greatest pressure during these months [of July, August, and September 1942] was from agriculturalists who needed labor. Before the harvest season was over, we had in the neighborhood of ten thosand [sic] workers out in the fields. In the very states from which had come the bust of anger at the April meeting at Salt Lake.")

The irony was nowhere more pronounced than in Park County, Wyoming, where the construction of the Heart Mountain Relocation Center led to boom-town conditions in the surrounding towns, and the demand for milk, groceries, dry goods, and various services brought a great deal of revenue into the local economy and tax revenue into state coffers. See Muller, "Apologies or Apologists?," pp. 481–83.

18 See War Relocation Authority, WRA: A Story of Human Conservation, p. 11; Jack Carberry, "Hostile Group is Pampered"; and Jack Carberry, "Food Is Hoarded for Japs."

19 War Relocation Authority, WRA: A Story of Human Conservation, pp. 47–50; Commission on Wartime Relocation and Internment of Civilians, Personal Justice Denied, pp. 178–79.

20 Memorandum, Calvert L. Dedrick to Colonel Miller, June 10, 1943, NARA College Park, RG 107, Entry 183, Box 33 ("The Congressional committee investigations of the WRA are certainly motivated in part by the publicity value of an investigation of the Japanese in the United States. We may expect more rather than fewer such investigations. Already the problem has been attacked by a Subcommittee of the Senate Military Affairs Committee [Senator Chandler], and by the Dies Committee of the House.").

21 War Relocation Authority, *WRA: A Story of Human Conservation*, pp. 111–16; Spicer et al., *Impounded People*, p. 169.

22 War Relocation Authority, *WRA: A Story of Human Conservation*, pp. 112, 115.

23 Kenneth D. Ringle, "The Japanese Question in the United States," June 15, 1942, NARA Washington, RG 210, Entry 116, Box 511, pp. 30–36.

24 War Relocation Authority, *WRA: A Story of Human Conservation*, p. 46.

25 John DeWitt, quoted in ibid., pp. 59–60.

26 Ibid., pp. 60–61; Dillon Myer to the Secretary of War, June 8, 1943, p. 2, JERS, reel 22, frame 206.

27 Transcript, War Relocation Authority Conference, Denver, Colorado, January 30, 1943, JERS, reel 22, frames 570, 573; War Relocation Authority, *WRA: A Story of Human Conservation*, p. 61.

28 See Morton Grodzins, Notes of Interview with Dillon S. Myer, September 29, 1943, JERS, reel 22, frame 401 (after disturbances at Manzanar and Poston, "the Project Directors really put the screws on" top WRA officials for segregation of the "troublemakers") (pp. 570–71).

29 R. B. Cozzens to D. S. Myer, January 7, 1943, JERS, reel 22, frame 187. It is noteworthy that in this letter on the question of whether WRA should segregate "disloyal elements" from the general internee population, Cozzens said, "definitely yes"—"[i]f the term 'disloyal elements' can be expanded to include troublemakers and agitators."

30 Grodzins, Notes of Interview with Dillon Myer, reel 22, frame 403, p. 5. For a short time late in 1942 and early in 1943, the WRA created so-called isolation camps at Moab, Utah, and Leupp, Arizona, to house "troublemakers" who participated in disturbances at the WRA's relocation centers. See War Relocation Authority, *WRA: A Story of Human Conservation*, pp. 179–80. Dillon Myer confessed that these camps were illegal, and they were disbanded before the end of 1943. See Grodzins, Notes of Interview with Dillon Myer, p. 6.

31 Dillon Myer to Secretary of War, June 8, 1943, pp. 5–6, NARA Washington, RG 210, Entry 16, Box 469 ("I agree that, in view of the importance which has been attached to segregation by the War Department and by other agencies and individuals who are guided by the War Department position in this matter, public acceptance of the loyal evacuees will no doubt be facilitated by a program of segregation.").

32 Henry L. Stimson to Dillon Myer, May 10, 1943, p. 1, JERS, reel 22, frame 97.

33 Dillon Myer to the Secretary of War, June 8, 1943, NARA Washington, RG 210, Entry 16, Box 469.

34 Scott Rowley to Philip M. Glick, May 25, 1944, NARA Washington, RG 210, Entry 16, Box 231.

35 Philip M. Glick to Scott Rowley, July 4, 1944, NARA, RG 210, Entry 16, Box 231.

36 Biographical information about Maurice Walk is scarce. The information presented here comes from "Maurice Walk Centennial Scholarship Fund: Honor-

ing 100 Years of Excellence," Campaign Record of the University of Chicago Law School (Winter 2002), p. 30.

37 323 U.S. 214 (1944).
38 323 U.S. 283 (1944).
39 Maurice Walk to Philip M. Glick, September 8, 1943, JERS, reel 24, frame 75.
40 Philip M. Glick to Maurice Walk, September 11, 1943, JERS, reel 24, frames 76–77.
41 Maurice Walk to Philip M. Glick, September 22, 1943, JERS, reel 24, frame 79. Glick responded by accepting Walk's resignation. See Philip M. Glick to Maurice Walk, September 28, 1943, JERS, reel 24, frame 80.

CHAPTER FIVE

1 Memorandum for the Solicitor General re: The Leave Program of the War Relocation Authority, October 9, 1944, pp. 8–10, 52–55, Charles Fahy Papers, FDR Presidential Library, Hyde Park, N.Y., Box 36.
2 War Relocation Authority, WRA: A Story of Human Conservation, p. 41.
3 Memorandum for the Solicitor General, October 9, 1944, pp. 11–14.
4 Telephone conversation, General DeWitt and General Gullion, January 14, 1943, CWRIC Records, reel 7, p. 8218; telephone conversation, Colonel Bendetsen and Mr. Braun, January 22, 1943, CWRIC Records, reel 7, p. 8214.
5 Muller, Free to Die for Their Country, p. 49.
6 War Relocation Authority, WRA: A Story of Human Conservation, p. 55 ("Since the Army was going to obtain from the male Nisei of draft age the very kind of information which WRA needed for leave clearance, why not broaden the registration program to take in all adult residents at the centers and turn it into a mass leave clearance operation?"). See also Morton Grodzins, Notes of Interview with Philip M. Glick, October 12, 1943, p. 2, JERS, reel 22, frame 411 ("The idea of registering for leave clearance with army registration was just a convenient method of killing two birds with one stone."); Memorandum, Thomas W. Holland to Donald Sabin et al., April 12, 1943, NARA Washington, RG 210, Entry 16, Box 286 ("I do not see how any individual in this country can carry with him a better endorsement than this [JAJB] recommendation"; JAJB approval will give the WRA "something of greater strength to rely on" than its own internal leave clearance system.).
7 Memorandum, Adjutant General's Office to Assistant Chief of Staff, G-2, and Director, Bureau of Public Relations, January 20, 1943, pp. 1–2, NARA College Park, RG 389, Box 1756.
8 War Relocation Authority, WRA: A Story of Human Conservation, p. 55. The registration teams were on their way to the centers by February 6, 1943, and began the work of registering the internees by February 10.
9 Robert K. Thurber, "History of Leave Clearance Operations," April 1945, pp. 4–5, JERS, reel 38, frame 166.
10 War Relocation Authority, WRA: A Story of Human Conservation, p. 56 ("To the

great majority of the Issei . . . this question was not only unfair but almost impossible to answer in the affirmative. It called upon them to renounce the only nationality they had, in the face of the known fact that they could not possibly acquire citizenship in the United States."); Thurber, "History of Leave Clearance Operations," p. 56.

11 Key sources include Weglyn, *Years of Infamy*, pp. 134–35; Commission on Wartime Relocation and Internment of Civilians, *Personal Justice Denied*, pp. 191–97; and Spicer et al., *Impounded People*, pp. 142–61. Brian Hayashi offers a slightly different interpretation of the registration episode, emphasizing both Japanese American agency and government coercion. See Hayashi, *Democratizing the Enemy*, pp. 145–47.

12 Stanley Arnold to John Hall, February 17, 1943, CWRIC Records, reel 8, pp. 9157–58.

13 Roger Daniels suggests that the phrasing of Question 28 was largely an administrative blunder on the part of the military. The phrasing of the question came from a form that the military had earlier used for *alien* volunteers. See Daniels, *Asian America*, p. 251. In that context, the language about forswearing allegiance to foreign powers made sense. Applied to the U.S. citizen Nisei, however, the language was just insulting.

14 Muller, *Free to Die for Their Country*, p. 57.

15 Spicer et al., *Impounded People*, p. 147.

16 War Relocation Authority, *Evacuated People*, pp. 18, 128; Muller, *Free to Die for Their Country*, p. 54.

17 War Relocation Authority, *Evacuated People*, p. 157. It should be noted that part of the explanation for the high numbers lay in the fact that Issei fathers often made the repatriation decision for their entire families.

18 Ibid., p. 164.

19 Memorandum, William P. Scobey to John J. McCloy, March 16, 1943, p. 2, NARA College Park, RG 107, Entry 183, Box 47.

20 War Relocation Authority, *WRA: A Story of Human Conservation*, p. 62 ("In a letter of April 8 to the Director of WRA, Senator Chandler reported that at the hearings conducted by his subcommittee 'those interrogated held the opinion that those who answered "no" to the loyalty question and those otherwise determined to be disloyal should be placed in internment camps.' ").

21 Ibid., p. 63. Tule Lake had been a relocation center from 1942 until the middle of 1943; WRA converted it to use as a segregation center primarily because registration revealed that of all ten of the WRA centers, Tule Lake had the largest population of "disloyals."

CHAPTER SIX

1 John J. McCloy to Francis Biddle, February 4, 1943, NARA College Park, RG 107, Entry 183, Box 47.

2 Memorandum, J. A. Ulio to Assistant Chief of Staff, G-2, War Department General Staff, January 20, 1943, p. 2, NARA College Park, RG 389, Entry 480, Box 1756.

3 Japanese-American Branch, Office of the Provost Marshal General, "History of the Japanese Program," 1945, p. 15, NARA College Park, RG 389, Entry 480, Box 1756.

4 Ibid., pp. 13–14.

5 Memorandum, J. A. Ulio to Assistant Chief of Staff, January 20, 1943, pp. 2–3.

6 John J. McCloy to J. Edgar Hoover, May 11, 1943, CWRIC Records, reel 8, p. 9118.

7 JAJB Minutes, July 15, 1943, p. 2; J. Edgar Hoover to John J. McCloy, May 22, 1943, CWRIC Records, reel 8, pp. 9116–17; Thomas W. Holland to Robert Frase, August 11, 1943, NARA Washington, RG 210, Entry 16, Box 286 (explaining background of FBI's discomfort with public statements about clearance of internees).

8 JAJB Minutes, July 15, 1943, pp. 2–3; J. Edgar Hoover to John J. McCloy, May 22, 1943, CWRIC Records, reel 8, pp. 9116–17.

9 Memorandum, Thomas W. Holland to E. M. Rowalt, April 16, 1943, NARA Washington, RG 210, Entry 16, Box 286 ("From the start of this thing I have been apprehensive of an essentially military Board taking over the leave work of the WRA, and that view still stands. . . . [I]t is possible that the members of the Board may feel that I am not cooperative with their efforts and that I am too fearful of adverse results. . . . [I]t would be better if you were to designate another member of the staff to represent WRA on the Joint Board."); JAJB Minutes, June 8, 1943, p. 1 (Robert Frase replaces Thomas Holland); JAJB Minutes, September 9, 1943, p. 1 (Robert Frase leaves; replaced by Robert Thurber).

10 Japanese-American Branch, Office of the Provost Marshal General, "History of the Japanese Program," p. 38.

11 Ibid., p. 40.

12 Speech, Lt. Col. Claude B. Washburne, Officer-in-Charge, WDC Civil Affairs Division, March 21, 1944, pp. 11, 15, 19–29, NARA College Park, RG 389, Entry 480, Box 1725; see also Memorandum, Victor W. Nielsen to Karl R. Bendetsen, April 22, 1943, CWRIC Records, reel 7, pp. 7502–4.

13 Japanese-American Branch, Provost Marshal General's Office, "History of the Japanese Program," p. 48.

14 Ibid., p. 49.

15 "Training Lecture on Persons of Japanese Ancestry Delivered as Part of Second Series of Lectures of November 1943 (Second Service Command)," n.d., pp. 6, 8, 9, 10, NARA College Park, RG 389, Entry 480, Box 1725.

16 Lieutenant Colonel Claude B. Washburne, "Concerning the Loyalty of Japanese-Americans," March 21, 1944, pp. 10–11, NARA College Park, RG 389, Entry 480, Box 1725.

17 Ibid., p. 32.

18 Japanese-American Branch, Office of the Provost Marshal General, "History of the Japanese Program," p. 72.

19 Seltzer and Anderson, "After Pearl Harbor."

20 Dedrick's willingness to do this work and possibly to share confidential Census Bureau information with the military have been sharply criticized. See ibid.

21 Memorandum, Calvert Dedrick to Colonel Miller, June 10, 1943, pp. 1–2, NARA College Park, RG 107, Entry 183, Box 33.

22 Ibid.

23 An indication to "refer" meant that the official screening the file was required to refer the file to his superior for a subjective review.

24 Presumably the Knights of Columbus.

25 It is not clear why a registrant would lose two points *twice* for being an amateur radio operator—once here and once in Question 15.

26 "Japanese-American Schedule for Rating, Referral, or Rejection, P.S.D.," March 24, 1943, NARA College Park, RG 389, Entry 480, Box 1732.

27 His case would be scored as follows: 3-plus for entire education in the United States; 1-minus for one trip to Japan; 2-minus for four years of Japanese language school in the United States; 3-minus for having a sister in Japan; 1-plus for having a brother in the U.S. Army; 1-plus for being a registered voter; 1-minus for reading the *Rafu Shimpo*. His total score would be 2-minus.

28 JAJB Minutes, April 8, 1943, p. 2.

29 "Questionnaire Analysis Manual," n.d., NARA College Park, RG 389, Entry 480, Box 1732.

30 Calvert Dedrick, "Memorandum for the Record," April 28, 1943, pp. 1–2, NARA College Park, RG 389, Entry 480, Box 1732.

31 Ibid., p. 2.

32 Telephone conversation, Captain Hall and Dillon Myer, May 6, 1943, p. 3, NARA College Park, RG 107, Entry 183, Box 32.

33 Telephone conversation, Dr. Dedrick and Captain Hall, May 7, 1943, pp. 1–2, NARA, RG 107, Entry 183, Box 32.

34 See JAJB Minutes, May 6, 1943, p. 3.

35 *Gunji kyoren* was a four- to seven-year program of military training that was compulsory for male middle and high school students in Japan. See "Training Lecture on Persons of Japanese Ancestry Delivered as Part of Second Series of Lectures of November 1943 (Second Service Command)," pp. 9–10. The JAJB slightly modified its approach to *gunji kyoren* on June 10, 1943, deciding that it would not count as an automatically disqualifying factor if the internee completed his *gunji kyoren* training before 1930. See JAJB Minutes, June 10, 1943, p. 2; and JAJB Minutes, May 6, 1943, p. 3.

36 JAJB Minutes, June 8, 1943, p. 2.

37 JAJB Minutes, May 25, 1943, p. 2. Also on the list were certain protests or

qualifications to the registration question about military service: "Protests against a separate unit for Japanese-Americans"; "Answer of 'Yes, if my civil rights are restored' to Question 27" (ibid.). However, the JAJB ended up attaching very little significance to internee responses to the registration question about military service because of concerns about the lack of uniformity in how the question was presented to internees at the ten different WRA camps.

38 JAJB Minutes, May 27, 1943, p. 3.

39 JAJB Minutes, June 3, 1943, p. 2.

40 Ibid.

41 "Training Lecture on Persons of Japanese Ancestry Delivered as Part of Second Series of Lectures of November 1943 (Second Service Command)," p. 2.

42 JAJB Minutes, May 20, 1943, Appendix I, p. 2.

43 In mid-June of 1943, General DeWitt informed Assistant Secretary of War John J. McCloy that the Civil Affairs Division had turned up new derogatory information in 492 of the first 1,000 cases referred to the WDC by the Joint Board. See JAJB Minutes, June 22, 1943, p. 1. On August 3, 1943, Dr. Dedrick reported to the JAJB that only a third of the cases referred to the WDC for record check were coming back with "no additional information" (JAJB Minutes, August 3, 1943, p. 3). In the view of some within the WRA, the Civil Affairs Division's findings of derogatory information were "so high as to raise serious doubts as to the validity of the criteria [it] was applying" (Memorandum, Frank Sweetser to Robert Frase, August 24, 1943, JERS, reel 22, frame 211).

44 JAJB Minutes, August 3, 1943, p. 1.

45 JAJB Minutes, p. 2. The list in the text is not complete; it contained a total of twelve "major factors."

46 Ibid. pp. 2–3. The entire list of minor factors contained seventeen items.

47 Ibid.

48 JAJB Minutes, May 12, 1944, p. 2.

49 JAJB, "Final Statistical Report," NARA College Park, RG 389, Entry 480, Box 1725.

50 JAJB Minutes, April 8, 1943, p. 2.

51 Telephone conversation, Capt. James Hall and Dillon Myer, April 9, 1943, p. 2, NARA College Park, RG 107, Entry 183, Box 32.

52 Ibid., pp. 2–3.

53 Ibid., p. 4.

54 JAJB Minutes, April 15, 1943, p. 2.

55 JAJB Minutes, April 22, 1943, p. 1.

56 Telephone conversation, Capt. James Hall and Mr. Rowalt, April 16, 1943, NARA College Park, RG 107, Entry 183, Box 32.

57 JAJB Minutes, March 2, 1944, p. 5.

58 Telephone conversation, Capt. James Hall and Dillon Myer, May 6, 1943, p. 2, NARA College Park, RG 107, Entry 183, Box 32.

59 Telephone conversation, Capt. James Hall and Dr. Calvert Dedrick, May 6, 1943, NARA College Park, RG 107, Entry 184, Box 32.

60 Ibid. p. 2 ("I've got three votes on the Board—3 out of 5.").

61 JAJB Minutes, May 6, 1943, p. 2.

62 JAJB Minutes, June 29, 1943, p. 2; JAJB, "Progress Report, February 26 through July 26, 1943," NARA College Park, RG 389, Entry 480, Box 1725.

63 JAJB Minutes, June 29, 1943, p. 2.

64 Ibid., pp. 2–3.

65 JAJB Minutes, July 13, 1943, p. 2.

66 Japanese-American Branch, Office of the Provost Marshal General, "History of the Japanese Program," p. 19.

67 JAJB Minutes, November 30, 1943, pp. 4–5.

68 Dillon Myer to Francis Biddle, August 27, 1943, NARA College Park, RG 389, Entry 480, Box 1740; Francis Biddle to Dillon Myer, September 27, 1943, NARA College Park, RG 389, Entry 480, Box 1740.

69 JAJB Minutes, November 4, 1943.

70 JAJB Minutes, August 24, 1943, p. 2. See also Japanese-American Branch, Office of the Provost Marshal General, "History of the Japanese Program," p. 19 ("The WRA, having no security responsibility, and acting through its field agents, ignored the spirit of the directive of 20 January 1943 and aided the Japanese in obtaining any employment possible regardless of the nature of the work.").

71 JAJB Minutes, August 5, 1943.

72 Japanese-American Branch, Office of the Provost Marshal General, "History of the Japanese Program," pp. 20–22.

73 JAJB Minutes, March 2, 1944, pp. 1–2.

74 Ibid. See also Clarence R. Harbert, Memorandum, March 27, 1944, NARA College Park, RG 389, Entry 480, Box 1733.

75 Clarence R. Harbert, Memorandum, March 27, 1944, p. 2, NARA College Park, RG 389, Entry 480, Box 1733.

76 Ibid.

77 Ibid.

78 Memorandum, Col. Alton C. Miller to Lt. Col. Harrison A. Gerhardt, March 30, 1944, NARA College Park, RG 389, Entry 480, Box 1733. This was not the first time these agencies ran into trouble in disseminating information about Nisei workers in war industries. Almost a year before the Cleveland Steel episode, WRA director Dillon Myer sought the War Department's permission to release to the press five photographs of Nisei workers at the G. & N. Manufacturing Company and the Master Chrome Company in Cleveland. Research revealed, however, that *none* of the Nisei workers in the photographs had been approved for work in war plants by the JAJB. See John J. McCloy to Dillon S. Myer, June 30, 1943, CWRIC Records, reel 8, p. 9086; Dillon S. Myer to John J. McCloy, July 3, 1943, CWRIC Records, reel 8, p. 9085.

79   JAJB Minutes, July 29, 1943, p. 2.

80   Dillon S. Myer, "Relation with Other Government Agencies Federal, State, and Local," June 30, 1946, NARA Washington, RG 210, Entry 116, Box 469.

81   War Relocation Authority, *WRA: A Story of Human Conservation*, p. 58.

82   Morton Grodzins, Notes of Interview with D. S. Myer, January 22, 1945, p. 3, JERS, reel 22, frame 45.

83   Ibid.

84   Japanese-American Branch, Office of the Provost Marshal General, "History of the Japanese Program," pp. 59–66.

85   Ibid., pp. 62–63.

86   Muller, "Betrayal on Trial."

87   Reconstructing the deliberations and findings of the JAJB in individual cases is quite difficult. The Joint Board did not issue opinions summarizing its reasoning in individual cases or even record any oral deliberations in its minutes. Indeed, in most cases the JAJB did not even list the results of its deliberations by the name of the affected internee. In certain instances, however, the Board's minutes did include short lists of individuals whom it recommended for or against indefinite leave or war plant work—sometimes even with an indication that one or another member of the Board dissented from the ruling. And in a smaller number of cases, the Board recorded in its minutes that it had reversed an earlier ruling because of new information. It is this small number of individually designated cases that allow scrutiny of how the Board envisioned loyalty and disloyalty in real human lives.

    A word about confidentiality is also appropriate here. In a number of places, this book relates the stories of individuals such as Harry Iba whose cases came before one or another of the loyalty bureaucracies for adjudication. Whether to use these individuals' real names or pseudonyms presented a difficult question. On the one hand, issues of loyalty and supposed disloyalty remain quite sensitive for many in the Japanese American community, and I did not wish to sully any person's or family's reputation by drawing public attention to false suspicions of disloyalty from sixty years ago, even if those suspicions are reflected in publicly accessible archives. On the other hand, it is my strong view that none of the individuals whose files I summarize had anything to be ashamed of, and concealing their identities might amount to a small but intolerable collaboration with a baseless sixty-year-old inquisition. I resolved this issue by attempting to locate each individual or his or her descendants and, where I was successful, by sharing what I planned to write and indicating my willingness to use a pseudonym if that was the preference of the individual or his or her descendants. After intense effort, I succeeded in locating individuals only in two cases, neither of whom requested that I use a pseudonym.

88   All biographical information comes from the Evacuee Case File of Harry Iba,

NARA Washington, RG 210. All of the information in evacuee case files was available to the Japanese American Joint Board.

89 JAJB Minutes, August 19, 1943. As a technical matter, of course, the JAJB's vote was for the proposition that it "could not recommend indefinite leave at this time" for Iba. Such a vote meant, however, either that the Board had "come[ ] to the definite conclusion that the release of the individual from a relocation center on indefinite leave would tend to endanger the national security," or that the Board had "come[ ] to the conclusion that the derogatory information developed concerning the individual [was] of such a substantial, if not conclusive, nature that in its opinion the individual should not be released from a relocation center on indefinite leave without careful scrutiny of the individual and further investigation where appropriate" (John M. Hall to Dillon Myer, August 4, 1943, NARA Washington, RG 210, Entry 16, Box 286). In practical terms, a finding that the JAJB "could not recommend indefinite leave at this time" was a recommendation for continued confinement.

It should be noted that the War Relocation Authority later granted Iba leave clearance, notwithstanding the JAJB's adverse finding.

90 All biographical information comes from the Evacuee Case File of Hiroshi Hishiki, NARA Washington, RG 210.

91 JAJB Minutes, August 19, 1943.

92 All biographical information comes from the Evacuee Case File of Dorothy Ito, NARA Washington, RG 210.

93 JAJB Minutes, February 2, 1944.

94 The Board sent 20,236 of its 39,375 files to the Civil Affairs Division of the Western Defense Command for a record check. See Japanese American Joint Board, "Final Statistical Report," NARA College Park, RG 389, Entry 480, Box 1725.

CHAPTER SEVEN

1 Japanese-American Branch, Office of the Provost Marshal General, "History of the Japanese Program," 1945, pp. 10, 66, 72–73, NARA College Park, RG 389, Entry 480, Box 1756.

2 Evacuee Case File of Yukio Ikegami, NARA Washington, RG 210.

3 JAJB Minutes, August 19, 1943.

4 Evacuee Case File of Yukio Ikegami.

5 Evacuee Case File of Sho Horibe, NARA Washington, RG 210.

6 Ibid.

7 Telephone conversation, Captain Hall and an unidentified WRA official, October 13, 1943, pp. 1–2, NARA College Park, RG 107, Entry 183, Box 33.

8 Ibid.

9 Ibid. The conversation as actually transcribed reads as follows: "That brings up

another point which worries me a little bit that the PMGO when they come to a decision to remove they are unnaturally anxious to see that there are not more interned every time. Now that decision they make which is an important and vital decision in the life of the individual does not appear to be arbitrary and without basis." Plainly there are errors in transcription, as is often the case with transcriptions of recorded conversations in the records from this era. The word "interned" simply makes no sense in this passage, as the PMGO's removal of a person from a job at a war plant could not result in his, or anyone else's, internment. Any Nisei already in war plant work had already been granted indefinite leave by the War Relocation Authority, and an adverse ruling on war plant work by the PMGO could not force the internee to return to camp. Given that Captain Hall was talking about the PMGO's behavior in presenting cases to an appellate panel, he undoubtedly said that the PMGO was "anxious to see that *they were* not *overturned* every time," and the secretary preparing the transcription simply misheard the passage as a reference to internment.

10 Ibid. As it happened, the IERB did overturn Nisei war plant removals with some frequency. The records of a number of IERB adjudications in Nisei cases survive in Box 1734, RG 389, Entry 480, at the College Park, Maryland, branch of the National Archives. In these surviving cases, the IERB's rulings reflect a rather confused and indiscriminate method. In some cases the IERB authorized war plant employment for individuals whose records would not have warranted even an approval for indefinite leave by the Japanese American Joint Board. See, for example, the appeal of George Masaaki Sawada, Case No. 36109, April 24, 1944 (IERB overturns war plant removal of Nisei whose mother was a Shintoist, whose brother was a Japanese alien, whose father-in-law was interned as an enemy alien, whose wife lived in Japan from age five to age eleven, who was a member of Butoku-Kai [a military arts society], who was a kendo instructor, and who took three trips to Japan, the last of which, in 1940, was for the purpose of celebrating the 2,600th anniversary of the Japanese emperor).

11 Telephone conversation, Captain Hall and an unidentified WRA official, October 13, 1943, pp. 1–2, NARA College Park, RG 107, Entry 183, Box 33.

12 Ibid.

13 A group of cases from mid-1945 are located in the records of the Provost Marshal General's Office, in a file titled "Facility Employment" in NARA College Park, RG 389, Entry 480, Box 1721.

14 Case of Isamu Kamibayashi, April 27, 1943, NARA College Park, RG 389, Entry 480, Box 1721.

15 Case of Noboru Mitsuoka, March 5, 1945, NARA College Park, RG 389, Entry 480, Box 1721.

16 Case of Tashi Hori, January 26, 1945, NARA College Park, RG 389, Entry 480, Box 1721.

CHAPTER EIGHT

1   The conclusions of this study tend to undermine—or at least markedly soften—the intensely bitter assessment of the WRA and its director, Dillon S. Myer, in Drinnon, *Keeper of Concentration Camps*.

2   JAJB Minutes, May 20, 1943, p. 3.

3   Memorandum, John F. Embree to John H. Provinse, April 23, 1943, NARA Washington, RG 210, Entry 16, Box 286.

4   Dillon S. Myer to Major Stewart W. Mark, July 21, 1944, NARA Washington, RG 210, Entry 16, Box 286. For more on how the reinstatement of the draft triggered petitions for expatriation, see Muller, "Penny for their Thoughts," 134–35.

5   War Relocation Authority, Regulation 60.10, "Investigation for Leave Clearance in Doubtful Cases," July 20, 1943, JERS, reel 242, frames 41–43.

6   Philip M. Glick to Edgar Bernhard, June 30, 1944, p. 2, JERS, reel 23, frame 121.

7   It is very difficult to believe that this was not a typographical error. Seven is a much higher point award than any other feature on the chart, positive or negative. In all likelihood, an internee was probably to receive a "1," or perhaps a "2," for being a registered voter.

8   War Relocation Authority, "Analysis of Leave Clearance Applications—Citizens," NARA Washington, RG 210, Entry 16, Box 286. It is not clear that the project directors at all of the relocation centers actually used this point system. As an indication of the agency's general approach to the features of Japanese American life that suggested loyalty or disloyalty, the point system is nonetheless instructive.

9   He would receive 3-plus for having a brother in the U.S. Army; 1-minus for having a sister in Japan; 1-plus for attending an American high school and 2-plus for graduating; 1-minus for attending Japanese language school; no points for travel to Japan; no points for his reading preferences; no points for attending a Buddhist church; and presumably 2-plus for being a registered voter.

10 Memorandum, Edwin E. Ferguson to Edwin Bates, April 22, 1942, NARA Washington, RG 210, Entry 16, Box 237.

11 Undoubtedly the most Machiavellian proposal to surface within the WRA related to its leave policies was a suggestion by Edgar Bernhard, an attorney in the WRA's regional office in San Francisco. Looking for a way to defeat a habeas corpus challenge to WRA detention, Bernhard came up with the idea that even for the most worrisome of internees, the WRA should never deny indefinite leave at all: it should grant leave and then pass along to the internee's potential employer all of the derogatory information in its files, so that the employer would then decline to hire the internee. This way, the WRA would technically permit the internee to leave, but as he would have nowhere to go, he would have to stay in camp. See Edgar Bernhard to Philip M. Glick, September 25, 1943, pp. 8–9, NARA Washington, RG 210, Entry 16, Box 231. Glick rejected Bernhard's

proposal. See Philip M. Glick to Edgar Bernhard, October 8, 1943, NARA Washington, RG 210, Entry 16, Box 231.

12 Spicer et al., *Impounded People*, p. 149.

13 Dillon Myer to the Secretary of War, June 8, 1943, NARA Washington, RG 210, Entry 16, Box 469.

14 Spicer et al., *Impounded People*, p. 157.

15 Morris E. Opler, quoted in Drinnon, *Keeper of Concentration Camps*, p. 79.

16 Dillon Myer to John J. McCloy, June 8, 1943, p. 6, JERS, reel 22, frame 207.

17 The details of Okamoto's life and grievances come from documents in his Evacuee Case File. See RG 210, NARA, Evacuee Case Files, Case File of Kiyoshi Okamoto. His involvement with the Heart Mountain Fair Play Committee is described in Muller, *Free to Die for Their Country*, pp. 76–86.

18 "Summary of Leave Clearance Hearing Docket, Kiyoshi Okamoto," in Evacuee Case File of Kiyoshi Okamoto.

19 Memorandum, Guy Robertson to Dillon S. Myer, December 10, 1943, in Evacuee Case File of Kiyoshi Okamoto.

20 Guy Robertson to Kiyoshi Okamoto, March 29, 1944, in Evacuee Case File of Kiyoshi Okamoto.

21 Guy Robertson to Ray R. Best, March 31, 1944, in Evacuee Case File of Isamu Horino, NARA Washington, RG 210.

22 Interviewer's Summary Concerning Applicant for Leave Clearance, Evacuee Case File of Dorothy Ito, NARA Washington, RG 210.

23 Abe Fortas, the undersecretary at the Department of the Interior, made a similar suggestion early in March of 1944. At this point, the War Relocation Authority had been placed under the supervision of the Department of the Interior; Fortas was therefore acting in a supervisory role. He suggested the creation of a new interdepartmental board, much like the Japanese American Joint Board, that would clear internees for indefinite release from the WRA centers. Fortas did not think that the board was at all necessary from a security standpoint; he thought it necessary only as part of "a thorough public relations job" that would "promote public confidence" in the relocation program. See Memorandum, John M. Hall to John J. McCloy, March 2, 1944, NARA College Park, RG 107, Entry 183, Box 33. Fortas's idea was never implemented.

CHAPTER NINE

1 Figures on the whereabouts of Japanese American internees and former internees as of September 1, 1944, can be found in Robinson, *By Order of the President*, p. 224.

2 General DeWitt asserted the impossibility of separating "the sheep from the goats" in his *Final Report*.

3 Greg Robinson describes Myer's March 1943 proposal to Stimson in greater detail in *By Order of the President*, p. 183.

4 For more on Stimson's response to Myer, see ibid., 185–86.

5   Roosevelt, "Message to the Senate on the Segregation Program," pp. 384–85 (emphasis added).

6   Robinson, *By Order of the President*, p. 198.

7   Delos C. Emmons to John J. McCloy, September 15, 1943, CWRIC Records, reel 1, p. 230.

8   John J. McCloy to Commanding General, WDC, September 15, 1943, CWRIC Records, reel 1, p. 231.

9   The Supreme Court would decide the cases on December 18, 1944. See *Korematsu v. United States* and *Ex parte Endo*.

10 Dillon S. Myer to John J. McCloy, October 16, 1943, CWRIC Records, reel 1, pp. 811–12.

11 John J. McCloy to Delos C. Emmons, November 5, 1943, CWRIC Records, reel 1, pp. 808–10.

12 Delos C. Emmons to John J. McCloy, November 10, 1943, CWRIC Records, reel 1, pp. 806–7.

13 For more on the Tule Lake riots of late 1943, see Spicer et al., *Impounded People*, pp. 229–41; Weglyn, *Years of Infamy*, pp. 156–73; and Commission on Wartime Relocation and Internment of Civilians, *Personal Justice Denied*, pp. 208–12. Greg Robinson's account of the maneuvering that led to the WRA's shift to the Department of the Interior is thorough and excellent. See Robinson, *By Order of the President*, pp. 202–6.

14 Robinson, *By Order of the President*, pp. 211–13.

15 John J. McCloy to George C. Marshall, May 8, 1944, CWRIC Records, reel 1, pp. 792–94; George C. Marshall to John J. McCloy, May 13, 1944, CWRIC Records, reel 1, p. 791.

16 Robinson, *By Order of the President*, pp. 217–18; Irons, *Justice at War*, p. 272.

17 Robinson, *By Order of the President*, pp. 219–20.

18 Franklin D. Roosevelt to the Acting Secretary of State and the Secretary of the Interior, June 12, 1944, CWRIC Records, reel 1, p. 785.

19 Telephone conversation, John J. McCloy and Delos C. Emmons, June 13, 1944, CWRIC Records, reel 22, p. 24920.

20 Charles H. Bonesteel to John J. McCloy, July 3, 1944, CWRIC Records, reel 22, p. 24898. Peter Irons describes this exchange between McCloy and Bonesteel in *Justice at War*, p. 274.

21 Telephone conversation, John J. McCloy and Charles H. Bonesteel, July 14, 1944, CWRIC Records, reel 22, pp. 24846–47.

22 See *Ochikubo v. Bonesteel*, 57 F. Supp. 513, the federal district court decision rejecting Ochikubo's request for a preliminary injunction. The case was decided in federal rather than state court because the defendant removed the case from state to federal court.

23 Telephone conversation, John J. McCloy and Charles H. Bonesteel, July 14, 1944, CWRIC Records, reel 22, pp. 24847–48.

24 Charles H. Bonesteel to John J. McCloy, July 18, 1944, CWRIC Records, reel 22, pp. 24834–35.

25 Charles H. Bonesteel to John J. McCloy, July 31, 1944, CWRIC Records, reel 1, pp. 437–38.

26 Charles H. Bonesteel to Chief of Staff, War Department, August 8, 1944, CWRIC Records, reel 1, pp. 768–85.

27 Charles H. Bonesteel to John J. McCloy, September 21, 1944, CWRIC Records, reel 1, pp. 671–74.

28 Charles H. Bonesteel to John J. McCloy, October 25, 1944, CWRIC Records, reel 1, pp. 669–70.

29 John J. McCloy to Charles H. Bonesteel, October 31, 1944, CWRIC Records, reel 1, p. 668.

30 Robinson, *By Order of the President*, p. 227.

31 One document that vividly reflects the uncertainty about the whereabouts of the potential excludees is a December 8, 1944, letter from W. H. Wilbur to the War Department Chief of Staff, CWRIC Records, reel 1, pp. 641–42. For more on the time pressure that the Supreme Court's likely *Endo* decision created, see Henry L. Stimson to Grace Tully, December 13, 1944, CWRIC Records, reel 1, p. 620; Robinson, *By Order of the President*, pp. 213–30; and Irons, *Justice at War*, pp. 267–77.

32 Henry L. Stimson, Memorandum for the President, December 13, 1944, CWRIC Records, reel 1, pp. 625–31.

33 "Understanding of Interior, Justice and War Departments on Japanese Relocation Program," December 29, 1944, CWRIC Records, reel 1, pp. 607–10.

34 Ibid.

35 See Victor W. Nielsen to Lt. Col. Claude B. Washburne, May 25, 1944, CWRIC Records, reel 22, p. 25000; WDC Deputy Chief of Staff to WDC Chief of Staff, July 7, 1944, CWRIC Records, reel 22, p. 24897.

36 WDC, "Supplemental Report on Civilian Controls Exercised by Western Defense Command," January 1947, p. 601, NARA College Park, RG 499, decimal 319.1, Box 8.

37 "Present Procedure for Screening Japanese for Residence within the Evacuated Area," July 13, 1944, CWRIC Records, reel 22, pp. 24882–85.

38 Ibid.

39 Telephone conversation, Delos C. Emmons and John J. McCloy, June 12, 1944, CWRIC Records, reel 22, p. 24954.

40 Claude B. Washburne to Chief of Staff, WDC, July 7, 1944, CWRIC Records, reel 22, p. 24892.

41 Ibid.

42 Ibid.

43 "Proposed Statement of Policy re Evaluation of Japanese Exclusion Cases," August 8, 1944, CWRIC Records, reel 22, p. 25068.

44 Ibid.

45 Ibid.

46 "Proposed Statement of Policy re Evaluation of Japanese Exclusion Cases," September 8, 1944, CWRIC Records, reel 22, pp. 25059–60.

47 This "Machine Records" system is described in the WDC's "Supplemental Report on Civilian Controls Exercised by Western Defense Command," pp. 623–28. The system was a specific application of a technology in far broader use by the army during World War II. See Province, "IBM Punch Card Systems in the U.S. Army." For more on the "Total Information Awareness" system that the federal government created after September 11, 2001, see Safire, "You Are a Suspect," p. A35.

48 See WDC, "Supplemental Report on Civilian Controls Exercised by Western Defense Command," p. 615.

49 Ibid., pp. 630–31.

50 Memorandum, Captain Arthur B. Caldwell to Colonel Alton C. Miller, January 25, 1945, p. 4, NARA College Park, RG 499, decimal 319.1, Box 10. Five women alleged to be "agents, sub-agents, or operatives of enemy countries" were not included in this exemption, leaving them subject to individual exclusion.

51 Ibid., pp. 9–10.

52 Ibid., p. 9.

53 Ibid., p. 4.

54 Ibid., p. 10.

55 Ibid., pp. 5–7; WDC, "Supplemental Report on Civilian Controls Exercised by Western Defense Command," pp. 627–28.

56 Memorandum, Caldwell to Miller, pp. 7–9.

57 WDC, "Supplemental Report on Civilian Controls Exercised by Western Defense Command," p. 628.

CHAPTER TEN

1 Biographical information on George Ochikubo comes from the transcript of Ochikubo's Individual Exclusion Hearing, September 9, 1944, NARA College Park, RG 153, JAG (Army) Litigation Division, Records of Exclusion Cases, Ochikubo file, Box 9; from Ochikubo's trial testimony in *Ochikubo v. Bonesteel*, No. 3834-Civil, United States District Court for the Southern District of California, February 28, 1945, and March 1, 1945, NARA College Park, RG 153, JAG (Army) Litigation Division, Records of Exclusion Cases, Ochikubo file, Box 7; and from an FBI investigation report on Ochikubo, December 17, 1943, CWRIC Records, reel 8, pp. 9751–55.

2 Charles H. Bonesteel to John J. McCloy, July 31, 1944, CWRIC Records, reel 1, p. 437; Evacuee Case File of Ruth Shizuko Shiramizu, NARA Washington, RG 210.

3 Evacuee Case File for Masaru Baba, NARA Washington, RG 210.

4 John L. Burling, Memorandum for the File, July 15, 1944, CWRIC Records, reel 8, p. 9803.

5 Edward J. Ennis to Charles H. Carr, July 14, 1944, CWRIC Records, reel 8, p. 9802.

6 See Wechsler, "Toward Neutral Principles of Constitutional Law."

7 John L. Burling to Herbert Wechsler, July 18, 1944, CWRIC Records, reel 8, pp. 9743–44.

8 Telephone conversation, John J. McCloy and Charles H. Bonesteel, July 18, 1944, CWRIC Records, reel 22, pp. 24836–41.

9 Mooting Shiramizu's and Baba's cases was, it seems, already a foregone conclusion.

10 See "Memorandum of Conference in the Office of the Assistant Secretary of War—August 1, 1944," CWRIC Records, reel 8, pp. 9746–50.

11 Edward J. Ennis, "Memorandum for Mr. John L. Burling, Re: Shiramizu, et al. v. Bonesteel, et al.," August 14, 1944, CWRIC Records, reel 8, p. 9742.

12 Ibid.

13 Ibid.

14 Ibid.

15 Ibid. (emphasis added).

16 Charles H. Bonesteel to John J. McCloy, August 19, 1944, CWRIC Records, reel 8, pp. 9814–15.

17 Abe Goff, "Memorandum for the Files, Subject: Shiramizu, et al. v. Bonesteel, et al.," August 14, 1944, NARA College Park, RG 153, JAG (Army) Litigation Division, Records of Exclusion Cases, Shiramizu file, Box 11.

18 See Charles H. Carr to Edward J. Ennis, August 24, 1944, CWRIC Records, reel 9, p. 10290. Interestingly, Mrs. Shiramizu tried to refuse the letter. She explained to the military officer who delivered the letter that "she was not particularly interested insofar as her own personal return is concerned, but that she had brought legal action in order to restore the rights of her race which she felt had been improperly taken away" (Charles H. Bonesteel to John J. McCloy, July 31, 1944, CWRIC Records, reel 1, pp. 437–38). Her disinterest notwithstanding, the letter had the desired effect of mooting her case.

Sadly, the permission to return to the West Coast did little to help the grieving widow. She had a young child, no husband, and no income. What she had wanted was an end to the *mass* exclusion, so that she could return to the coast with her extended family. The prospect of returning alone as a single mother to a potentially hostile community was nothing short of frightening to her. Bitter and depressed, she decided to leave camp for Denver, Colorado, where she had some relatives. See Evacuee Case File of Ruth Shiramizu.

19 "Col. Hazzard, Captor of Aguinaldo, Dies"; "Col. Oliver Hazzard"; "How Funston Did It"; "Apache Indians to Trail Villa"; "Capt. R. T. Hazzard Kills Self"; "Historical Missions of the Seventh Cavalry Regiment."

20 "Colonel Hazzard's Talk to the School," April 30, 1945, NARA College Park, RG 499, WDC Central Correspondence file, decimal 350.001, Box 14.

21 All questions are from the transcript of the Individual Exclusion Hearing of George Ochikubo, September 9, 1944, NARA College Park, RG 153, JAG (Army) Litigation Division, Records of Exclusion Cases, Ochikubo file, Box 9.

22 Findings of Hearing Board, September 9, 1944, NARA College Park, RG 153, JAG (Army) Litigation Division, Records of Exclusion Cases, Ochikubo file, Box 9.

23 "Proposed Statement of Policy re Evaluation of Japanese Exclusion Cases," September 8, 1944, CWRIC Records, reel 22, pp. 25059–60.

24 Ibid. On February 9, 1945, Maj. Gen. H. C. Pratt reaffirmed Major General Bonesteel's individual exclusion order "after due consideration of the report of the Board of Officers" chaired by Colonel Hazzard. See H. C. Pratt, Memorandum, "Exclusion of George Ochikubo," February 9, 1945, NARA College Park, RG 153, JAG (Army) Litigation Division, Records of Exclusion Cases, Ochikubo file, Box 9.

25 *Ochikubo v. Bonesteel*, 57 F. Supp. 513.

26 Ibid., p. 516.

27 See Memorandum, H. C. Pratt to Chief of Staff, U.S. Army, January 8, 1945, CWRIC Records, reel 22, pp. 24735–41.

28 See *Ebel v. Drum* and *Schueller v. Drum*.

29 *Ebel v. Drum*, pp. 196–97.

30 Myron G. Cramer to Commanding General, WDC, February 14, 1945, CWRIC Records, reel 22, pp. 24742–44. As it turned out, Major General Cramer was not the only person arguing for a highly selective presentation of the record. On August 26, 1944, FBI director J. Edgar Hoover urged that if the lawyers were to submit the FBI's report on Ochikubo to the district court, they should excise the portion of the report in which the FBI agent concluded that he had found "no definite subversive activities" on Ochikubo's part. See J. Edgar Hoover to Herbert Wechsler, August 26, 1944, CWRIC Records, reel 9, p. 10287. "It is not thought that in the present trial the FBI should be placed in the position of expressing an opinion as to the presence or lack of subversive tendencies on the part of" Ochikubo, Hoover argued. Justice Department attorney John Burling, however, disagreed: "It is entirely clear that there is no military necessity for concealing the fact that the Bureau found no evidence of subversion and the case was closed" (J. L. Burling to Herbert Wechsler, September 8, 1944, CWRIC Records, reel 8, p. 9819).

31 By the time of trial, Ochikubo's case had been consolidated with those of two other Nisei who were contesting individual exclusion: Elmer S. Yamamoto, an attorney, and Kiyoshi Shikegawa, a fisherman. Naturally, the facts in each of these two excludee's files were somewhat different from Ochikubo's, but the legal issues their cases presented were identical.

32 Charles H. Bonesteel to Chief of Staff, War Department, August 8, 1944, CWRIC Records, reel 1, p. 769.

33 Brigadier General Wilbur's trial testimony of March 1, 1945, can be found at

NARA College Park, RG 153, JAG (Army) Litigation Division, Records of Exclusion Cases, Ochikubo file, Box 7.

34 It is possible that Brigadier General Wilbur was referring to the incendiary balloons that Japan launched toward the northwestern United States late in 1944 and early in 1945. See Mikesh, *Japan's World War II Balloon Bomb Attacks*.

35 Colonel Schweitzer's testimony of February 27, 1945, can be found at NARA College Park, RG 153, JAG (Army) Litigation Division, Records of Exclusion Cases, Ochikubo file, Box 7.

36 The trial transcript here reads "inclusive" rather than "conclusive." I have made the change to conclusive because the context makes it quite obvious that the court reporter here made an error in transcription.

37 To be sure, there is one reading of the military witnesses' testimony that would make it appear more misleading than outright fraudulent. On this view, the military witnesses were suggesting that the process of selecting individuals for exclusion had two robust and independent tracks—a mechanical track, which used rigidly fixed categories to identify some excludees, and a subjective track, which allowed the WDC to pluck out others for exclusion without using any firm standards.

The trouble with this gloss on the military witnesses' testimony is that the historical record contains no evidence of a genuinely functioning system of the second, subjective, sort. Given that the WDC was under great pressure to limit the number of individual excludees to 10,000, and that its mechanical categories themselves produced at least that number, it is difficult to see how the WDC could have actually implemented any system of subjective and standardless exclusion of the type that the witnesses described in more than a handful of cases. Indeed, to the extent that the WDC actually made such subjective decisions, it seemed to do so mostly in the cases of individuals who were suing it.

Thus, even if one gives the military witnesses at the *Ochikubo* trial the benefit of the doubt, their testimony was grossly misleading, in that they implied that the WDC operated a dual system of review, when for all intents and purposes it really operated just one.

38 See *Ochikubo v. Bonesteel*, 60 F. Supp. 916.

39 Peter Irons tells the story of this concealment in his seminal work *Justice at War*.

40 "Gist of Statement by Tel., JA to TJAG," January 22, 1945, NARA College Park, RG 153, JAG (Army) Litigation Division, Records of Exclusion Cases, Ochikubo file, Box 7.

41 See John H. Doughty to the Judge Advocate General, July 11, 1945, NARA College Park, RG 153, JAG (Army) Litigation Division, Records of Exclusion Cases, Ochikubo file, Box 8.

42 See Archibald King to Commanding General, WDC, September 28, 1945, NARA College Park, RG 153, JAG (Army) Litigation Division, Records of Exclusion Cases, Ochikubo file, Box 8.

43　H. C. Pratt to the Judge Advocate General, October 6, 1945, NARA College Park, RG 153, JAG (Army) Litigation Division, Records of Exclusion Cases, Ochikubo file, Box 8. General Pratt had more than one reason to want to establish this legal proposition. Not only did he want to do so for the benefit of future military commanders in future conflicts, he also wanted to do so for the benefit of his predecessor, Gen. John DeWitt, who at the time of the *Ochikubo* litigation was a defendant in a civil lawsuit in which a non-Japanese excludee was seeking tort damages for an unlawful application of force. See *DeWitt v. Wilcox*.

44　Telephone interview with George Ochikubo, DDS, June 30, 2006.

CHAPTER ELEVEN

1　On loyalty testing before and just after the American Revolution, see Hyman, *To Try Men's Souls*, pp. 61–95. Good sources on the Sedition Act include Miller, *Crisis in Freedom*, and Smith, *Freedom's Fetters*.

2　Klingberg, *Southern Claims Commission*.

3　For more on these prosecutions, see Peterson and Fite, *Opponents of War*.

4　Hyman, *To Try Men's Souls*, pp. 277–78.

5　"McCarthy era" is a misleading name for the period of intense Cold War anxiety over loyalty because the period began well before Wisconsin senator Joseph McCarthy rose to prominence.

6　The leading source on this huge loyalty screening system is Bontecou, *Federal Loyalty-Security Program*. For the text of Executive Order 9385, see Executive Order 9385, pp. 1937–91.

7　Bontecou, *Federal Loyalty-Security Program*, pp. 239–41.

8　In examining the differences between civilian and military modes of loyalty adjudication, this study follows in the tradition of Lucy Salyer's important comparative institutional assessment of administrative and judicial decision-making in cases involving the admission and deportation of Chinese in the late nineteenth and early twentieth centuries. See Salyer, *Laws Harsh as Tigers*. This study finds within the various civilian and military agencies of World War II some of the same sorts of conceptual and institutional cleavages that separated immigration administrators from federal judges in their evaluation of the cases of Chinese immigrants.

9　In this connection, it is interesting to note that most of the cases in which the Industrial Employment Review Board reversed war plant removals by the PMGO were cases in which the Nisei appellant *personally appeared* before the IERB.

10　Diary of Richard S. Nishimoto, March 13, 1944, JERS, reel 236, frames 281–82.

11　An excellent source on this study is Hirabayashi, *Politics of Fieldwork*.

12　Diary of Richard S. Nishimoto, March 13, 1944.

13　Fletcher, *Loyalty*, pp. 8–9, 40.

14　See Morse, "Blame and Danger"; Otto, "On the Ability of Mental Health Professionals to 'Predict Dangerousness' "; and Bauer et al., "Reflections on Dangerousness."

15 Grodzins, *Loyal and the Disloyal*.
16 Ibid., p. 14.
17 Ibid., p. 129.
18 Ibid., p. 197.
19 Ibid., p. 145.
20 Ibid., p. 207.
21 Suzuki, "For the Sake of Inter-university Comity," p. 96.
22 Grodzins, *Loyal and the Disloyal*, p. 130.
23 Ibid.
24 Ibid.
25 Ibid., pp. 130–31.
26 Executive Order No. 9835.
27 Philip M. Glick, "Outline of Procedure for Appointment of a Board of Prominent Civilians to Give Hearings on Request to Evacuees to Whom WRA Proposes to Deny Indefinite Leave," May 15, 1943, NARA Washington, RG 210, Entry 16, Box 286.
28 Dillon Myer to the Attorney General, October 16, 1943, NARA Washington, RG 210, Entry 16, Box 286. Wolfe sat on the Utah Supreme Court from 1935 to 1954, six of those years as chief justice. See "James H. Wolfe, 73, Ex-Justice in Utah," obituary.
29 Dillon Myer to the Attorney General, October 16, 1943.
30 Memorandum, J. Edgar Hoover to Ugo Carusi, October 26, 1943, NARA Washington, RG 210, Entry 16, Box 286.
31 "Civil Rights Group Called Red 'Front.' "
32 "Utah Chief Justice Cleared."
33 Elias, "USA's Muslims Under a Cloud."
34 See Waldman, "Prophetic Justice."

BIBLIOGRAPHY

PRIMARY SOURCES

Manuscripts and Archival Material

Berkeley, California

    Bancroft Library

        Japanese American Evacuation and Resettlement Records, 1930–74

            (on microfilm)

College Park, Maryland

    National Archives and Records Administration

        Records of the Department of Justice, Record Group 60

        Records of the Office of the Secretary of War, Record Group 107

        Records of the Office of the Judge Advocate General (Army), Record

            Group 153

        Records of the Commission on Wartime Relocation and Internment of

            Civilians, Record Group 220 (on microfilm)

        Records of the Office of the Provost Marshal General, Record Group 389

        Records of the U.S. Army Defense Commands (World War II), Record

            Group 499

Hyde Park, New York

    Franklin D. Roosevelt Presidential Library

        Charles Fahy Papers

Washington, D.C.

    National Archives and Records Administration

        Records of the War Relocation Authority, RG 210

Court Cases

DeWitt v. Wilcox, 161 F.2d 785 (9th Cir. 1947)

Ebel v. Drum, 52 F. Supp. 189 (D. Mass. 1943)

Ex parte Endo, 323 U.S. 283 (1944)

Ex parte Ventura, 44 F. Supp. 520 (W.D. Wash. 1942)

In re Ernest Wakayama, No. 2380-O'C, United States District Court for the Southern

    District of California, Central Division (1942)

In re Toki Wakayama, No. 2376-H, United States District Court for the Southern

    District of California, Central Division (1942)

In re Yokohama Specie Bank, Limited, 195 P. 2d 555 (Cal. Dist. Ct. App. 1948)

I.N.S. v. St. Cyr, 533 U.S. 289, 301 (2001)

Kawakita v. United States, 343 U.S. 717 (1952)

Korematsu v. United States, 323 U.S. 214 (1944)

Ochikubo v. Bonesteel, 57 F. Supp. 513 (S.D. Cal. 1944)

Ochikubo v. Bonesteel, 60 F. Supp. 916 (S.D. Cal. 1945)

Schueller v. Drum, 51 F. Supp. 383 (E.D. Pa. 1943)

Published Government Documents

DeWitt, John L. *Final Report: Japanese Evacuation from the West Coast, 1942*. Washington: Government Printing Office, 1943, portions reprinted at <http://www.sfmuseum.org/war/dewitt1.html> (accessed August 8, 2006).

War Relocation Authority. *The Evacuated People: A Quantitative Description*. Washington: Government Printing Office, 1946.

———. *WRA: A Story of Human Conservation*. Washington: Government Printing Office, 1946.

Presidential Materials

Executive Order 9066. *Federal Register* 7, no. 38 (February 25, 1942): 1407.

Executive Order 9385. *Federal Register* 12, no. 59 (March 25, 1947): 1935.

Roosevelt, Franklin D. "A Message to the Senate on the Segregation Program of the War Relocation Authority." In *Public Papers and Addresses of Franklin D. Roosevelt, 1943 volume*. New York: Harper and Brothers, 1950.

SECONDARY SOURCES

Books

Asato, Noriko. *Teaching Mikadoism: The Attack on Japanese Language Schools in Hawaii, California, and Washington*. Honolulu: University of Hawaii Press, 2005.

Austin, Allan W. *From Concentration Camp to Campus: Japanese American Students and World War II*. Urbana: University of Illinois Press, 2004.

Axel, Elof. *The Unfit: A History of a Bad Idea*. Cold Spring Harbor, N.Y.: Cold Spring Harbor Laboratory Press, 2001.

Azuma, Eiichiro. *Between Two Empires: Race, History, and Transnationalism in Japanese America*. New York: Oxford University Press, 2005.

Bontecou, Eleanor. *The Federal Loyalty-Security Program*. Ithaca: Cornell University Press, 1953.

Bracher, Karl Dietrich. *The German Dictatorship: The Origins, Structure, and Effects of National Socialism*. New York: Praeger, 1970.

Broszat, Martin. *The Hitler State: The Foundation and Development of the Internal Structure of the Third Reich*. London: Longman, 1981.

Commager, Henry Steele. *Freedom, Loyalty, Dissent*. New York: Oxford University Press, 1954.

Commission on Wartime Relocation and Internment of Civilians. *Personal Justice*

Denied: Report of the Commission on Wartime Relocation and Internment of Civilians.
Seattle: University of Washington Press, 2007.

Daniels, Roger. *Asian America: Chinese and Japanese in the United States Since 1850.*
Seattle: University of Washington Press, 1988.

——. *Concentration Camps USA: Japanese Americans and World War II.* New York: Holt,
Rinehart & Winston, 1970.

——. *Prisoners Without Trial.* New York: Hill and Wang, 1993.

de Nevers, Klancy C. *The Colonel and the Pacifist: Karl Bendetsen, Perry Saito, and the
Incarceration of Japanese Americans during World War II.* Salt Lake City: University of
Utah Press, 2004.

Drinnon, Richard. *Keeper of Concentration Camps: Dillon S. Myer and American Racism.*
Berkeley: University of California Press, 1987.

Fiset, Louis. *Imprisoned Apart: The World War II Correspondence of an Issei Couple.* Seattle:
University of Washington Press, 1998.

Fletcher, George P. *Loyalty: An Essay on the Morality of Relationships.* New York: Oxford
University Press, 1993.

Grodzins, Morton. *The Loyal and the Disloyal: Social Boundaries of Patriotism and Treason.*
Chicago: University of Chicago Press, 1956.

Hayashi, Brian M. *Democratizing the Enemy: The Japanese American Internment.* Princeton:
Princeton University Press, 2004.

Higham, John. *Strangers in the Land: Patterns of American Nativism, 1860–1925.* New
Brunswick: Rutgers University Press, 1988.

Hirabayashi, Lane Ryo. *The Politics of Fieldwork: Research in an American Concentration
Camp.* Tucson: University of Arizona Press, 1999.

Hosokawa, William. *JACL: In Quest of Justice.* New York: William Morrow, 1982.

——. *Nisei: The Quiet Americans.* New York: William Morrow, 1969.

Hyman, Harold M. *To Try Men's Souls: Loyalty Tests in American History.* Berkeley:
University of California Press, 1959

Ichioka, Yuji. *The Issei: The World of the First Generation Japanese Immigrants.* New York:
Free Press, 1988.

Irons, Peter. *Justice at War: The Story of the Japanese American Internment Cases.* Berkeley:
University of California Press, 1993.

Kashima, Tetsuden. *Judgment Without Trial: Japanese American Imprisonment during World
War II.* Seattle: University of Washington Press, 2003.

Kiyota, Minoru. *Beyond Loyalty: The Story of a Kibei.* Honolulu: University of Hawaii
Press, 1997.

Klingberg, Frank W. *The Southern Claims Commission.* Berkeley: University of
California Press, 1955.

Leighton, Alexander H. *The Governing of Men: General Principles and Recommendations
Based on Experience at a Japanese Relocation Camp.* Princeton: Princeton University
Press, 1946.

Mikesh, Robert C. *Japan's World War II Balloon Bomb Attacks on North America.*
Washington: Smithsonian Institution Press, 1973.

Miller, John C. *Crisis in Freedom: The Alien and Sedition Acts.* Boston: Little, Brown and Company, 1951.

Miyamoto, S. Frank. *Social Solidarity Among the Japanese in Seattle.* 1939. Reprint, Seattle: University of Washington Press, 1984.

Muller, Eric L. *Free to Die for Their Country: The Story of the Japanese American Draft Resisters in World War II.* Chicago: University of Chicago Press, 2001.

Peterson, H. C., and Gilbert C. Fite, *Opponents of War, 1917–1918.* Madison: University of Wisconsin Press, 1957.

Robinson, Greg. *By Order of the President: FDR and the Internment of Japanese Americans.* Cambridge: Harvard University Press, 2001.

Salyer, Lucy E. *Laws Harsh as Tigers: Chinese Immigrants and the Shaping of Modern Immigration Law.* Chapel Hill: University of North Carolina Press, 1995.

Smith, James Morton. *Freedom's Fetters: The Alien and Sedition Laws and American Civil Liberties.* Ithaca: Cornell University Press, 1956.

Spicer, Edward H., et al. *Impounded People: Japanese-American in the Relocation Centers.* Tucson: University of Arizona Press, 1969.

Svinth, Joseph R. *Getting A Grip: Judo in the Nikkei Communities of the Pacific Northwest, 1900–1950.* Tumwater, Wash.: Electronic Journals of the Martial Arts and Sciences, 2003.

Tateishi, John. *And Justice for All: An Oral History of the Japanese American Detention Camps.* New York: Random House, 1984.

Ten Broek, Jacobus, Edward N. Barnhart, and Floyd W. Matson. *Prejudice, War, and the Constitution.* Berkeley: University of California Press, 1954.

Thomas, Dorothy S., and Richard Nishimoto. *The Spoilage: Japanese-American Evacuation and Resettlement during World War II.* Berkeley: University of California Press, 1946.

Weglyn, Michi. *Years of Infamy.* New York: Morrow Quill Paperbacks, 1976.

Yoo, David K. *Growing Up Nisei: Race, Generation, and Culture among Japanese Americans of California, 1924–1949.* Urbana: University of Illinois Press, 2000.

Articles

Essays in Edited Collections

Austin, Allan Wesley. "Loyalty and Concentration Camps in America: The Japanese American Precedent and the Internal Security Act of 1950." In *Last Witnesses: Reflections on the Wartime Internment of Japanese Americans,* edited by Erica Harth. New York: St. Martin's Press, 2001.

Daniels, Roger. "Western Reaction to the Relocated Japanese Americans: The Case of Wyoming." In *Japanese Americans: From Relocation to Redress,* edited by Roger Daniels et al., 112–16. Seattle: University of Washington Press, 1992

———. "Words Do Matter: A Note on Inappropriate Terminology and the Incarceration of Japanese Americans." In *Nikkei in the Pacific Northwest: Japanese Americans and Japanese Canadians in the Twentieth Century,* edited by Louis Fiset and Gail M. Nomura, 190–214. Seattle: University of Washington Press, 2005.

Suzuki, Peter T. "For the Sake of Inter-university Comity." In *Views from Within: The Japanese Evacuation and Resettlement Study*, edited by Yuji Ichioka, 95–123. Los Angeles: UCLA Asian American Studies Center, 1989.

Periodicals

Abbott, Roger S. "The Federal Loyalty Program: Background and Problems." *American Political Science Review* 42, no. 3 (1948): 486–99.

Bauer, A., et al. "Reflections on Dangerousness and Its Prediction—A Truly Tantalizing Task?" *Medicine and Law* 21 (2002): 495–517.

Bernstein, Marver H. "The Loyalty of Federal Employees." *Western Political Quarterly* 2, no. 2 (1949): 254–64.

Morse, Stephen J. "Blame and Danger: An Essay on Preventive Detention." *Boston University Law Review* 76 (1996): 113–55.

Muller, Eric L. "Apologies or Apologists? Remembering the Japanese American Internment in Wyoming." *Wyoming Law Review* 1 (2001): 473–95.

———. "Betrayal on Trial: Japanese American 'Treason' in World War II." *North Carolina Law Review* 82 (2004): 1759–98.

———. "A Penny for Their Thoughts: Draft Resistance at the Poston Relocation Center." *Law and Contemporary Problems* 68 (2005): 119–57.

Otto, Randy K. "On the Ability of Mental Health Professionals to "Predict Dangerousness": A Commentary on Interpretations of the 'Dangerousness' Literature." *Law & Psychology Review* 18 (1994): 43–68.

Parrish, Michael E. "A Lawyer in Crisis Times: Joseph L. Rauh, Jr., the Loyalty-Security Program, and the Defense of Civil Liberties in the Early Cold War." *North Carolina Law Review* 82 (2004): 1799–1839.

Seltzer, William, and Margo Anderson. "The Dark Side of Numbers: The Role of Population Data Systems in Human Rights Abuses." *Social Research* 68, no. 2 (Summer 2001): 339–71.

Thomas, Dorothy Swaine. "Some Social Aspects of Japanese-American Demography." *Proceedings of the American Philosophical Society* 94, no. 5 (October 19, 1950): 459–80.

Volpp, Leti. "Obnoxious to Their Very Nature: Asian Americans and Constitutional Citizenship." *Asian Law Journal* 8 (2001): 71–85.

Waldman, Amy. "Prophetic Justice." *The Atlantic Monthly* 298, no. 3 (October 2006): 82–93.

Wechsler, Herbert. "Toward Neutral Principles of Constitutional Law." *Harvard Law Review* 73 (1959): 1–35.

Newspapers

"Apache Indians to Trail Villa." *Iowa City Citizen*, April 7, 1916.

"Capt. R. T. Hazzard Kills Self." *The Chehalis (Wash.) Bee-Nugget*, September 9, 1921.

Carberry, Jack. "Food Is Hoarded for Japs in U.S. While Americans in Nippon Are Tortured." *Denver Post*, May 23, 1943.

——. "Hostile Group Is Pampered at Wyoming Camp." *Denver Post*, April 24, 1943.

"Civil Rights Group Called Red 'Front.'" *New York Times*, August 31, 1947.

"Col. Hazzard, Captor of Aguinaldo, Dies." *San Francisco Examiner*, January 21, 1960.

"Col. Oliver Hazzard." Obituary. *San Francisco Chronicle*. January 21, 1960.

Elias, Marilyn. "USA's Muslims Under a Cloud." *USA Today*, August 10, 2006.

"How Funston Did It." *New York Times*, March 29, 1901.

"Internees Hired by Ickes for Farm." *New York Times*. April 16, 1943.

"James H. Wolfe, 73, Ex-Justice in Utah." *New York Times*, March 29, 1958.

"Resolution of Policy towards the Japanese at Heart Mountain Relocation Center." *Cody (Wyo.) Enterprise*, May 5, 1943.

Safire, William. "You Are A Suspect." *New York Times*, November 14, 2003.

"Utah Chief Justice Cleared." *New York Times*, March 14, 1953.

Films

Abe, Frank. *Conscience and the Constitution*. 60 min. Independent Television Service, 2000.

Omori, Emiko. *Rabbit in the Moon*. 85 min. New Day Films, 1999.

Web Sites

"FBI Reports on Kendo in Seattle and Portland before World War II," *Journal of Combative Sport* (November 2003). <http://ejmas.com/jcs/jcsart_power_1103.htm> (accessed August 4, 2006).

"Final 'Buffalo Six' Member Pleads Guilty." <http://www.foxnews.com/story/0,2933,87264,00.html> (accessed August 4, 2006).

"Historical Missions of the Seventh Cavalry Regiment." August 2004. <http://www.first-team.us/journals/7th_rgmt/7thndx01.html> (accessed August 7, 2006).

"'I Plead Guilty,' Taliban American Says." <http://archives.cnn.com/2002/LAW/07/15/walker.lindh.hearing/> (accessed August 4, 2006).

Kendo America. "About Kendo." <http://www.kendo-usa.org/abtken.htm> (accessed August 4, 2006).

National Japanese American Historical Society. "The Military Intelligence Service (MIS) 1941–1952." <http://www.njahs.org/research/mis.html> (accessed August 5, 2006).

Province, Charles M. "IBM Punch Card Systems in the U.S. Army." <http://www.pattonhq.com/ibm.html> (accessed August 7, 2006).

Seltzer, William, and Margo Anderson. "After Pearl Harbor: The Proper Role of Population Data Systems in Time of War." *Statisticians in History*, March 2000. <http://www.amstat.org/about/statisticians/index.cfm?fuseaction=PaperInfo&PaperID=1> (accessed August 6, 2006).

"Two Plead Guilty in Oregon Terror Case." <http://www.cnn.com/2003/LAW/10/16/terror.suspects/> (accessed August 4, 2006).

"What Is Kodokan Judo?" <http://judoinfo.com/whatis.htm> (accessed August 4, 2006).

ACKNOWLEDGMENTS

This book was several years in the making, and I got lots of help along the way.

The University of North Carolina at Chapel Hill, my home institution, has been very supportive of this project. When he was dean, Gene Nichol was kind enough to award me the George R. Ward Professorship at the School of Law at the moment when I was gearing up to start the research for the book. Not only did that boost my confidence, but the stipend that came along with it helped me travel to the various archives around the country that held documents I needed to review. I was also fortunate to receive a W. N. Reynolds Research Leave from the University of North Carolina for the spring semester of 2005. This additional semester of relief from my teaching duties gave me much-needed time for both research travel and writing.

The faculty and staff of the Katherine R. Everett Law Library at the University of North Carolina School of Law are extraordinary. For several years I peppered them with one odd interlibrary loan request after another, and they never so much as blinked. I am lucky to have the assistance of such a dedicated and professional group. Nick Sexton, Jim Sherwood, and former staff member Samantha Agbeblewu deserve special mention.

For several years, I taught a seminar on law and loyalty to upper-level UNC law students, and I have no doubt that their enthusiasm and interest helped sustain my commitment to this project. I also have no doubt that their reactions to the material we read—including, one semester, an early draft of this manuscript—helped me deepen and broaden my thinking.

I am also indebted to a remarkable group of archivists at the National Archives, without whose guidance and assistance I could not have written this book. These include Aloha South, the expert on War Relocation Authority records at the downtown branch of the archives in Washington, D.C.; Fred Romanski, the expert on Justice Department records in College Park, Maryland; and Wilbert Mahoney and Kenneth Schlessinger in the Modern Military Records unit in College Park. The staff of the FDR Presidential Library in Hyde Park, New York, were also helpful during my visit there. I had valuable assistance in obtaining the photographs that appear in the book from Susan Snyder at Berkeley's Bancroft Library, Kelly Haigh in the Special Collections Division at UCLA's Charles E. Young Research Library, and Dace Taube of the Regional History Center at the University of Southern California.

My colleagues on the faculty at the University of North Carolina School of Law have been quite helpful to me at various points in the research and writing of this book. Joe Kennedy deserves special mention; in this project, as in all things, he has been a dispenser of sound advice. Hiroshi Motomura has also been very generous with his time and guidance, about the book and all manner of other things.

I have had very fruitful correspondence about matters I touch on in the book with the historians Roger Daniels and Greg Robinson. I am lucky to know these scholars and to have the benefit of their expertise. Roger Daniels deserves a special note of gratitude, not just for his help with this project, but for the work of his entire career. I am quite sure that I would not be in a position to do the work that I do if he had not done so much to develop the field and open it to new scholars.

While I did not seek financial support from the California Civil Liberties Public Education Program for this project, I have twice received grants from them in the past in connection with earlier work, and that support continues to benefit my work in this field, in direct and indirect ways. It is a marvelous program, and I am grateful for its generosity.

Along the way, valuable information, encouragement, and support of various kinds have come from Gene Akutsu and his family, John Allore, Margo Anderson, John Q. Barrett, Mary Caviness, Mary Dudziak, Sally Greene, Chuck Grench, Art Hansen, Tom Ikeda, Tetsuden Kashima, Yosh and Irene Kuromiya, Steve Lowry, Scott Marlow, Kristine Minami, George Nozawa, Katy O'Brien, Dan Pollitt, Harry Scheiber, William Seltzer, Bob Sims, Barbara Takei, Kenji Taguma, Frank and Sadie Yamasaki, Sara Yamasaki, Marshall Yount, and my fellow board members of the Heart Mountain Wyoming Foundation. I received excellent feedback on a couple of the book's chapters from the participants in the Triangle Legal History Seminar, including especially its founders, Adrienne Davis and Ed Balleisen.

My biggest debt of all is to my family, whose support sustains me in everything I do—my brother David and his family, my brother-in-law Peter Branden and his family, my parents-in-law, Ann and Alex Branden, my loving and generous parents, Joan and Jim Muller, my beautiful and inspiring and brilliant daughters, Abby and Nina, and—last, but the opposite of least—my wife, Leslie Branden-Muller. She is the one who really makes the whole thing possible.

mass exclusion in, 91; Democrats gain House seats in 1944 in, 96. *See also* Tule Lake Segregation Center

Carter, John Franklin, 15, 16

Chandler, Albert B. ("Happy"), 26, 156 (n. 20), 159 (n. 20)

Children, exemption from individual exclusion process of, 105

"Chinese menu" approach, 52, 65

Christianity: conversion of Japanese Americans to, 10; in Dedrick's point system, 47; in Dedrick's color-coding system, 50; in War Relocation Authority point system, 76, 77

Citizenship: and Nisei, 9, 11; renunciation of American, 102, 105, 125, 130. *See also* Dual citizenship

Civil Affairs Division (Western Defense Command): records on Japanese Americans, 42, 52, 139; racial prejudice in, 44; on Japanese informants as untrustworthy, 48; in Dedrick's color-coding system, 49, 51–52, 162 (n. 43); and War Relocation Authority, 54; supporting role of in loyalty adjudication, 83; and Provost Marshal General's Office, 95, 96; in original process for individual exclusion, 98; and Washburne's loyalty assessment proposal, 100–102, 104

Civil rights: wartime rights versus, 60; as issue in registration process, 73–74; Okamoto addresses question of, 80; Wirin lawsuits raise question of, 93

Civil War, 135–36

Clark, Chase, 21

Cleveland Steel Products Company, 58–59

Cody (Wyoming), 25

Cohn, Roy, 136

Cold War, 1, 136, 145

Colorado: relocation center in, 22;

Amache Relocation Center, 23 (ill.), 34 (ill.)

Color-coding system, 49–52

Concentration camps, 2, 149 (n. 2), 150 (n. 6)

Constitution of the United States: Fourteenth Amendment on citizenship, 9; civil liberties versus wartime powers, 60; and Pratt on exclusion orders as unreviewable, 123. *See also* Civil rights

Cramer, Myron C., 123–24, 173 (n. 30)

Daniels, Roger, 10, 25, 153 (n. 24), 159 (n. 13)

Dedrick, Calvert L.: data analysis for Provost Marshal General's Office, 44, 46; on Japanese Americans as a threat, 46; point system of, 46–49; color-coding system of, 49–52, 61, 162 (n. 43); "ham-and-eggs" approach to classification of, 50, 52; on War Relocation Authority's "white" category proposal, 54

Defense work. *See* War plant work

Demonstrations: at Poston and Manzanar relocation centers, 26, 31, 38; government response to, 31, 38; violent protests at Tule Lake Segregation Center, 88

De Witt, John L.: Japanese American disloyalty assumed by, 5, 17–18, 19, 28, 32–33, 84, 101, 138; authority to remove people from military zones, 17, 84; Nikkei forced into assembly centers by, 21; on military service for Nisei, 24, 32–33; on segregation of the disloyal, 26–27; leaves Western Defense Command, 86

Dies, Martin, 26, 156 (n. 20)

Disloyal, segregation of the. *See* Segregation of the disloyal

Hall, Pierson M., 122, 130, 131, 132
"Ham-and-eggs" approach to classification, 50, 51, 52, 65
Harbert, Clarence, 58, 59
Hawaii, 18, 86
Hazzard, Oliver Perry Morton, 117–19, 130
Heart Mountain Relocation Center: local attitude toward, 25; military recruitment at, 36; Okamoto's draft resistance movement at, 80–81; economic effect of, 156 (n. 17)
Hirabayashi, Gordon, 131
Hishiki, Hiroshi, 62–64
Holland, Thomas W., 59, 160 (n. 9)
Hoover, J. Edgar, 16, 40–41, 146, 173 (n. 30)
Hori, Tashi, 71–72
Horibe, Sho, 68–69
House Subcommittee on Un-American Activities, 26, 136, 146, 156 (n. 20)
Hughes, James, 55, 56

Iba, Harry, 61–62, 165 (n. 89)
IBM punch cards, 103–4, 106, 171 (n. 47)
Ickes, Harold, 58, 88–89, 90
Idaho: governor of opposes Japanese American relocation to, 21; relocation center in, 22; Minidoka Relocation Center, 36
IERB (Industrial Employment Review Board), 69–70, 166 (n. 10), 175 (n. 9)
Ikegami, Yukio, 68
Indefinite leave, 31; Japanese American Joint Board on, 34, 53@-54; in Dedrick's color-coding system, 49; War Relocation Authority disregarding Japanese American Joint Board findings on, 55–56; as irrevocable, 56; war plant work by internees on, 56–59

Individual exclusion: ceiling placed on number of excludees, 7, 97, 98, 104–5, 106, 129–30, 174 (n. 37); system that Western Defense Command wanted, 7, 83, 95, 98–104; system actually used by Western Defense Command, 7, 83, 104–6, 125; Western Defense Command system tested in federal court, 7, 83, 127–30, 132; Bonesteel's support for, 92, 94–96; shift from mass exclusion to, 96–98; Ochikubo hearing for, 116–22; in *Ochikubo v. Bonesteel* trial, 122–33
Industrial Employment Review Board (IERB), 69–70, 166 (n. 10), 175 (n. 9)
Interior Department, 88, 97, 168 (n. 23)
International Harvester Company, 70–71
Internment of Japanese Americans. *See* Japanese American internment
Isolation camps, 157 (n. 30)
Issei: population of in 1941, 9; presumed to be loyal to Japan, 9; Japanese Associations of, 10; little English spoken by, 12; on Japanese education for their children, 12, 152 (n. 14); Japanese nationalism of, 12–13, 152 (n. 18); uncertainty about remaining in United States, 13; in FBI report on Nikkei loyalty, 16; forced into assembly centers, 21, 155 (n. 1); segregation of the disloyal considered, 26, 27; WRA-126 form for, 35; and Question 28 of loyalty questionnaire of 1943, 35, 36, 158 (n. 10); repatriation requests in 1943, 36–37
Ito, Dorothy, 64–65

JACL. *See* Japanese American Citizens League
JAJB. *See* Japanese American Joint Board

Japanese-American Branch (Provost Marshal General's Office): responsibilities of, 40; staff of, 41; as Japanese American Joint Board information source, 41–42; on Western Defense Command's records on Japanese Americans, 42; racial prejudice in, 44; Dedrick's point system used by, 46–48, 75–76; Dedrick's color-coding system used by, 49–52; not moving as fast as War Relocation Authority wants, 54; in war plant cases, 57; War Relocation Authority criticized by, 60–61, 163 (n. 70); approach to Nisei loyalty of, 67, 139

Japanese American Citizens League (JACL): as Nisei organization, 10; super-patriotic creed of, 14; military service for Nisei supported by, 23–24, 32; in Dedrick's point system, 47; and Ochikubo lawsuit, 111 (ill.), 117

Japanese American internment: lower levels of government in, 2; racism in, 5, 7, 17–20; and election of 1944, 6; assembly centers for, 21; farm labor during, 22, 31, 155 (n. 7), 156 (n. 17); and pressures for freedom, 22–25; and pressures for confinement, 25; and loyalty as criterion for freedom or confinement, 28–30; Japanese Evacuation and Resettlement Study and, 141; "internment" as euphemism, 149 (n. 2); works on, 150 (n. 11). See also Individual exclusion; Mass exclusion; Relocation centers; Segregation of the disloyal

Japanese American Joint Board (JAJB), 39–65; in loyalty bureaucracy, 3; intended as meeting point for other agencies, 3; interagency conflict in, 3; functions of, 6, 34–35, 39–40,

139; dissolution of, 6, 57, 83; establishment of, 34; members of, 34, 40; FBI withdraws from, 40–41; sources of information of, 41–44, 139; organizing and processing data, 44–61; language for recommending against indefinite leave, 53–54; fissure between War Relocation Authority and military members of, 53–61; War Relocation Authority disengages from work of, 55; War Relocation Authority disregards findings of, 55–56; human consequences of errors of, 61–65, 139; Nielsen proposes review board similar to, 99; recommends against leave clearance for Ochikubo, 110; biases affect loyalty adjudication by, 140; on loyalty versus racial pride, 142; behavior prediction as task of, 143; reconstructing deliberations of, 164 (n. 87)

Japanese Americans (Nikkei): none convicted of spying or sabotage, 4, 61, 150 (n. 10); presumption of disloyalty of, 5; population in 1941, 9; before the war, 9–14; Carter-Munson study of loyalty of, 15–16; enemy alien draft status for, 22; lessons to be learned from loyalty assessment of, 135–47. See also Issei; Japanese American internment; Nisei

Japanese Association of Los Angeles, 11 (ill.)

Japanese associations, 10

Japanese Evacuation and Resettlement Study (JERS), 141, 144

Japanese language schools, 12; Army Intelligence on, 18; Army Service Commands on, 43; Washburne on, 44; in Dedrick's point system, 47, 48; in Dedrick's color-coding system, 49, 50; Los Angeles Nippon Institute, 63; in War Relocation Authority point system, 76; in Nielsen's loyalty evaluation system, 99; in Bonesteel's policy statement of August 8, 1944, 102; Ochikubo attends, 108

JERS (Japanese Evacuation and Resettlement Study), 141, 144

Jinshu Kyokai, 108

Jus soli, 11

Kamibayashi, Isamu, 70

Kawakita, Tom, 153 (n. 27)

Kendo, 12, 47

Kibei, 13–14; Carter-Munson loyalty study on, 15; in Military Intelligence Service, 23; segregation of the disloyal considered, 26, 27; number of, 153 (n. 24)

Kido, Saburo, 111 (ill.), 117

Klingberg, Frank W., 136

Korematsu, Fred, 30, 87, 122, 131

Korematsu v. United States, 30, 87

Lafrenz, William F., 117

Leave (furloughs): War Relocation Authority loyalty assessment related to, 6, 78; for agricultural work, 22, 31, 156 (n. 17); for gaining judicial acceptance of detention, 24–25; types of, 31; inefficiency of process for, 31–32; combining army registration with, 33, 158 (n. 6); War Relocation Authority point system for, 75–76; Gila River Relocation Center loyalty review process for, 81–82. *See also* Indefinite leave

Los Angeles: Japanese Association of Los Angeles, 11 (ill.); Los Angeles Nippon Institute, 63

Loyal and the Disloyal, The: Social Bound-aries of Patriotism and Treason (Grozdins), 144

Loyalty: during second Red scare, 1, 4, 136–37; as criterion for freedom or confinement for Japanese Americans, 28–30; panics about, 135–37; versus racial pride, 141–42; dangerousness as less ambiguous than, 141–45; from nonbetrayal to devotion, 142–43; national versus group, 144–45. *See also* Loyalty bureaucracy; Loyalty questionnaires of 1943

Loyalty: An Essay on the Morality of Relationships (Fletcher), 142

Loyalty boards of 1950s, 1, 137, 145

Loyalty bureaucracy: components of, 2–3; unique characteristics of, 137–38. *See also* Japanese American Joint Board (JAJB); Provost Marshal General's Office (PMGO); War Relocation Authority (WRA); Western Defense Command (WDC)

Loyalty oaths, 135, 137

Loyalty question. *See* Question 28

Loyalty questionnaires of 1943: midlevel government officials evaluate, 1–2; purposes of, 5–6; background of, 31–33; registration process and, 35; contents of, 35–36; and failure of registration program, 36–38; "high mortality of loyalty" due to, 38; and Japanese-American Branch, 41; in Dedrick's color-coding system, 45 (ill.), 49; Ochikubo's response to, 109, 119, 121; works on Japanese American reaction to, 149 (n. 3). *See also* Question 27; Question 28

Machine Records (punch-card) system, 103–4, 106, 171 (n. 47)

Magazines: in Dedrick's loyalty point system, 48; read by Nisei, 62, 63, 64

Nativism, 19, 117

Nielsen, Victor W., 99

Nikkei: defined, 9. *See also* Japanese Americans (Nikkei)

Nisei: population in 1941, 9; as birth-right American citizens, 9, 11; assimilation of, 9–14; English spoken by, 10; Japanese American Citizens League of, 10; dual citizenship of, 11–12, 99, 105, 151 (n. 11), 152 (n. 12); in martial arts programs, 12; in Japanese schools, 12, 18, 43, 44, 47, 48, 49, 50; and Japanese nationalism, 13; travel to Japan by, 13–14; education in Japan for, 13–14, 153 (n. 24); Carter-Munson study of loyalty of, 15–16; officials urging of to engage in war effort, 16; Western Defense Command assumes disloyalty of, 16–18; searches of homes of, 17 (ill.); as only American citizens presumed disloyal, 20; force of into assembly centers, 21; pressures on presumption of disloyalty of, 21–30; enemy alien draft status for, 22; segregation of the disloyal among considered, 26, 27; loyalty as criterion for freedom or confinement of, 28–30; DSS-304A form for male, 35; and Question 28 of loyalty questionnaire of 1943, 36, 38; repatriation requests of in 1943, 36–37; Japanese American Joint Board approach to loyalty of, 39–65; Dedrick's point system stacked against, 48–49; in war plant work, 57–59, 138, 163 (n.78); and human consequences of Japanese American Joint Board errors, 61–65, 139; Provost Marshal General's Office's approach to loyalty of, 67–72, 138; removal of from war plant work, 69–72; War Reloca-

tion Authority's approach to loyalty of, 73–82, 138, 139; Western Defense Command's approach to loyalty of, 83–106, 138; sterling record of those released, 138; scholarship on prewar life of, 151 (n. 6). *See also* Kibei; Military service for Nisei

Nishimoto, Richard, 141

Nokai, 68

Ochikubo, George, 107–10; registration form of, 37 (ill.); summary form of loyalty case of, 45; at Topaz Relocation Center, 107, 109–10, 119, 121; volunteers for army, 109; photograph with his lawyer, 111 (ill.); Bonesteel refuses to allow return of, 113, 115, 122; individual exclusion hearing of, 116–22; military intelligence data collected on, 120 (ill.); after the war, 133. See also *Ochikubo v. Bonesteel* (1944)

Ochikubo v. Bonesteel (1944): mass exclusion challenged in, 7, 107, 110, 115–16; reaction of Bonesteel to, 93; and government delays, 111–16; moved to federal court, 112; mooting of considered by government, 112–14; espionage and sabotage defense considered by government in, 113, 114, 115, 140; social resistance defense considered by government in, 113, 114–15; preliminary injunction sought in, 116, 122–23; trial of, 122–33; federal court's authority as issue in, 123–24, 131–32; main issues to be litigated in, 124; misleading testimony by military at trial of, 127–30, 140–41, 174 (n. 37); federal court rejects, 131, 169 (n. 22); Pratt insists on appeal of, 132–33, 175 (n. 43); as about making law, 133

Office of Naval Intelligence (ONI): prewar surveillance of Issei by, 9; Ringle report on Nikkei loyalty for, 15–16; on Japanese American Joint Board, 34, 40; on Ito case, 65; Western Defense Command loyalty system requires data from, 104

Okamoto, Kiyoshi, 80–81

ONI. *See* Office of Naval Intelligence

Oregon, military zone in, 17

Pacific Coast. *See* West (Pacific) Coast

Paternal jus sanguinis, 11

PMGO. *See* Provost Marshal General's Office

Point system, 46–49

Poston Relocation Center: protests at, 26, 31, 38; administrators at disagree on meaning of disloyalty, 29; Nishimoto at, 141

Powell (Wyoming), 25

Pratt, Henry: becomes Western Defense Command commander, 97; on exclusion orders as unreviewable, 123, 131–32; Ochikubo exclusion order reaffirmed by, 130, 173 (n. 24); in *Ochikubo v. Bonesteel* ruling, 131; *Ochikubo v. Bonesteel* appealed by, 132–33, 175 (n. 43)

Prejudice, anti-Japanese, 14, 95. *See also* Race

Protest. *See* Demonstrations

Provost Marshal General's Office (PMGO), 67–72; in loyalty bureaucracy, 3; and conflict with other agencies, 3; coherent definition of loyalty lacking in, 3; on Japanese American Joint Board, 3, 6, 34, 40; determining war plant work eligibility as responsibility of, 6, 40, 53, 57, 67–72; approach to Nisei loyalty, 6, 67–72, 138, 165 (n. 90); and Bendetsen on Nisei disloyalty, 33, 154

(n. 12); on language for recommending against indefinite leave, 53; separation from War Relocation Authority, 57–60; on publicizing Nisei war plant workers, 58, 59; and Industrial Employment Review Board, 69–70, 166 (n. 10), 175 (n. 9); War Relocation Authority's approach to loyalty compared with that of, 73, 77–78; moves into background of loyalty adjudication, 83; and Bonesteel's request for files on Japanese Americans from, 95, 96; on Western Defense Command's individual exclusion system, 105; as having little experience of Japanese Americans, 138–39; biases affect loyalty adjudication by, 140; on loyalty versus racial pride, 142; behavior prediction as task of, 143. *See also* Japanese-American Branch

Question 27 (loyalty questionnaire of 1943), 35; Nisei reaction to, 35–36; Nisei answers to, 63, 64, 71; Ochikubo's answer to, 109

Question 28 (loyalty questionnaire of 1943), 35; Issei reaction to, 35, 36, 158 (n. 10); Nisei reaction to, 36; Nisei answers to, 38, 62, 63, 64, 70, 71; in Dedrick's color-coding system, 50; segregation associated with "no" answer to, 56; in Provost Marshal General's Office's approach to loyalty, 73; in War Relocation Authority's approach to loyalty, 73–75, 79; in Western Defense Command's individual exclusion system, 105, 125, 130; Ochikubo's answer to, 109; response to evacuation and answer to, 145; source of phrasing of, 159 (n. 13)

Race: Japanese American internment as system of racial oppression, 2; in assumptions of Nikkei disloyalty, 5, 7, 16, 17–20, 138, 154 (n. 12); pride in, taught in Japanese language schools, 12, 43; loyalty investigators' racism, 42–44; Dedrick's racism, 46; in Hazzard's view of Japanese, 117–18; loyalty versus pride in, 141–42; as basis for predicting behavior, 143–44

Rafu Shimpo (newspaper), 49, 77, 161 (n. 27)

Red scare, second, 1, 4, 136–37

Registration questionnaires. *See* Loyalty questionnaires of 1943

Religion: Shinto, 43, 47, 76. *See also* Buddhism; Christianity

Relocation centers: characteristics of determined by state officials, 2; run by War Relocation Authority, 3, 21; establishment of, 21–22; Amache Relocation Center, 23 (ill.), 34 (ill.); Manzanar Relocation Center, 26, 31, 38; demonstrations and protests at, 26, 31, 38, 88; segregation of "troublemakers" at, 27; military service for Nisei calls into question, 32–33; resistance to loyalty questionnaire of 1943 at, 36; Minidoka Relocation Center, 36; "relocation" as euphemism, 149 (n. 2). *See also* Gila River Relocation Center; Heart Mountain Relocation Center; Poston Relocation Center; Topaz Relocation Center; Tule Lake Segregation Center

Relocation offices, 32

Repatriation and expatriation requests: registration process accompanied by, 36–37; in Dedrick's point system, 48; in Dedrick's color-coding system, 50; in Provost Marshal General's Office's approach to loyalty, 73; in War Relocation Authority's approach to loyalty, 74, 75; in Nielsen's loyalty evaluation system, 99; in Western Defense Command's individual exclusion system, 105, 125, 130

Rhett, John T., 117

Ringle, Kenneth D., 11 (ill.), 15–16, 26

Robertson, Guy, 81

Robinson, Greg, 85

Roosevelt, Franklin D.: as having little to do with internment's defining features, 2; and intelligence on loyalty of Japanese Americans, 5; Japanese American internment and election of in 1944, 6; Carter-Munson study of Nikkei loyalty ordered by, 15; Executive Order 9066 of, 17, 84, 114, 131; letter endorses ending mass exclusion, 85, 87; delays ending mass exclusion, 90–91, 111; on distributing Japanese Americans throughout United States, 90–91, 93–94; McCloy meets with, 91; meeting with Bonesteel about mass exclusion, 93–94; mass exclusion ended by, 96; reelection in 1944, 96; negative view of Japanese Americans, 154 (n. 6)

Rowley, Scott, 29, 142

Sabotage and espionage: no Japanese American convicted of, 4, 61, 150 (n. 10); Bonesteel on decreased risk of, 94, 124; as *Ochikubo v. Bonesteel* defense, 113, 114, 115, 140; theme of in Wilbur's testimony at *Ochikubo v. Bonesteel* trial, 125–27

Salt Lake City Conference (1942), 21, 24

Salyer, Lucy, 175 (n. 8)

Sawada, George Masaaki, 166 (n. 10)

Schweitzer, Harold W., 127–30

War plant work: eligibility for as Provost Marshal General's Office responsibility, 6, 40, 53, 57, 67–72; Japanese American Joint Board to advise on, 34–35, 39; in Dedrick's color-coding system, 49; and War Relocation Authority, 54–55; internees on indefinite leave in, 56–59; Nisei workers in, 57–59, 138, 163 (n. 78); Nisei workers removed from, 69–72

War Relocation Authority (WRA), 73–82; coherent definition of loyalty lacking in, 3; conflict with other agencies, 3; in loyalty bureaucracy, 3; on Japanese American Joint Board, 3, 6, 34, 40, 41, 160 (n. 9); purposes of loyalty assessment of, 6; control of evacuated Nikkei shifted to, 21; relocation centers established by, 21–22; on military service for Nisei, 23–24, 32–33; habeas corpus suits against, 24, 78, 87, 97, 167 (n. 11); press and public criticism of, 26; and loyalty as criterion for freedom or confinement, 28–30; "all out" relocation strategy of, 32, 33, 54; cooperates with military on loyalty questionnaires, 34, 39; on Dedrick's color-coding system, 50, 51; fissure with military members of Japanese American Joint Board, 53–61; on clearing "white" cases for war plant work, 54–55; disengages from Japanese American Joint Board work, 55; disregards Japanese American Joint Board findings, 55–56; separation from Provost Marshal General's Office, 57–60; approach to Nisei loyalty, 73–82, 138, 139; point system of, 75–76; moves into background of loyalty adjudication, 83; on ending mass exclusion, 84–85; Tule Lake

protests lead to criticism of, 88; Western Defense Command's veto power over, 88; under Department of Interior, 88, 168 (n. 23); Ochikubo granted leave clearance by, 110; as coming to know Nisei well, 139; biases affect loyalty adjudication by, 140; on loyalty versus racial pride, 142; behavior prediction as task of, 143; and review board for segregees, 145–46. See also Leave (furloughs); Myer, Dillon S.; Segregation of the disloyal

Wartime Civilian Control Administration (WCCA), 21

Washburne, Claude B., 44, 99, 100–102, 104

Washington, military zone in, 17

Washington, George, 135

WDC. See Western Defense Command

Wechsler, Herbert, 112–13, 115, 116

West (Pacific) Coast: Japanese American population in 1941, 9; anti-Japanese prejudice on, 14, 95; Carter-Munson study of Nikkei loyalty on, 15–16; military zones created on, 17; mass exclusion of Japanese Americans from, 17, 22, 84; Nikkei forced into assembly centers on, 21; mass exclusion ended on, 84; ceases to be theater of operations, 88; ending mass exclusion opposed on, 89; Marshall fears violence if mass exclusion is ended on, 89; other groups move into Japanese neighborhoods on, 95, 99. See also California

Western Defense Command (WDC): in loyalty bureaucracy, 2–3; coherent definition of loyalty lacking in, 3; conflict with other agencies, 3; three approaches to Japanese American loyalty of, 6–7, 83; individual exclusion system actually used by, 7, 83, 104–6, 125; individual exclusion system wanted by, 7, 83, 95, 98–104; individual exclusion system of tested in federal court, 7, 83, 127–30, 132; Nisei disloyalty assumed by, 16–18; Wartime Civilian Control Administration of, 21; approach to Nisei loyalty of, 83–106, 138; and genesis of large-scale individual exclusion program, 84–98; as committed to mass exclusion, 85–86; Emmons becomes commanding officer of, 86; veto power of over War Relocation Authority, 88; Bonesteel becomes commanding officer of, 91; Pratt becomes commanding officer of, 97; in transition to individual exclusion, 97–98; original process of for individual exclusion, 98; policy statement of August 8, 1944, 102–3, 125; revised policy statement of September 8, 1944, 103, 121, 125; Machine Records (punch-card) system of, 103–4, 106, 171 (n. 47); Hazzard trains hearing officers of, 117–18; in *Ochikubo v. Bonesteel* trial, 122–33; as having little experience of Japanese Americans, 138–39; biases affect loyalty adjudication by, 140; on loyalty versus racial pride, 142; behavior prediction as task of, 143. *See also* Bonesteel, Charles H.; Civil Affairs Division (Western Defense Command); De Witt, John L.; Emmons, Delos C.; Pratt, Henry

"White" category, 49, 50, 51, 54–55

Wilbur, William H., 125–27, 129, 130, 132

Wirin, A. L.: files lawsuits on behalf of internees, 93, 110, 111; photograph with Ochikubo, 111 (ill.); preliminary injunction sought by, 116; at Ochikubo's individual exclusion hearing, 117; at *Ochikubo v. Bonesteel* trial, 127–28, 129, 130

Wolfe, James H., 146

Women, exemption from individual exclusion process of, 105, 125, 129

World War I, 136

WRA. *See* War Relocation Authority

WRA-126, 35

Wyoming: relocation center in, 22. *See also* Heart Mountain Relocation Center

Yamamoto, Elmer S., 173 (n. 31)

Yasui, Minoru, 131

Young Men's Buddhist Association, 70, 71

H. EUGENE AND LILLIAN YOUNGS LEHMAN SERIES

Lamar Cecil, *Wilhelm II: Prince and Emperor, 1859–1900* (1989).

Carolyn Merchant, *Ecological Revolutions: Nature, Gender, and Science in New England* (1989).

Gladys Engel Lang and Kurt Lang, *Etched in Memory: The Building and Survival of Artistic Reputation* (1990).

Howard Jones, *Union in Peril: The Crisis over British Intervention in the Civil War* (1992).

Robert L. Dorman, *Revolt of the Provinces: The Regionalist Movement in America* (1993).

Peter N. Stearns, *Meaning Over Memory: Recasting the Teaching of Culture and History* (1993).

Thomas Wolfe, *The Good Child's River*, edited with an introduction by Suzanne Stutman (1994).

Warren A. Nord, *Religion and American Education: Rethinking a National Dilemma* (1995).

David E. Whisnant, *Rascally Signs in Sacred Places: The Politics of Culture in Nicaragua* (1995).

Lamar Cecil, *Wilhelm II: Emperor and Exile, 1900–1941* (1996).

Jonathan Hartlyn, *The Struggle for Democratic Politics in the Dominican Republic* (1998).

Louis A. Pérez Jr., *On Becoming Cuban: Identity, Nationality, and Culture* (1999).

Yaakov Ariel, *Evangelizing the Chosen People: Missions to the Jews in America, 1880–2000* (2000).

Philip F. Gura, *C. F. Martin and His Guitars, 1796–1873* (2003).

Louis A. Pérez Jr., *To Die in Cuba: Suicide and Society* (2005).

Peter Filene, *The Joy of Teaching: A Practical Guide for New College Instructors* (2005).

John Charles Boger and Gary Orfield, eds., *School Resegregation: Must the South Turn Back?* (2005).

Jock Lauterer, *Community Journalism: Relentlessly Local* (2006).

Michael Hunt, *The American Ascendancy: How the United States Gained and Wielded Global Dominance* (2007).

Michael Lienesch, *In the Beginning: Fundamentalism, the Scopes Trial, and the Making of the Antievolution Movement* (2007).

Eric L. Muller, *American Inquisition: The Hunt for Japanese American Disloyalty in World War II* (2007).